REAL PROCESS

JOHN W. BURBIDGE

Real Process:

How Logic and Chemistry Combine in Hegel's Philosophy of Nature

UNIVERSITY OF TORONTO PRESS
Toronto Buffalo London

© University of Toronto Press Incorporated 1996
Toronto Buffalo London
Printed in Canada

ISBN 0-8020-0897-6

Printed on acid-free paper

Toronto Studies in Philosophy
Editors: James R. Brown and Calvin Normore

Canadian Cataloguing in Publication Data

Burbidge, John, 1936–
Real process : how logic and chemistry combine
in Hegel's philosophy of nature

(Toronto studies in philosophy)
Includes bibliographical references and index.
ISBN 0-8020-0897-6

1. Hegel, Georg Wilhelm Friedrich, 1770–1831.
2. Philosophy of nature.   3. Logic.   4. Chemistry –
Philosophy.   I. Title.   II. Series.
B2949.N3B8 1996   113'.092   C96-930229-0

University of Toronto Press acknowledges the financial assistance to its
publishing program of the Canada Council and the Ontario Arts Council.

This book has been published with the help of a grant from the Humanities
and Social Science Federation of Canada, using funds provided by the Social
Sciences and Humanities Research Council of Canada.

FOR ELIZABETH AND LEA

Contents

II   Philosophy of Nature

Preface

No scholarly work is produced in isolation. While serving as external examiner for Mark Peterson's thesis 'Volcanoes in the Sky,' I became intrigued with Hegel's handling of chemistry. Dietrich Engelhardt's *Hegel und die Chemie* not only exhaustively set the context, but also provided parallel texts of the three original editions of the *Encyclopaedia*, together with Nicolin and Pöggeler's 1959 edition. Discussions with Dietrich von Engelhardt, Cinzia Ferrini, H.S. Harris, Wolfgang Bonsiepen, and Trevor Levere contributed background and enlightenment. The opportunity to read papers on this and related topics at the Conference on Hegel and Newtonianism, organized in Cambridge by Michael Petry, at the Hegel Societies of Great Britain and America, at a meeting of the 'Tübinger Kreis' in Lübeck, and at the Centre for the History and Philosophy of Science at the University of Toronto tested the waters. Comments from the anonymous reviewers of the University of Toronto Press provided me with useful feedback. The resources of the Hegel Archiv in Bochum, made available to me through the courtesy of Dr Helmut Schneider, were invaluable, and were mined twice – once for the early works on chemistry that Hegel used and once for secondary literature. The Robarts Library in Toronto, the Vatican Library, the Biblioteca di Filosofia of the Villa Mirafiori in Rome, and Trent's Bata Library all contributed material. Funding for the project was provided by the Social Sciences and Humanities Research Council of Canada in the form of a research grant, and by Trent University in the form of a sabbatical leave. To all I extend my thanks.

References in the notes cite only author or editor and title. Full publication details will be found in the Bibliography. *HGW* refers to the critical edition, G.W.F. Hegel, *Gesammelte Werke* (Hamburg: Meiner). I use *Phän* to identify the *Phenomenology of Spirit*, *WL* for the *Science of Logic*, paragraph numbers for the *Philosophy of Nature* and shorter *Logic*; (Miller) indicates the comparable pages in the English translations of these works. The lecture notes inserted into the *Philosophy of Nature* (the additions) are identified by the name of their editor, Michelet, to remind the reader that they do not necessarily represent Hegel's considered opinion. All translations are my own.

HALFWAY LAKE
THE FEAST OF THE TRANSFIGURATION, 1995

REAL PROCESS

1

Hegel's System

'Knowing is actual, and can be expounded, only as science, that is, as *system*.'[1]

I

Hegel's philosophy is a system. By that we mean that each stage is derived from its predecessor and leads to its successor, so that the complete set of components forms an integrated structure.

Hegel's handbook for his lectures, the *Encyclopaedia of the Philosophical Sciences in Outline*, sets out the schema of such a system. His disciples added excerpts from student lecture notes to the various theses, and then gave the whole package the title 'System of Philosophy.' Generations have since assumed that this work presented the definitive picture of Hegel's view of the universe.

It is not so clear, however, in what way Hegel's philosophy is systematic. Some have set it out in a series of triplets,[2] or adopted the alien terminology of thesis, antithesis, and synthesis.[3] On this reading, Hegel, like Procrustes, forced the various bits of information into a threefold pattern that functioned recursively (to use computer jargon), and was applied to its own products.

Others, like E.E. Harris, start from another statement in the preface to the *Phenomenology*: 'The truth is the whole.'[4] Hegel's thought becomes systematic when any particular concept is shown to be finite and partial, demanding that it be sublated into a larger whole. The system is driven teleologically, ever moving towards its all-encompassing end or purpose.

Still others talk as if the system uses some kind of deduction.[5] From accepted premises, using logical rules, one derives conclusions that are necessary.

These positions agree in that the clue to any systematic philosophy lies in its logic: the patterns of reasoning that lead disciplined thought from one stage to the next. Yet Hegel included the philosophy of nature within the total purview of his vision. This, too, was to be organized in a coherent and integrated way. Nature is the realm of human experience and scientific investigation. For all that humans might exploit it for their own purposes, it presents a given that is not completely malleable to the preconceptions of thought.[6]

To comprehend nature philosophically is to take this realm of contingent experience and organize it according to logical principles. So what Hegel said about nature could not be simply the product of second-order reflections on natural science and natural phenomena. Once nature became the object of philosophy, what was said about it had to be systematic.[7]

This demand poses the primary puzzle for interpreters of Hegel's philosophy of nature. How much is driven by logical concerns, and how much responds to empirical fact? If it is primarily logical, then it is claiming the ability to derive natural phenomena from strictly a priori principles; there is no need to appeal to experience. But then new scientific evidence may well falsify the theory.[8] If, however, it is empirical, then it is in danger of losing its systematic status. For, as time passes and scientific investigation uncovers new information about the natural order, any logical structure will be broken into pieces. In either case, philosophy will have to abandon its claims to systematic knowledge.

This dilemma underlies the examination of Hegel's philosophy of chemical phenomena undertaken here. He appears to be conscious of both the Scylla of a priori deduction and the Charybdis of simple observation of facts. Unlike Schelling, he does not presume to tell science what experiments it should next undertake. Unlike the chemists of his day, he submits explanatory hypotheses to critical examination on the basis of logical principles.[9] Whether he is justified in believing that he has grasped the horns of the dilemma is a question that can only be answered by a careful examination of his actual procedure.

I shall focus this study on a single query: Why does Hegel have two separate discussions of chemical process? One, in the *Science of Logic*, talks in abstract terms about objects and syllogisms. The other, in the *Philosophy of Nature*, refers to galvanism and combustion, acids and alkalis, mixture and chemical union. Were the system a priori, the latter discussion would simply be included in the former as a footnote, illustrating how the logic is instantiated. Instead the two find themselves in quite different systematic locations. In the *Logic*, chemism comes after mechanism and before finite teleology. In the *Philosophy of Nature*, mechanics has been left far behind. It is the physics of light, colour, and electricity that precedes chemical process, while organisms, with the self-maintaining dynamic of life, follow; in this context finite teleology does not surface in any significant way.

At the same time, both sections discuss the use of a medium or catalyst to transform one-sided chemical objects into neutral products; both consider the way such neutral products can be analysed into their component elements. Nor is the similarity simply at the level of abstractions. In both the *Logic* and the *Philosophy of Nature*, Hegel uses water to illustrate the neutral medium of chemical process, and points to the implicit teleology when an oxide adjusts its internal proportions so that it can unite with another substance.

I shall use the differences and the similarities between the two discussions of chemical process as a frame for unravelling our puzzle about Hegel's systematic intent. By unpacking the detail in these two sections, and by identifying the various arguments he uses, we can determine how each of the discussions of chemical process is systematic in its own terms and how the two are related within a total picture.

However, 'Chemism' is not the only chapter of the *Science of Logic* in which Hegel discusses topics relevant to chemical phenomena. In the chapter 'Real Measure' he covers such concepts as neutralization, elective affinity, and the measurement of determinate proportions, all of which appear again in the paragraphs from 'Chemical Process' in the *Philosophy of Nature*. Here, too, we have a logical analysis to compare and contrast with his handling of natural phenomena.

The choice of chemical process as the focus of our attention enables us to distinguish the systematic nature of the *Science of Logic* from that of the *Philosophy of Nature* within a limited and manageable frame of reference. It has another advantage as well. Hegel's lifetime coincided with the emergence of modern chemistry. When he was born in 1770, Stahl's phlogiston theory was orthodoxy, and chemists were only beginning to isolate particular chemical substances. When he died in 1831, the basic foundations of modern chemistry were in place.[10]

There are four significant aspects in the development of chemistry over this period, all of which play a part in our story.

In the first place, chemists in Britain, France, Sweden, and elsewhere were breaking down substances into constituents, which were identified for the first time. From Joseph Priestley and Scheele in the 1770s, who isolated vital air (or oxygen) as well as other gases, to Humphrey Davy's and Berzelius's use of the Voltaic pile in the 1810s and 1820s to decompose alkaline and pebble earths, these sixty years saw the identification of the basic set of what we now call the chemical elements: substances such as hydrogen, potassium, chlorine, and strontium were all 'discovered' during this period.

In the second place, Lavoisier's experiments with combustion showed that fire took oxygen from the air and combined it with an original, combustible substance. The phlogiston theory (which said that fire burnt off phlogiston, leaving a pure radical) was challenged at its roots and gradually withered away. By the turn of the century, what had previously been called metallic earths were known to be oxides, and the 'anti-phlogiston' theory (as it was known) had triumphed.

In the third place, the development of the battery, or voltaic cell, enabled chemists to break up compounds that had before appeared to be simple substances. This device confirmed the composition of water, already discovered by Cavendish. But it also decomposed alkalis and the halogen compounds like fluoric and muriatic (hydrochloric) acid into their constituents and was used as well to oxidize metals.

In the fourth place, more accurate measurements made it possible to determine the exact quantity of each constituent that went into a fully saturated compound. These were found to combine in ratios that followed a simple progression. For the first time chemistry became amenable to mathematical calculation and the use of equations.

Many of these developments were going on while Hegel was teaching in Jena, Nürnberg, and Berlin; lecturing regularly on the philosophy of nature, and publishing sections of his system. He delighted in informing his students of what was current in the world of chemistry. If there is an a posteriori aspect to his systematic philosophy, then, he should have been amending the system in light of new scientific discoveries as they occurred. We have here a 'litmus test' for use in identifying the role of empirical data in the system.

I apply this test in two ways. In the first place, I look at how he changed his mind through various versions of these texts. The chapter 'Real Measure,' from the *Science of Logic* of 1831, is a major reworking of the first edition of 1812. Although 'Chemism,' in its full form, has only one version (from 1816), it underwent some revisions in the three editions of the *Encyclopaedia Logic*. Similarly 'Chemical Process' went through two reprintings of the *Philosophy of Nature*. A consideration of these changes over time provides a distinctive kind of insight into Hegel's systematic project.

In the second place, both the chapter on real measure and the paragraphs on chemical process have remarks, appended by Hegel to the systematic analysis. These take up applications of the principles discussed in a more relaxed way, offering another view of the relation between the empirical achievements of chemistry and Hegel's philosophical project. From them we catch a glimpse of his overall purpose and what he was hoping to achieve.

II

A system cannot function simply on a global scale; it also has to work in detail. Each stage must follow from what precedes and justify or establish what comes after.

The intricate paragraphs of the larger *Science of Logic* indicate that Hegel took this demand very seriously. A fine-grained pattern leads from concept to concept. For all of the schematic quality of the *Encyclopaedia*, he was concerned here, too, with transitions. Invariably he required several paragraphs for the key moves to new stages, while covering straightforward developments in a more cursory fashion.

To investigate this detail is not easy, since the texts we have at our disposal do not allow an unequivocal interpretation. For Hegel's logical analyses we have the *Science of Logic*, a three-volume exploration of the way thinking, in fact, thinks. While Hegel added comments and remarks that discuss how these pure concepts have come to be applied in philosophy or science, the systematic core is a thicket of abstract vocabulary, used in a careful, technical way. To unravel that thicket so that each branch and twig is given its due significance is an uncertain and difficult task. Yet it is inescapable if we want to understand how one logical concept, when consistently thought through, leads on to another.

A different problem arises in the *Philosophy of Nature*. We do not have a fully articulated text. Instead, Hegel summarized his position in a number of distinct theses, each of which was given oral elaboration in his lectures. These theses are telegraphic in character, condensing the point made into a sentence or two of compact prose. Hegel at times adds a remark or two, but these, like those in the *Logic*, apply the point being made to current discoveries in science; they do not explain the systematic advance.[11]

Most editions of the *Philosophy of Nature* include – in addition to Hegel's Remarks – a digest drawn from lecture notes taken by his students. These digests are, however, quite unsatisfactory, since Michelet, the editor of this part of the 'System of Philosophy,' collected student notes from lectures Hegel had given,[12] incorporated Hegel's own notes for lectures in

1805, and collated them into segments that would correspond to the paragraphs of the 1830 *Encyclopaedia*.[13] Such collated summaries are highly unreliable, particularly with regard to the sciences, where developments are continual. In addition, by cutting and pasting to fit the themes of specific paragraphs, Michelet left out the connections that indicated Hegel's systematic intent. Only recently has an edition of the 1819 lecture series been published in its integrity.[14] While others have been promised, there is as yet no evidence that they will appear in the near future.

Even with a more accurate record, however, the lectures, aimed at an undergraduate audience, spent more time in illustrating the basic theses of the text with recent experimental developments than in exploring the systematic transitions from stage to stage. Hegel may use a term drawn from the logic to suggest why a move must be made; but this would be understood only by someone who had been totally immersed in the logic, and could thus recognize the implicit transitions that thought inevitably makes. Many of his students did not have that background.

Despite all these difficulties that Hegel has put in our way, I nonetheless attempt an explication of what is going on both in his *Logic* and in his *Philosophy of Nature*. Any such interpretation requires a governing principle. My assumption is that Hegel was not consciously advancing his system as an idiosyncratic vision, against all comers. He claimed that he was only making explicit the inherent rational nature of the universe.[15] Philosophers, he would say, do not advance different systems that represent a wide range of diversity; rather they undertake the common task of exploring the way reason functions in pure thought, in nature, and in society. If their conclusions can be called in question, that critique does not stem from alternative presuppositions arbitrarily espoused but from the inherent logic of sound reasoning.

My interpretation grants him this claim. If it be true that he is developing the way reason itself functions, I cannot resort to interpretations that make him adopt arbitrary and implausible positions. Ultimately, what he says should make sense to careful, disciplined thought. Any failure in this regard must be established, not by opposing contrary positions adopted without argument, but from logical flaws in the process itself.[16]

The approach I am proposing, then, assumes that the abstract vocabulary of the *Logic* and the telegraphic prose of the *Encyclopaedia* are articulating a rational discourse. Each term has been chosen because it says just what Hegel wanted to say, and no more. Wherever the text does not fit our interpretative prejudgments, it is our task to rethink, to see if there is more (or less) going on than we at first imagined. While it is easy to dismiss the text because we think we know better, that is not how we discover what an author intended to say.

III

The principle of interpretation just adopted leads into a consideration of what Hegel was doing in his *Logic*. That work was to be the explication of what happens when thought thinks through its own operations; it explores the nature of reasoning conscious of its own dynamic. Since Hegel's claim to a systematic philosophy ultimately depends on this theory of logical reasoning, we need to spend a bit of time on what it means to think logically.

Thinking is a distinctive mental operation that can be distinguished from imagining or representing. For many people words evoke images. When they hear 'tree,' for example, a picture of a tree, often a very specific one, occurs in their mind's eye. Some assume that the picture is what the word means. Others, however, have no such picture. They understand the meaning of the word without imagining any particular application. These two responses reflect three different mental operations that are often found in the same person – and frequently combined into a single complex act. The first operation is simply imagining: having a mental picture that illustrates the term being used. The second operation is pure thinking: being able to use the term correctly and define it in other words. The basic definitions of good dictionaries are based on this kind of thinking. The third involves a bit of both, for it involves thinking the meaning of the concept or word only to the extent that it is instantiated in something outside the mind. It represents the meaning in a particular way. This could involve using images, or it can use another reflective operation we call reference. For this third act of representing, the meaning of a term is at least in part fleshed out by the way that term functions in the actual world.

Hegel distinguished between these three. The first he called imagination, and its content, a picture; the second he called thinking, and its content, a concept; the third, both process and content, he called representation. Logic is concerned only with the second. Imagination and representation do not have any way of establishing the connection between items in their domain – between pictures or between representations. Indeed empirical philosophy, which bases its epistemology entirely on such operations, can only justify connections by appealing to a mechanical kind of association: because one image or representation has been experienced next to, or reminds us of, another, it evokes the image or representation of that other in the mind. Any connection is contingent on the psychological history of the person in question.

Thinking, however, develops in another way. A concept starts out as something rather general and indefinite. Thought's first task is to fix it more exactly: to define it. In so doing, however, it finds that the original meaning changes; for the new fixed determinations exclude or leave unexplored other, contrary, possibilities. To work out the original meaning fully, thought must, in the second place, not only define its constituent terms but also these other features. Finally, all the various aspects need to be woven together in a complex concept that has its own distinctive character. As a single complete thought, this new, distinctive character can be taken on its own; it becomes a new general, as yet indefinite, concept.

Hegel names these three steps *understanding, dialectical reason, and speculative reason.*[17] They advance through a kind of waltz. Once speculation integrates the various moments into a network of mutual implications, they collapse into a simple concept that then becomes the renewed focus of understanding's precision.

None of these moves of thought appeal to pictures or items represented in thought. They work simply with what we would colloquially call the 'meaning' of the terms being thought. They are thus quite abstract. For those of us who work more naturally with images or objects of representation, it is a hard discipline constantly to put these aside and think nothing but the basic thoughts, defining what they mean, and noticing carefully how that meaning subtly changes. Since thoroughgoing conceptual analysis is not easy, this kind of abstract logical activity makes Hegel's *Science of Logic* notoriously difficult to read, and leads most commentators to rely on the references to the history of philosophy or to contemporary affairs to represent what is going on.[18]

We need to notice something else about this description of rational thought. Pure thinking (or conceiving) is dynamic; it moves from original definition through various stages that refine the meaning to a new complex concept.

Influenced by the tendency of representation to refer a term to a specific content, some philosophers have argued that concepts do not change; they are fixed.[19] The task of analysis is to disclose this eternal, unchanging thought in its pure form. This led Descartes and his successors to talk about clarity and distinctness as virtues of thought. Such adjectives assume that, just as light discloses all the characteristics of a pre-existing visual object, so thinking unveils something already there and determinate, which we call a concept.

Hegel, however, was not a Platonist, separating a form from its use. He was closer to Aristotle. There is no concept that is not conceived; the operation of conceiving determines a concept, so that it moves from being general and indeterminate to being particular and determinate. We usually call this process 'understanding what we mean.' Were we to reflect carefully on what goes on there, we would realize that such understanding subtly changes the concept so that its definition alters.

To elucidate the pattern of pure thinking, then, involves not only concepts, but conceiving; not terms, fixed and determined by understanding, but the dynamic processes by which thought moves: first from general to particular; then from one particular to another; and finally to the network of relations that interconnect the particulars within a more encompassing concept.

If the abstractness of pure thinking is one of the hurdles that Hegel puts in the way of his interpreter, then, the dynamic of thinking is a second. Used to a more static discourse, we read a paragraph as if it were dwelling on a single point, spelling out its presuppositions and implications. But Hegel frequently describes a development of thought. The end of a paragraph has moved on from where it started. The intermediate sentences do not portray a static scene, but narrate a sequence.

It is frequently difficult to catch that dynamic because of the constraints of written language. Nouns are supposed to signify entities, and so we tend to read them as descriptive. But infinitives and gerunds are nouns that express processes and operations. In reading them we should be thinking meanings that are dynamic and active. Those dynamic meanings are then integrated by the syntax of the sentence into a single, complex operation. As a result, when we come to a period, we must go back and discover the dynamic process that moves through the several distinct clauses and phrases of the sentence. In other words, we must rethink Hegel's thoughts. That is the foundation of a Hegelian mode of interpreting.[20]

IV

Thinking is never easy. The temptation is to take short cuts. Either we find some kind of formula that offers an overview, or we simply translate Hegel's dense vocabulary into something equally obscure and often more difficult to understand. There are a number of good discussions of Hegel's *Logic* from a bird's eye view. But if we are going to investigate the systematic nature of his philosophy, we need to immerse ourselves in the detail.

To be sure, the *Logic* as a whole is so rich that a detailed analysis would take much longer than any reasonable person would want to spend. Nevertheless, at least some parts need to be explicated sufficiently to show how Hegel allows thought to follow its own path through a series of concepts in the manner we have suggested. Only if that development has some kind of inevitability – such that each concept is both the presupposition for its successor – and the implication of its predecessor – can there be any hope of establishing his philosophy as a system.

In what follows, I take the two chapters of the larger *Logic* connected with chemistry – on real measure and on chemism – and talk them through. Starting, rather arbitrarily, where the chapter starts, I trace a path of thinking, suggesting how general and indeterminate concepts become determinate; how thoughts of other possibilities arise and are explored; and how the set of various terms that emerge come to be interconnected and interrelated. I undertake nothing more than an *exposition de texte*, paraphrasing each sentence in conceptual language such that the inherent rational pattern can be exposed.

Hegel uses abstract terms to name both the content and the process of thought. Thinking the content is assumed; for who would be reading the *Science of Logic* who were not themselves actively thinking through and conceiving what was written down? As an aid to understanding, however, I explicitly employ the language of thinking. Hegel himself discusses some of these terms in the *Logic*: the transition or passing over from one concept to another, reflection on what has just occurred, conceiving or understanding a concept so that it is fully determined. Along with Hegel, I avoid the subjective vocabulary of 'clear' and 'distinct.' But I do use such terms as 'precise,' 'define,' 'consider,' 'implication,' and 'integration' – none of which are part of his terminology – because they retain a strictly conceptual sense in English. And I suggest the dynamic conceptual activity by using 'we' to represent the community of rational thinkers.

While I strive to use as little technical vocabulary as possible, and in that way to suggest the inherent rationality of the logical development, it is still incumbent on the reader who wants to test the validity of my reading to sit down with Hegel's own text (preferably German) and compare it with what I have to say.[21] My exposition is, after all, falsifiable precisely to the extent that it fails to do justice to every nuance of Hegel's carefully designed German.[22]

V

The second half of our study concerns the eleven paragraphs Hegel devoted to chemical process in the *Philosophy of Nature*. Here we do not have the discursive prose of the larger *Logic*, but rather condensed summaries to be elaborated in lectures. The paragraphs are short theses, often of less than four (albeit complex) sentences. There are four added remarks, three of which contain extensive discussions of contemporary chemistry.[23] There is no logical development, no argument justifying the transition to a new stage. Here we must resort to other tactics for our investigation.[24]

For the sake of simplicity I limit myself to the final text Hegel published: the edition of 1830. Because the remarks Hegel added to this text are applications of the theoretical points being made, I consider them separately and in less detail, though I use material from them when it throws light on the basic text.

Since here we do not have full-fledged descriptions of the systematic or inferential process, my approach is, of necessity, different from that followed with regard to the larger *Logic*. In the *Encyclopaedia* Hegel relied on technical terms. Their meanings, defined in the *Logic* or earlier in the *Philosophy of Nature*, were to carry the development forward. Although the syntax of the sentence combined those terms in a distinctive way, much was still left unspecified. As well, Hegel did not appeal to detailed scientific and natural phenomena in his general descriptions of nature. He provided these in his lectures. The brief summary texts of the section on chemical process were to be fleshed out with reference to other material, both systematic and empirical.

This, then, provides the framework for the following commentary. Both the German text of 1830 and a fairly literal translation are provided. Then expository notes discuss key terms and their significance within the previous systematic discussion. Others provide relevant background from contemporary scientific texts. Finally, a commentary identifies how logical thought and natural science combine in the systematic development.[25]

Deliberately I have not drawn out implications from Hegel's thought for contemporary science or contemporary philosophy. Modern science is a complex field, and I am not competent to comment on its achievements and methods. The material here is offered to philosophers of science as a historical case-study in which a priori concepts and a posteriori experience are both used to explain nature. I leave it to them to decide whether there is anything here that can prove instructive in understanding our contemporary systems of thought and shifts in paradigms.[26]

Prior to entering into the substance of our discussion, however, some background would not be amiss. The possibility of a critical philosophy of nature was first adumbrated in Kant's *Metaphysisches Anfangsgrund der Naturwissenschaften*, but it became a full-blown discipline in its own right at the hands of Schelling. Hegel entered into Schelling's project when he arrived at Jena to resume academic studies; once Schelling left, he took over responsibility for courses in the area, and even developed a draft manuscript on the philosophy of nature, before turning to the *Phenomenology of Spirit* and the final system. In the next chapter I summarize these developments, paying particular attention to the role chemistry played in them.

2

The Background

Any philosophy of nature has a fundamental problem: How can the thinking of philosophy do justice to the facts of experience? Kant presented the challenge in a definitive way: thought involves concepts, and concepts, being general, express only possibilities. In sensation we encounter facts, and facts are singular and actual. As contraries, singular actuals and universal possibles do not intersect. So where thought follows its own logic it can construct consistent theories, but these have no truth unless one can show how concept and fact correspond. In other words, explanations of nature are impossible without some point of contact between thought and immediate experience.[1]

I

Kant devoted his *Critique of Pure Reason* to resolving this problem. But he discussed specifically scientific explanations in a shorter treatise, *The Metaphysical Principles of Natural Science*. There he applied the principles developed in the *Critique* to the concept of 'body' to show how at least mechanics could offer genuine knowledge of nature.

For Kant space and time provide the hinge between concept and fact. Since *all* sensible intuitions occur in space and time, the singular actuals of experience are already organized by them, as the framework of intuition in general. So concepts can legitimately be used to describe our experience of nature when they fit with appropriate spatial and temporal relations. Further, mathematics articulates the necessary relations involved in space and sequence. So natural science can determine what is necessary (in that its contrary is not possible) when its concepts are matched by mathematical descriptions.

Since any natural science will be scientific only when it can show the necessity of its laws and explanations, an empirical investigation not amenable to mathematical descriptions cannot hope to be scientific. This condemns not only introspective psychology, but also chemistry to being just skilled manipulations of experience:

Therefore, so long as there has been found for the chemical working of matter no concept which can be constructed [mathematically], that is, no law for the parts' drawing together or apart can be derived, according to which (perhaps in proportion to its density or some such) their movement with its results can be made intuitive in space a priori and so articulated (a demand that will be satisfied with difficulty, if ever), chemistry can become nothing more than a systematic craft, or experimental account, never a proper science. For its principles are strictly empirical and allow no articulation a priori in intuition, and hence cannot in the least make comprehensible the theoretical possibility of the axioms of chemical appearances, since they are not amenable to the application of mathematics.[2]

For mechanics, however, Kant can develop its a priori conditions by deriving from the categories of quantity, quality, relation, and modality those principles that are amenable to mathematical instantiation. These define the conditions for matter as substance extended in space. They involve movement, attractive and repulsive forces, and the laws of conservation, inertia and reaction. Necessity emerges once the action and reaction of attractive and repulsive forces are shown to be equal.

Yet chemistry, too, involves attraction and repulsion. Affinity draws bodies together into a union so close that it transforms their qualities; and chemical reduction separates substances out of such unions and reconstitutes them as independent.[3] Kant justifies his exclusion of chemistry from the range of sciences by pointing out that chemical attraction does not involve a transmission of motion, as in mechanics, but rather alters the bond between materials. As reflecting a range of degrees within a continuum, this alteration cannot be accurately measured, since it is not possible to determine empirically the ultimate units of a continuum. So the relations involved in the bond cannot be constructed with mathematical necessity, and chemistry cannot become a rigorous science.

II

Kant's conclusions set the stage for the ensuing discussion. They were challenged from two sides. First, Fichte pointed out that the sources of necessity in Kant – the basic conceptual categories – were, ultimately, contingent facts. Second, Schelling discovered an intellectual intuition into what matter actually is in the passivity of sensation. Since both of these developments were important for Hegel's philosophy of nature, we shall look at each briefly.

Kant had provided no independent proof for his twelve-fold table of categories. They were postulated from the contingent fact that traditional logic had organized judgments in terms of quantity, quality, relation, and modality. Since, however, these concepts are to establish necessity in natural science, a stronger justification is required.

To provide what was needed, Fichte combined two aspects of Kant's philosophy: first, that categories were a function of conceiving, or understanding; second, that moral decisions presuppose free agency.

Since in its categorical use conceiving is as unconditioned an activity as moral willing, Fichte pointed out that knowing too presumes a free agent. Working from this fundamental insight, Fichte derived the categories systematically from the basic structure of free will.

There is, first of all, agency as such; it expresses singularity, reality, substance, and possibility. Second, there is that which agency acts upon and which offers resistance to its dynamic. Here we generate not only particularity, negation, cause, and actuality, but also the otherness of nature. Third, neither of these moments can be absolute, since, as direct opposites, each would then destroy the other; they are both parts of a more comprehensive, genuinely absolute, dynamic. With this third moment Fichte had universality, limitation, reciprocity, and necessity.[4]

This systematic derivation of the categories, however, was based ultimately on an unproved assumption. In the same way that Kant had justified only the *belief* in human freedom as the necessary condition of moral decisions, so Fichte's first three principles were simply the *fundamental presuppositions* of any knowing whatsoever. Were knowledge an illusion, they would become simply figments of an arbitrary construction. So in the last analysis, science is grounded in a primordial act of faith.[5] We have no final assurance that there is a reality that corresponds to our concepts.

III

While Schelling developed and extended Fichte's science of knowledge in his transcendental philosophy, he also responded to the ultimate uncertainty at its core. Kant had shown that conceptions without intuitions were empty, and that the categories of thought can justify the necessity of science only when they are matched by an appropriate intuition. It was because Fichte had ignored the whole question of intuitions that he was reduced to relying on faith. A reconsideration of the contact we have with reality in direct experience would not only remove the appearance of arbitrary conviction, but also make possible a philosophy of nature.[6]

In addition to space and time, claimed Schelling, there is a third a priori characteristic of intuition. Whereas the former two describe its universal form, the latter identifies its essential content. Schelling's argument went something like this:[7]

If we are active in conceiving, we are passive in intuiting; but we are aware of that passivity because it occurs within the context of an alien, prior activity. We are, so to speak, forced to be passive. So in every moment of sensible intuition we have an immediate sense not only of the resistance, but also of the persistence of an alien reality. What both resists and persists is a dynamic of repulsive and attractive forces, or matter. Common to all sensation then, and so a priori, is an intellectual awareness of this actuality of matter.[8]

Indeed, matter is known to have the same threefold structure that Fichte had shown to hold for free agency: the move from universal to particular, or real agency; the move from particular to universal, or passive resistance; and the undifferentiated union of the two, or matter absolute. Because these were not only functions of conscious agents but also characteristics of matter, Schelling called them potencies.[9] Since this intuition makes us aware of general possibility rather than singular actuality, it satisfies Kant's criterion for being called intellectual rather than sensible.

From this appeal to intellectual intuition, Schelling was able to draw three implications for his philosophy of nature. First, this insight expands the range of a priori scientific principles beyond mechanics to chemistry. Second, the threefold structure, as inherent in all matter, offers a clue for explaining natural phenomena. Third, by recognizing the similarity in structure and the opposition in content between the self's free agency and dynamic matter, we can move beyond the relativism and ultimate contingency of both transcendental philosophy and natural science and unite them in a comprehensive, undifferentiated absolute. I shall look briefly at each.

1 / Since the a priori of intuition extends beyond the forms of space and time to the actuality of matter's constitution, philosophy is not just dependent on mathematics to provide a link between concepts and intuitions. In establishing the grounds for a genuine science it can justify not only mechanical motion but also the chemical composition of bodies where elective affinity expresses both the attraction between some bodies and the repulsion between others.

Here, as Kant recognized, it was a question not of quantity, but of quality. Unlike Kant, however, Schelling was not limited to the schema provided by mathematics. Because of his a priori insight into the actuality of matter, he could articulate a universal and necessary framework for chemistry. Copying Kant's a priori derivation of the principles of mechanics, Schelling developed twenty-four theorems. The first, for example, states that 'no chemical process is anything other than a reciprocal action of the basic forces of two bodies.'[10]

2 / The second thrust of Schelling's philosophy of nature was to consider natural phenomena as they were described by the scientists: combustion, light, heat, air, electricity, and magnetism. As he proceeded he found the prevailing mechanistic and atomistic theories to be unsatisfactory, and the phenomena to fit more closely with the pattern of three potencies.

In combustion the active principle of oxygen was balanced by a passive combustible element, which (in common with J. Richter and other chemists of the time) he identified with heat.[11] Indeed, light and heat were related as pure agency to pure passivity, since heat was bound light and light was free heat. At another level electricity represented the activity of nature, magnetism its passive moment, and chemism the undifferentiated union of both.[12] The hierarchy of levels continued, because magnetism, electricity, and chemism were all activities; space with its three dimensions was passive; while the organism, as reproductive, irritable, and sensitive, was their undifferentiated union.

So the intellectual intuition into the dynamic nature of matter grounded Schelling's explanations of natural phenomena, and justified his repudiation of atomism and mechanism by offering a more comprehensive, theoretical framework.

3 / Schelling argued that this was not just the arbitrary proposal of a peculiar philosopher by setting the whole study of nature in a larger context.

We have already remarked on the intuitive link between the agency of the self and the dynamic of matter. These two represented the first two potencies: the freedom of the self expresses activity; the regularity of matter embodies passivity. So the two moments, investigated by transcendental philosophy and the philosophy of nature respectively, were opposites within a genuinely comprehensive reality that incorporated both into an undifferentiated union – what Schelling called 'the absolute.' Intellectual intuition was the way this absolute found expression in knowledge.

So the fundamental compatibility of all nature, all history, and all reality, as shown by their shared pattern of three potencies, was to establish the ultimate validity of Schelling's philosophy of nature.[13]

IV

When Hegel came to develop his own philosophy of nature, he drew on the work of his predecessors. Like Fichte, he saw the need for a systematic derivation in which each moment or stage emerged from its predecessor. Like Schelling, he was not content with simple postulation or faith. Ultimately all reality was one, and both nature and thinking about nature were moments within that unity.[14]

He did not, however, achieve a satisfactory integration of these two concerns easily. In 1803–4, he lectured on the philosophy of nature, and some fragments from his notes are still available.[15] In 1804–5 he started writing a 'Logic, Metaphysics and Philosophy of Nature,' which moved from the basic principles of thought to the metaphysical structure of reality before venturing into the discussion of nature.[16] While this manuscript broke off just as it comes to organism, in 1805–6 Hegel lectured on the whole philosophy of nature as well as the philosophy of spirit.[17]

He was not to return to a fully systematic handling of the philosophy of nature until the first edition of the *Encyclopaedia of the Philosophical Sciences* in 1817. By that time, however, his approach had changed significantly. We can suggest the nature of the changes in the following way: Hegel started with too undifferentiated a union between the logic of thinking and the phenomena of nature. That union had to be matched by an equally rigorous non-union or distinction between thought's activity and nature's passivity before he would be able to achieve a satisfactory resolution of the problem – a union of union and non-union.

In 1804–5, Hegel's absolute was not the undifferentiated union of Schelling. It acted on, or related to, itself. A more proper designation was self-determining spirit. Spirit was not a simple identity of activity and passivity, but rather itself active in differentiating the various moments of its own life, in establishing them on their own as distinct. From this perspective, active thought and the givens of nature became two different ways absolute spirit determined itself.[18]

In this early system, the first section, or logic, explored the categories of quality, quantity, and relation, concluding with cognition as the proportion between being and thinking. For thought to know something, it must be able to construct a model out of defined parts and then use that construction to prove what is to be known.

The second section investigated the most universal forms of cognition: the metaphysical principles that undergird all reality. Following Schelling's pattern of identity, exclusion, and ground, Hegel moved through the laws of thought and the metaphysical objects of soul, cosmos, and God to the cognitive and practical ego. He concluded with the idea of spirit absolute, as that which has nothing other than itself to refer to since it has integrated knowing and acting.

Within the self-referential dynamic of spirit, nature was distinguished as the moment of opposition, a restricted determination of its unrestricted determining. At the same time, the logic had articulated the rational principles that would characterize not only spirit, but also this alien product of its own activity. So philosophical thought, following the cognitive demands of the logic, could construct a model to represent the basic organization of matter, and then show how natural processes reproduced this conceptual structure.

In other words, since nature and logical idea were both moments within absolute spirit, and spirit explicitly referred to itself, the idea could derive natural principles by means of pure thought and then confirm its conclusions with reference to what actually happened in nature. This derivation using construction and proof would lead to a genuine cognition of nature.[19]

The construction of matter started from the ideal principle of self-maintenance, in which light is transmuted to heat and heat to light. This process, however, must become real and corporeal so that its self-maintaining dynamic infinitely reconstitutes itself. Such a metaphysical infinite would involve three moments: first, it would be on its own account; second, it would give itself a structure; and third, it would reconstitute itself as identical with itself in its structure.

So in the same way that geometry drew lines and constructed figures to prove its theorems, the philosophy of nature exploited logical principles in constructing the framework of matter. There would be a simple self-equivalence, or nitrogen gas; there would be a differentiation between structured moments, or oxygen gas and hydrogen gas; and there would be a reconstituted self-equivalence, or carbon dioxide gas.

When one removed the fluidity or heat from these gases,[20] one was left with the pure elements of nitrogen, oxygen, and so on. From a logical point of view, these four elements made up a process, moving from nitrogen through the differentiated moments of oxygen and hydrogen to carbon dioxide which, as self-equivalence, was the same as nitrogen.[21]

On the basis of this discussion of the chemical elements, Hegel 'constructed' the physical elements of fire, air, water, and earth, going on to list the various sorts of earths: metals, alkaline earths, pebble earths, and what we now know to be metallic oxides.

The other side of cognition – the moment of proof – involved the use of inferences or syllogisms, in which middle terms brought together two extremes. Chemical process, as a mediated union of differentiated substances, reflected this logical structure and so displayed the full pattern of cognition. By converting metals to fluidity, heat transformed the static to the dynamic. Then, using water and air as mediating or middle terms, it oxidized not only metals but also combustible substances like sulphur, generating a chemical differentiation between acids and bases. When these latter substances were brought together in a liquid they produced salts, a reconstituted form of earth. So here too we have an infinite dynamic that moved from simple self-equivalence (metals) to differentiated structure (acids and bases) and back to reconstituted self-equivalence (salts). This time it was not a construct of pure thought but a process present in nature. The process fitted with the construction, however, for oxygen and hydrogen, as abstract differentiation, were the essential moments in differentiating acids from bases.[22]

The most complete embodiment of this dynamic was the galvanic process, since it started out from metals (or earth) and by means of electricity (fire) and a liquid (water) generated oxygen gas and hydrogen gas (air) in the course of reconstituting a different kind of earth in the metal oxides and hydrates. As a single infinite and self-identical dynamic that could maintain itself indefinitely, 'the galvanic process is now the picture of the organic process; it is the fire that generates itself through itself.'[23] Hegel thus set the stage for his construction and proof of organic life.

In this presentation, there was no clear separation of logical argument and empirical phenomena. The inherent unity of idea and nature in absolute spirit justified a rational construction of phenomena like oxygen gas and metallic earths, and a conflation of proof and chemical process into a single theoretical discussion. In this way, working from the conviction that both thought and external reality were moments that absolute spirit distinguished within its own dynamic, Hegel extended the systematic concerns of Fichte into the realm of natural philosophy. It was, in a sense, the 'reconstituted self-equivalence' of the two 'differentiated' moments represented by Fichte and Schelling. But it also appeared as if Hegel was 'deducing' natural phenomena from strictly logical principles.

V

Hegel did not stay with this identification of nature and idea that used construction and proof. Very shortly he abandoned using methods of cognition as the foundation for his philosophy. In its place he proposed a 'phenomenological' pathway to absolute knowing. This kind of knowing involved making absolute claims, discovering that they were relative, and incorporating that relativity into a reconstituted absolute claim. What was called cognition was only one instance of these absolute claims.[24] This then required a distinction between an explication of the purely theoretical principles of such knowing, in the *Science of Logic*,[25] and a comprehension of the nature that confronts thought in the contingency and finitude of sensible experience.[26]

A manuscript, dated by the editors of the critical edition to 1807–8, shows that Hegel was moving in that direction shortly after completing the *Phenomenology*. It portrays mechanism, chemism, life, and cognition as theoretical concepts developed on strictly logical grounds. Here we have a text that anticipated parts of the third book of the *Science of Logic*, even though finite teleology had not yet obtained its distinctive location between chemism and life.

By this time chemical process was a logical concept, not a phenomenon in nature; it was analysed into a structure of syllogisms where extremes, characterized simply as universal, particular, or singular, were mediated to produce integrated conclusions. I shall have occasion to refer to this text again when discussing the logic of chemism. What is of interest, however, in the light of later developments, is that it talked of chemical combination or union, but not of separation; and it described that one process in terms of three different syllogisms, respectively mediated by particularity, singularity, and universality.[27]

Such, in brief, are some stages that the philosophy of nature adopted in the time between Kant's *Critique of Pure Reason* and Hegel's *Science of Logic*. Curiously enough, when we look back over this historical development, we find what Hegel at the time called an infinite structure.[28] It started with Kant who, in the basic principles of natural science, had a simple conjunction of rational concept and sensible intuition. These two moments broke apart into Fichte's systematic derivations of the categories and Schellings's intellectual intuition into the actuality of matter. The opposing perspectives were reintegrated by Hegel into a single philosophical argument that united theoretical construction and proof with empirical phenomena. The next stage would be to counter this moment of union within absolute spirit with a balancing moment of non-union. Logical thought and the philosophy of nature needed to be articulated as distinctive disciplines, each with its own systematic method: logical derivation on one side, thoroughgoing empirical observation on the other. Only where both union and non-union were taken seriously could one have an adequate knowledge of spirit.

Rather than being the presupposition of the philosophy of nature, then, in Hegel's mature system absolute spirit would be its final consummation. How the union and non-union of logic and nature contributed to that achievement provides a sub-text for the following study.

I

SCIENCE OF LOGIC

A / REAL MEASURE

3

Specific Quantity

Our first logical discussion will be an *exposition de texte* of the chapter, 'Real Measure,' from the second edition of the *Logic* of 1831. This concept is significant, for it was by developing the right forms of measurement that natural science had broken free from its Aristotelian past. On this basis, Kant, as we have seen, relegated chemistry to a systematic craft because it was not subject to quantitative analysis. However, one of his students, J.B. Richter, showed that accurate measurements could determine the standard proportions of an acid and a base that combine to form a salt; in other words, chemistry, was finding a way of measuring real bodies. As an intellectual operation that was central to all scientific endeavours, this kind of measuring needed to be examined as a key aspect of logical thinking.

This section was considerably revised from the first edition of 1812.[1] Since in due course I shall be using the third edition of the *Encyclopaedia* of 1830 published only a year previously, as my primary text for the *Philosophy of Nature*, it is appropriate to use this final version as the basis for the following systematic discussion. In due course, however, I shall consider the changes made to the earlier text.[2]

Hegel's *Science of Logic* was originally published in three books: *The Doctrine of Being*, *The Doctrine of Essence*, and *The Doctrine of Conceiving*. 'Measure' is the third and final section of the first volume, preceded by 'Determination' (or 'Quality') and 'Magnitude' (or 'Quantity'). Since it involves applying quantities to qualities, its analysis served as a mediating third to Hegel's consideration of 'Quality' and 'Quantity.' Within this section there are three chapters: 'Specific Quantity,' 'Real Measure,' and 'The Coming to Be of Essence.'

Since the *Science of Logic* is intended to be systematic, each chapter starts from where the previous one stopped; it uses as components in its argument concepts and terms that have been discussed earlier. To set the stage for our discussion of real measure, then, it is necessary to review the immediately preceding development and suggest its rationale in a schematic way.

In its most elementary form 'measure' means that some quantifiable quality is quantified. We say that something *has* a measure; in this sense the ancients used to say that everything is measured. Such a sense is vague, however, and relatively indeterminate. So thought needs to move on from this unsatisfying stage by distinguishing some feature that is quantifiable from whatever is used to quantify. The latter becomes a standard for measuring the former: a yardstick used to measure extended bodies.

That relation too is conceptually incomplete. For the ruler, itself quantifiable, has been quantified arbitrarily; there are no natural measures. At the same time it is some quality of the thing being measured that determines what kind of measuring is appropriate. The two sides – the measuring and the measured – are of the same order; both, for example, are extended. So it is a matter of indifference which one serves as the rule and which is to be measured against that standard. To move forward in the *logic* of measuring, we should have two sides that are qualitatively distinct. A single unit of one kind of thing can then be used to set a limit within which we count the number of units of the other kind of thing.

Hegel illustrates this new type of measuring by referring to the measurements of velocity and acceleration in which units of time are used to measure the distance in space travelled. In these assessments, one distinguishes some quality taken as unity or basic (for example, time) from another that is then counted or numbered (space). The two are then brought together in a proportion or ratio, where the former is the denominator and the latter the numerator. So we talk of kilometres per hour or feet per second squared; the first is a direct ratio, the second a ratio of powers.

(To stay with the illustrations, however, makes it difficult to see how thought moves from stage to stage. For the images and representations of the illustrations reveal no connections that link one thought to the next. On the level of example there is no reason why we should move from yardsticks to velocity and acceleration or from these to specific gravity. In a systematic development, there are shifts to different kinds of measuring, and these come about only by focusing on the specific *meaning* of 'measuring' at each point, and how its imprecision needs to be rectified.)

At the present stage, one kind of quantifiable quality is used to measure another that is qualitatively distinct from the first. These two qualities, however, are simply diverse and have no inherent relation to each other. So this act of measuring is affected by the arbitrary decision not only of what serves as a basic unit, but also of what qualities one takes both to measure and to be measured. We can remove some of this contingency by making the two aspects, the one that measures and the one that is measured, two distinct qualities of the same thing. We would then have a way of measuring what the thing really is.[3]

This move involves a return to the initial sense of measure, in which everything *has* a measure. But that concept is no longer vague and imprecise. Now the measurement of anything involves a ratio (or proportion) between two of its own qualities. When we use one quality of a thing to measure another, we focus on it as a qualified entity. So we are measuring something real, or – to put it more neatly – we have a real measure.

From this perspective, we see that the earlier kind of measuring uses the abstractions we call space and time and ignores the particular thing that was moving or accelerating. The concept 'measure' as presently understood has, however, developed to the stage where we can use it for chemical bodies. Hegel is ready to explore the logical principles underlying Richter's proposals for chemical measurements.

4

When Two Measures Are Combined

Hegel now considers what happens when we measure things rather than abstract quantifiable features.[1] Since we have moved from applying an external standard or rule to using one quality to measure another quality of the same thing, we begin by considering what kind of measure would be appropriate for this kind of measuring: we need to have two quantifiable qualities that can be related in a ratio. Further, to be a genuine measurement, the association of the two qualities must be intrinsic to the thing itself.

One of the qualities is used to measure the other. It provides the units against which the other quality is counted or numbered – the denominator. Since those units are, to some extent, arbitrarily determined, the quality itself should be something obvious on the surface of the thing to be measured. What is then counted to provide the numerator in the ratio can then be more distinctive; it is the quality that constitutes the thing's reality.[2] By putting these numbers in a ratio, we measure the specific character of the thing: it is the number of units of the core quality that are found in one unit of the superficial quality. This ratio *specifies* what a thing is like. When we say, for example, that the *specific* gravity of gold is 197, we mean that there are 197 units of mass for each unit of volume.

Because only the superficial quality is abstract while the other is inherent and immediate, the ratios are simple and direct. There can be no introduction of powers to one side of the proportion, since that can occur only when both are abstract and are determined by an external calculation. As a direct ratio, then, the measurement can be expressed in a simple exponent.

The exponent that specifies (or measures) the thing comes from the ratio between a unit of the surface quality and the corresponding quantity of the inherent quality. It is, in some sense, peculiar to that entity. But this attempt to measure the entity on its own is inherently incomplete; for it is a matter of indifference what we use as a unit of the abstract quality. That unit acquires significance only when it becomes a standard, used as the denominator for measuring other things as well. Since it is superficial, and not inherent, it is amenable to, and indeed requires, such an extension if it is to be a reliable standard. In other words, one can specify a thing in this way only by comparing it with something else.

We have reached this recognition that some sort of comparison is necessary by reflecting on this kind of measuring in general. To establish it systematically, however, we must show how it is implied by the conceptual content itself. We start by reviewing that content.[3]

Measuring, at this stage, produces an exponent that expresses a ratio between two quantities, one arbitrarily set as the unit denominator, the other as the numerator. This ratio is to specify what the thing really is – how it is determined. But it is only a number; the thing is quite indifferent to what that number is, since the latter is arbitrary, depending on which basic units we started with. In other words, as mere numbers, the quantities have no essential relation to this particular entity.

In its turn an entity is alterable. External conditions such as heat and pressure, for example, can change its density. Indeed, as we know from chemistry, when combined with other bodies, an entity can change into something else entirely. Since the first ratio no longer holds, it has become another distinct entity. It has acquired a different specific ratio – a new distinctive measurement.[4]

So we are now thinking of two things, one which has the original measurement and another which does not. In this context what distinguishes one from another is not another quality, or another kind of measuring. Rather the two qualities that together made up the ratio of the first thing, simply have a different ratio in the second. Measuring produces different exponents.

Both entities are alterable, however; the change can be shown by measuring their direct relation, or combination. When combined, each maintains itself and retains something of its distinctive measurement; yet each has passed over from what it originally was and has become something else; it has altered. So the measurement of the combination must also adjust. Its specific ratio is identical with neither of those that measured the original entities.[5] However, to satisfy our concern to measure the quality that specifically defines the thing we started with, we can connect the ratio it has in combination, with the ratio it had originally.

This leads to a complex picture. In the first place, because they are distinct, each thing has its specific measurement, and it retains this definition of what it is like. In the second place, however, we combine them. The combination is different from either one on its own, so they are qualitatively altered when they are put together. (We have already noted that the measurements are abstract and in some sense indifferent to the thing.) So the measurement of the combined product produces a different set of figures – a different ratio – from either of the original pair. The change in the exponent when the thing is considered first on its own and then in combination now offers a more developed way of specifying what that original thing is. We first measure it on its own and then in combination; these two figures are finally related in a new, second-order ratio.[6]

(In the first edition, Hegel calls the process, in which two quantitatively distinct entities are combined into a compound that removes their difference, neutralization. And he shows how a priori thought can anticipate such a process. It cannot tell in advance what particular numbers will emerge; that can only be determined empirically. Yet it can know that there will be a change, and that observation will be needed to decide what that change is in fact.)

One might think that we could determine the exponent of the combined product in an a priori way: all we need do is add together the figures for each of the two qualities – the two numerators and the two denominators – and then combine them in a new ratio. That would be appropriate if we were working with pure quantities – abstract numbers. But these are measurements of things, indeed measurements of two different ways in which a thing can be qualified. One of those qualities was superficial, obvious enough for breaking it up into units, but not applying to the thing as it really is. The other quality (in Hegel's example, the mass or weight) was the key defining factor, specifying the thing on its own account. All that we can anticipate in the combination is that the figures for the second, inherent, quality can be added together; the superficial figures are not so definitive that they continue to hold. As a result, the ratio or measurement that specifies the combined product cannot be calculated in advance on the basis of figures derived from the two original entities, but must be ascertained through a new measurement.[7]

The variability that occurs in the exponent when things are combined means that the new measurement is significant. It specifies or determines the original thing in a new way. The initial ratio or exponent only considered what it was on its own. To distinguish this thing from others we need to take into account as well what happens when it is combined with them. So for a more accurate measurement, we measure the thing on its own, independently measure the combined product, and then relate the two measurements. This second-order ratio defines the qualitative character of the original thing more precisely than the first order ratio could do; for it spells out what it is in relation.

In summary, Hegel has been showing how a comparison between measurements is logically required in that the numbers used in the original measurement were abstract and external. The numbers were indefinite because they were not inherent. They become useful for defining, not when they are taken on their own, but when they are related in proportions or ratios; this precision is increased when we can establish ratios of ratios, incorporating reference to other things. This increasing complexity is how we overcome the arbitrariness of numbers.[8] In other words, a single set of numbers is not enough to specify precisely what a thing is. One needs to move to relations between sets.

5

Measuring Involves Series of Measured Ratios

1 / Even the refined definition of what it means to measure real things turns out to be inadequate. Spelling it out in detail exposes indeterminate moments that need to be resolved. So Hegel moves on to a more complicated logical analysis.[1]

He starts by recalling a discussion that took place much earlier in the *Logic* when discussing the concept 'something.' There one thing was distinguished from another, not by some quantifiable measurement, but simply by its quality. When a quality changed, the thing became something else. Within that analysis, were two things to be combined so that the combination manifested a third quality, both the originals would be dissolved or cancelled; they remain only notionally in the combined entity.

This reminder is used to offer a contrast with the current stage in the logical development.[2] Because the numbers used in measuring are abstract and indifferent to their context, they are not affected by any change in the thing, in the way a simple quality is. The original measurement remains, and (as we have seen) can be combined with another measurement to produce a second-order ratio. This latter proportion uses the measurement of the original thing as denominator and the measurement of the product of its combination with something else as its numerator.

The original measurement was to specify the qualitative nature of a thing; this second-order mode of measuring is just a more sophisticated way of specifying that same quality. The latter remains unaffected by the variation in numbers and continues to be the focus, despite the changes that take place when the thing is combined with something else. The initial quality determines not only the measure generated by the neutral product but also the second-order ratio that combines the two first-order ones. But this means in turn that the second-order ratio is just as abstract, external, and indifferent to the quality as the first order one was. Since the thing remains in some sense independent of its measurement, it could combine just as easily with things other than the one originally considered.

Entertaining such possibilities is an inevitable and legitimate move for thought once it realizes that a particular kind of measuring is in some sense arbitrary and incomplete. Because the initial combination is not exhaustive and final, we see that a full specification of the initial thing can be achieved only by thinking through what happens in *all* possible combinations that the original thing is involved in.[3]

2 / There is no way to know when we have exhausted all of these possibilities. Instead we have a number of combinations, each of which specifies the original thing further by means of a second-order ratio. In other words, the thing is uniquely defined by a diversity of such ratios.[4] Each of these ratios is the product of a comparison. That comparison has not been introduced from the outside by an arbitrary act of reflection. It is intrinsic, for an independent entity has actually combined with a number of other entities to generate neutral products. Neutralization is, so to speak, the way an independent thing *compares itself* with its counterparts in reality. Only by making the comparison intrinsic in this way can the measuring hope to specify the initial quality as it really is.[5]

The quality of something, then, is measured by the set of diverse numbers that are the exponents of a range of second-order ratios. The thing being measured is the common element that unites all these figures into a single perspective. Since each number specifies only a part of what its specific quality is, a complete measurement would require an exhaustive collection of all possible ratios of this sort.

Even now, however, we cannot be certain that we have uniquely specified the independent thing. That can only be achieved by setting it beside another thing, which generates a different range of exponents when it is combined with the same set of opposite entities. The different numbers that emerge would show how the two things are distinct. By comparing the two sets of exponents we might then capture what is qualitatively unique about each.

The trouble is that the two sets of numbers are not really comparable. In the first case, the second-order exponent is derived by taking the first-order ratio of the original thing as the denominator (or basic unit), and then calculating the comparable figure for the neutralized product (which becomes the numerator). In the second case, however, we are using a different denominator: the first-order ratio that characterizes the *second* thing. So the exponents that result for its second-order ratios share nothing in common with those that emerge in the first case. The two sets are simply different, in a quite indeterminate way. To be sure, we have a diverse set of numbers, but the numbers measure apples and oranges and cannot legitimately be put on the same plane. To establish a clear relationship between the two things we need something common that is single and self-contained.

Any basis for comparison needs to reflect the specific nature of both things being compared. Yet all that we have to go on are the particular measurements we already have. We are not justified in calling to our aid any other, as yet unspecified, quality or characteristic. So we must think back over the path we have taken to see if there is anything they share.

In fact, each of them has been combined with the same set of opposite entities. So, if we can establish a fixed order within this set so that the exponents are listed in a determinate sequence, then we shall have the basis for a viable comparison. Once the exponents are set out in order in this way, they cease to be a diverse mixture and become a constant series.[6] Then, by measuring the relation between any two members of the series, we can generate third-order ratios for each the two things to be compared, and use these figures to compare them.

This way of comparing is different from the one that developed earlier. There two things were combined into a neutral product. That was not possible once we moved to ratios of a second order, for now we have two entities that are not only independent, but share nothing in common other than the fact that they combine with the same kinds of things. They are indifferent to each other; each one generates its own set of exponents. Only because these exponents are derived from a shared range of opposites, can they be arranged in an order that is common to both. Since this ordered series makes comparison possible, it has to be the unit, the denominator so to speak, of the third-order ratios, while the numerators are the intervals between the items in the series.

We can barely breathe a sigh of relief from settling that difficulty, before we are confronted with another: what about all those other things that entered into the neutral combinations in the first place? As yet, they have not been specified at all. The comparison just achieved depended on two factors: (a) the two things were indifferent to each other and so could not combine into a neutral product, and (b) they combined with the same set of opposites. In contrast, these opposites are neither indifferent to the original things; nor do they share the same possibilities of combination. As well, there is no reason to limit the number of neutral combinations into which they can enter to the two already mentioned. In other words, when they are measured, each one of those opposites has a first-order ratio, which can be taken as the basic unit (or denominator) for determining a set of second-order ratios (derived from its interaction with a group of things that includes our original two). Then, once again, these ratios can be ordered into a series that enables this set of opposites to be compared amongst themselves at the third level.

Once again the picture is getting complicated. For now there are two intersecting series that involve three orders of ratios. At the most basic level is the ratio of a single entity by which an abstract quality is used to measure what it is within itself. (Our example was specific gravity.) This basic entity is then combined with something else, which has its own specific measurement. So at the second level there is the ratio between the measurement for the original entity (as denominator) and the measurement for the neutral product (as numerator). This second level expands into an ordered series of exponents that reflect different possibilities of neutral combination. The ordered series becomes a constant, used for comparing things that are (a) indifferent to each other, yet (b) combine with the same set of opposites. Finally there is a contrary range of things – the opposites – which have among themselves a standard of comparison based on the way they combine with the first group. In the middle of this network are a number of basic ratios for neutral combinations that serve two functions: they act as numerator *both* for the second-order exponents of the original side *and* for the second-order exponents of the opposite side.[7]

Both sides are a series of entities or units. In the total picture, each member of each series serves three different functions, which taken together help us measure what it is specifically. First, we want to determine what it is in itself, so we take it as the basic unit and relate it to the comparable figures for all its neutral combinations with things on the other side. Second, it helps to generate the exponent when the figure on the other side is taken as basic. Third, it can be used to situate itself within an ordered series that the other side can use for the sake of comparing its various members with each other. In this latter case, its relations with other members of its own side provide the numerator for a third-order ratio. The result is that we do not have a simple plurality, but two complementary series that intersect with each other.[8]

This increasing complexity in the kind of measurement evolves because at each stage measuring has been bedevilled by contingency. Its particular limitation suggests other, unexplored, possibilities: combinations with other entities, other things susceptible to the same set of combinations, and so on. There is something arbitrary about just this number or just this comparison. In each case thought takes into account what is missing and suggests a way of overcoming the problem, so that it builds on what has already been achieved.

There is another kind of inadequacy, however: the simple can become lost in the complex. Our original purpose was to specify the basic quality of something. The indefinite was to be rendered definite. But the complexity that has led us to third-order ratios has not dispersed the imprecision, but only made it more acute. To escape such a lack of precision we moved to measuring things rather than mere aspects in the first place. Now that we have two series of things facing each other, we have a similar problem. For each thing has an indefinite range of possible combinations with members of both the opposite series and its own.

So we come to one of the more difficult moments in Hegel's logical analysis, where we move from one type of measuring to a different type altogether. The examples we have been using are not just expanded and elaborated, but are replaced by other, quite different, examples. Like the moves from a simple ruler to velocity and from velocity to specific gravity, this move cannot be represented, only conceived. For thought must work through the limitations of the previous mode of measuring and identify what characteristics its replacement requires. Representation is impotent when faced with such a challenge; only thought is plastic enough to undergo such a metamorphosis.[9]

3 / The moves so far in our analysis have been gradual and incremental. Now, however, Hegel suggests that things turn upside down. Thought reflects on what has so far been worked out and discovers that it is quite different from what we were trying to achieve. The complex of intersecting series has failed to satisfy our aim of measuring the quality of a particular thing. So we review the progress thus far to see if we can find the potential for a new beginning.

Hegel prepares the way for this inversion by recalling an earlier discussion in his chapter 'Quanta.' Whenever one wants to figure out a degree of intensity, one does so only by considering some other degrees as well which, together with the first, make up a range of numbers.[10] Here, in a similar way, to specify precisely the initial measurement of something, we have had to take into account a whole series of numbers that express ratios. We have moved from considering something on its own, to considering it in relation.

In both cases, however, the meaning of the original concept is affected, and has turned into the opposite of what was intended. There, degree (which started out representing *intensive* magnitude) was converted into a set of numbers that expressed *extensive* magnitude. Here in measuring we started out using numbers to characterize an unmediated and obvious relationship between two qualities of a thing. As immediate, it was a matter of indifference whether we looked at anything else; the numbers should serve on their own. However, the numbers were not able to specify what the qualitative relationship really was, since any quality distinguishes something from something else, and numbers are purely abstract. So if we wanted to specify our original measurement, we had to relate it to appropriate measurements derived elsewhere. These different measurements would help us distinguish the basic quality. What happened as a result was that measuring the simple quality of a thing produced an increasingly complex series of numbers, involving reference to a wide range of other things – first, those kinds of things it can combine with; second, those it is indifferent to but with which it shares the same possibilities of combination; and third, the ordered series of both sets of things. As in the discussion of degree we started out with something simple, but ended up with a whole range of numbers that together are supposed to spell out precisely what that simplicity is.

The difference from the discussion of degree, however, lies in the fact that the original simple measurement does not just dissolve into complexity. It has continued to be significant, since it still serves as a denominator in a second-order ratio, and so, incorporated into the exponent of that ratio, becomes a determining factor in the third-order ratios as well. It plays a role throughout the network of numerical relations. The original number is not cancelled but reaffirmed.[11]

Recall that the original immediate measurement was of the inherent qualitative character of the thing, measured against a superficial unit. The reaffirmation of its significance is a recognition that the quality measured in this way is not something transient and unimportant, but rather a critical feature of the whole operation. That quality not only makes the thing into something on its own account, but also distances it from everything else. It is something exclusive.

Only by taking into account this exclusive nature of the thing's basic quality are we able to use the whole series of exponents (by which we compare one thing with another) to specify precisely how each thing is distinguised from the others. The difference between them is not simply quantitative, but qualitative. Because of this original quality the thing prefers some combinations to others.

This insight is derived, not from any despair about the abstract nature of numbers, but from the need to retain the initial measurement throughout the whole process. Only by recognizing how important it is to the whole logical analysis, do we discover its real significance. Within the complexity of the complementary series of exponents, this number acquires a unique, defining status, distinguishing this thing from all of the others.

So we are not thereby turning our back on the quantitative. We have come to this insight by doing full justice to the quantitative character of measuring. In the first place, the original independent entity was combined with a plurality – an indefinite number – of things that were qualitatively different; it did not really matter with which one of that plurality it was combined, or whether, indeed, it was combined with any. This appeal to a range of indifferent quantitative possibilities was essential for getting at the distinctive character of the thing to be measured.

In the second place, however, the original quality being measured was something specific and exclusive. Its distinctive character was not totally indifferent to whatever it came in contact with, but distinguished between those things it could, and those things it could not, combine with – between the first objects of comparison and the second. Out of the whole numerical range of possible combinations it has preferences.

This means, however, that one combination rules out others, and indeed can cancel a neutralization that has already occurred in favour of one more appropriate to its specific character. The measurement of any such preferred combination would be more definitive of a specific quality than simply listing the total range of possible ratios.

Out of the indefinite plurality of three orders of ratios, there has now emerged one actual combination that excludes the others. One out of a number of options has been 'selected' or 'chosen.' So the original thing does not simply have an affinity for a set of things on the other side; it 'elects' some things over others. 'Elective affinity,' an expression current in the chemistry of Hegel's day, captures the kind of measuring we are now interested in.

6

Elective Affinity

The concept of elective affinity, of preferring one combination to another, can be applied to spheres other than chemistry. Hegel pointed out that the same kind of measured relation occurs in harmonics: a tone can be both basic (or dominant) and secondary (or harmonic); but once a harmony has been established, it is exclusive. So the concept is flexible and can be used in different contexts.[1] Any of the applications we use in our more relaxed moments, however, are secondary; they are not part of its logical meaning.

Nonetheless the concept of chemical object does provide an appropriate reference for this section. As we shall see when we come to discuss 'Chemism' (from the third book of the *Logic*), a chemical object is not immediately indifferent to its surroundings in the way a mechanical one is; nor is it self-contained like an organism. Rather, an object is called 'chemical' when it inherently refers to something else; it *is* the capacity to combine with another for which it has a preference.[2]

Elective affinity can be discussed in the chapter on 'Real Measure' because a chemical reaction is not simply qualitative; it can be measured. In addition, the opposite member in any combination is not a simple entity, but one from a set of alternatives. So, on the one hand, it is a matter of indifference which one is actually neutralized; on the other, once that combination has been effected, it excludes others that are less preferred. This whole network of meanings is included in 'elective affinity': the term refers to a measured ratio that is one out of an indifferent range, yet excludes the others of that range.[3]

Earlier we noted that simple affinity closely associated a qualitative aspect with a quantitative one. The particular quality of an entity was defined by the neutral combinations it made with members of an opposite series of things. Those members were differentiated from each other not by anything qualitative but by the specific quantity of each that was required for a complete combination. All those numbers made up a totality that measured the quality of the original thing.[4]

When affinity becomes exclusive – as in elective affinity – the measurement in question is no longer merely quantitatively different from other combinations. It has become qualitative and distinctive. In addition to the simple differences in extensive magnitude that distinguish the various combinations, something else is added. The original entity selects from among the members of its opposite series. The pure indifference of quantity has fallen away. The exclusive nature of the resulting connection is measured, not as an extensive magnitude, but as an intensive one. Our initial thing unites *more strongly* with one of its opposites than with another.[5] The measure used for the degree of intensity is the ratio that generates this particular combination. In other words, the same exponent serves for both the intensive and the extensive measurement.

Unfortunately the fact that we can shift from one way of reading the measurement to another does not help us with the task of articulating the exclusive *quality* of the combination. As far as the simple numbers are concerned, it is a matter of complete indifference whether there is only one neutral product, or whether our original entity combines in appropriate proportions with a bunch of other things as well. The figure is the same in both cases and, so, does not distinguish between them.

We cannot rest content with the measurement's ambiguity, however. Since the measuring is to determine what is qualitatively distinct, the exponent that results from the act of measuring is supposed to be exclusive. The number is not just one out of a series; for the intensive relation of more and less has become the basis for rejecting other options. The preference for one combination over others is a function of something more than just quantitative magnitude. It reflects the particular components that make up the compound.

There is, however, another side to this kind of measuring. Each of the components that enters into the exclusive compound has, in addition, the character of being something indifferent and somewhat independent. It could combine with several other things; with each of them it would establish a specific and determinate proportion. These, however, have been rejected. Only when this possibility of other combinations is present is the elective affinity understood to be exclusive. So the full meaning of the concept involves switching back and forth from the intensity of this particular combination to the indifferent possibility of alternative combinations, each of which has its own level in a range of preference. Each ratio is simply one in a range of quantities on the one hand; but on the other it measures a specific and exclusive combination of components.

Measuring elective affinity has turned out to be a rather complex concept. When focusing on the quantitative result, we realize that it is not enough and we have to shift to the qualitative, exclusive aspect, which distinguishes this combination from other possible ones. When we pay attention to the latter moment, we recognize that it, too, is not the total picture, since the thing being measured combines with these others in definite proportions, which are only quantitatively distinct from the measurement in question. The quantitative and the qualitative moments in the meaning of this concept shift back and forth.

In this alternation, some of the secondary combinations could turn out to be, not indifferent options, but other exclusive and qualitative neutralizations with their own degree of preference. So elective affinity involves a ratio that shifts from being a simple quantity to measuring a qualitatively distinct combination, and back again. To resolve this internal tension in its meaning we need to look at the specific nature of each such measurement.[6]

7

The Nodal Line

We have been working through the logic of measuring. The more adequate kind of measurement does not apply an external standard, but uses a superficial feature of a thing to measure something intrinsic; the two are combined in a ratio, where the first is taken as the unit, or denominator, and the other is counted out to establish the numerator. We have looked at several ways in which such measurements need to be refined if they are to capture the specific quality of the thing; the most recent was the ratio that measures the specific combination that it prefers over other possibilities – what we have called elective affinity. We now look more closely at that particular ratio and the function it plays.[1]

This exclusive ratio does not measure the relation this combination has to other combinations but, rather, the relation between the two things combined. The neutral product is not some indeterminate kind of integration, but one that, in being exclusive, is made up of just these components.[2]

Hence the particular unity that constitutes an elective affinity is something on its own account; we need not refer to any other combination. This means, however, that there is no ground or reason for its distinctive characteristic. The exclusive nature of this compound is simply a given, determined by the particular qualitative entities that enter into it. So we measure elective affinity by measuring the particular amount of each of these elements.[3]

But reflection opens up the possibility that those two elements could combine in other proportions. Since, as a simple given, we could not justify the uniqueness of the original neutralization, we have no reason to exclude such considerations.

For, when we consider the quantitative aspect of the measurement, we note that there is a simple numerical relation; this proportion can vary along a continuum: as the numbers change, other combinations could emerge. When we consider how these ratios are related to each other, the comparison is not as arbitrary as it was when we were comparing combinations of different entities; all of these fractions are derived from the same two elements.

However, each of the elements has its own independent life, amenable to entering into all kinds of other compounds. The exclusive compound, then, could be broken up into its components that could then be recombined in other proportions. There is nothing to prevent one ratio from being replaced by another.[4]

The measurement of the ratio for any specific elective affinity, based as it is on the qualities of its components, is not as exclusive as it was at first made out to be. For it is indifferent to the possibility of other combinations of the same elements. Both as a simple quantity, and as defined by these basic components, it is indeed amenable to such a change.

The neutral combination, then, can be distinguished from the numbers used to measure it. The latter aspect reflects the quantitative character of the measurement; the former, as the relation of two elements, is qualitative, a foundation that persists. In contrast to the formal status of numbers, it is a material being. Indeed, the same material being continues as the proportions vary. Any distinctive quality or neutralization that emerges from a certain proportion is measured by those numbers from the continuum that specifically apply to it.

For all that the measurement of an exclusive compound specifies something on its own account, it does not rule out the possibility of other combinations of those same elements. Indeed, by sharpening the distinction between the quantitative measuring and the qualitative measured, the numbers now emerge as in some sense arbitrary. So we could entertain the possibility of other ratios, some of which also measure saturated, or neutral, compounds of the same two elements. Each exponent of these ratios will specify the inherent nature of a neutral compound; yet because those numbers are equally arbitrary, they also leave open the possibility of further saturated compounds of the same basic elements.

The set of affinities we generate in this way are quite different from the earlier set. There we had two, qualitatively distinct series; an independent entity from one could be combined with a whole range of possible alternatives on the other side, while preferring some to others. In this case the various affinities emerge from one and the same basic substratum, using the same basic elements, albeit in varying proportions. Since any particular saturation is exclusive, its measurement separates itself from all other possible ratios of these things, even though some of those proportions will activate qualitatively distinct neutral compounds, which can also be measured. In the continuous quantitative series, measurements of actual neutralizations alternate with ratios that are only numerically different.

What we have, then, is a scale of more and less that is not a simple sequence, but a line of nodes. The appropriate image would be a string with a series of knots tied in it – the knots being the proportions that generate neutral compounds and, so, measure something real; the string is the continuum of ratios.[5]

Let us review where we are. We have a proportion that can be measured – a proportion between real things that have themselves combined into a neutral entity, qualitatively distinct from anything else. This measurement is self-contained; but it is at the same time nothing but a proportion between two numbers. So it is in some sense external to what is being measured and amenable to having the precise quantities of the basic materials altered. Within a range, a change in proportion should not really affect the nature of the initial compound. The extra amount of one or the other element is simply irrelevant. But there comes a point at which the simple change in quantity turns into a change in quality. The new proportion generates a new species of compound, distinguished qualitatively from the one that went before. Something new, with its own distinctive determination, has emerged, and the proportion it represents is no longer an arbitrary set of numbers that is varying from a base, but an actual measurement, specifying a distinctive quality. A new determinate ratio has replaced the earlier one.

The two are related, nonetheless. The first one was the basis for setting up the second, partly in that the two compounds have the same elements, and partly because they stand on a single quantitative continuum. At the same time a critical difference has intervened. The qualitative characteristics of the new compound entity bear no relation to those of the original one. They are simply indifferent to each other. This difference in quality, despite the quantitative continuum, reflects the way numbers are external to the things they measure; at the same time, we cannot explain it by appealing to a different content, as we could when talking of elective affinity.

In other words, the second compound, as qualitatively new, cannot be derived from what went before; it simply pops up, unmediated. Were we to attempt an explanation, we could only say that it was implicit in the gradual movement towards the new integrated compound. But this would say nothing more than that it in fact occurred when the numbers changed.

Rather than being an explanation, such a statement is nothing more than a tautology.

Lacking any satisfactory justification, any new qualitative compound is subject to the same logical analysis that the earlier one went through, so the whole process can be extended indefinitely.[6]

We need to analyse this way of measuring more closely. The transformation from one quality to another happens through a steady, continuous change of quantity. Altering the ratios towards a point of qualitative shift is, when considered quantitatively, simply introducing a difference of more or less – a gradual change. Yet it is only what is superficial in the alteration, not what is qualitative, that is gradual. A quantitative ratio that is infinitely close to the one that precedes is nonetheless qualitatively distinct from it; for another entity altogether emerges.

Looking at the process from the qualitative rather than the quantitative side, the gradual progress that is supposed to have no inherent limit is radically broken. This break is not relative to anything that has gone before; it is absolute. The new quality comes into being on the basis of a purely quantitative (and so indifferent) change; it is simply indeterminately other than the one that disappeared. Hence the qualities have no relation at all to each other; the qualitative change is a leap.

People try to explain the qualitative transformation conceptually by appealing to the gradual change. But really, a gradual alteration of a ratio is a matter of relative indifference. It is quite contrary to anything qualitative. Whether the two distinct neutral compounds are considered simply as states of affairs or as independent things, the concept of gradual change does nothing at all to help us understand the production of qualitative difference – the replacing of one thing by another. It specifies no limit that separates the one from the other.

Since there is no qualitative boundary the two share – at least to the extent that thought can anticipate it – they are simply external to each other. So we are far removed from even a minimal account that would enable us to understand the relation. From this perspective no explanation is possible. We cannot conceive what is involved; it is immeasurable.[7]

8

What Cannot Be Measured

Hegel starts this section with a review of the present stage of the argument.[1] The measurement of an exclusive combination, or elective affinity, can be considered on its own account; it has been established as self-contained. Nonetheless, being quantitative, it is still affected by the external and the indifferent; it is susceptible to increases and decreases on a scale of changing ratios. At some point in the course of gradual change, a quality that has been specified by one such ratio is transformed into something qualitatively different – a leap that, paradoxically, cannot be measured or explained. A minor variation in quantity condemns a measured quality to extinction. In other words, magnitude is that characteristic by which, for all that a thing appears to be fixed and invulnerable, it can yet be attacked and indeed destroyed. Paradoxically enough, not only the thing is destroyed, but also the possibility of measuring in quantitative terms. For there is no way of quantifying the qualitative metamorphosis.

What has emerged in this analysis is the concept of what cannot be measured or explained – the measureless. Let us examine this term more closely.

When considered on its own, apart from any context, 'measureless' suggests that any use of quantity is meaningless: to use numbers would introduce a determination that is quite incapable of specifying the thing. But in the context of the nodal line, this indifferent determination of quantity is, at the same time, something that specifies. The transformation of one quality into another is defined as immeasurable, even though it takes place at a certain point in the continuum. In other words, the abstract term 'measureless' has been converted into a way of describing what has happened qualitatively. One measuring ratio slips over into another, new one. The qualitative transformation is something measureless, even though the point of change can be specified as a particular ratio. So we have a concept that names the transformation of specific existing entities into others that are equally specific and distinct. But the two terms of this transformation are described by ratios that remain strictly quantitative, close neighbours on a continuum, and so are useless to explain what has happened in the move from one quality to the other.

The measureless aspect extends even further, since we need not stop with one qualitative transformation. Because this one lacks an explanation, there is no limit that restricts what other kinds of transformations are possible, and how many. So the process could continue into a measureless infinity.

When we reflect on the *pattern* of this on-going process (rather than on the range of its extension), we find a double movement. Varying the quantity destroys a particular quality, together with the ratio that measures it; and the new quality disrupts and controverts the continuity whereby quantities gradually change. The endless repetition of this process involves moving back and forth in a kind of circle, where each aspect – qualitative and quantitative – cancels the other, only to be cancelled in turn by that other. Such a conceptual pattern is also infinite. This time, however, we do not have an indefinitely extended line, but a self-contained circular movement that continues without reference to anything else.[2]

This is the third time Hegel has discussed infinity in the course of the *Logic*. The first time was qualitative infinity, in which a finite thing is defined by its limit and the infinite is what lies beyond the limit. Thought simply moves over from the first to the second, and the former disappears when the latter emerges. In other words, in coming to terms with its own limit, the finite changes into the infinite.

The second time was quantitative infinity as a way of defining number;[3] here infinity names a continuum that can always stretch further. In this second case, the beyond is already inherent in the way a finite number functions: any quantum points beyond itself.

In the measureless infinity, there is a bit of both; each of the earlier kinds of infinity cancels, and goes beyond, its opposite. The qualitative disappearance into what is simply beyond disrupts the quantitative continuum, whereas the quantitative continuum suggests that the qualitatively other is not really a beyond. The concept of the measureless infinite puts the qualitative infinite in a dynamic tension with the quantitative and vice versa.

When Hegel started out discussing measure, he was using a very general and imprecise concept. A quantity was used to specify a quality. Quantity and quality were both unmediated concepts – neither one reflectively defined. That original simple immediacy has now been dissolved, and we have a thoroughly worked out definition of the way quantity and quality interact in a process of measuring.

Except we no longer have a process of measuring. We are instead thinking of a network of meanings in which, rather than specifying each other, quantity and quality cancel each other at the very point where they are to define what is critical and distinctive. We must collect this network of meanings, which makes up the concept of the measureless, into a synthesis and consider it all together. By reflecting on the whole picture, we can determine the basic principles involved and can get at the ground or reason for the apparent contradiction.[4]

Within the concept of the measureless as it has now developed, one quality passes over into another even though the only quantitative change is a minor alteration in the determinate magnitude. Since the substratum being measured remains fundamentally the same, the qualitative change is something external and rather indifferent; it does not fundamentally alter the basic reality. So the change collapses the different qualities into a single description of a single thing. Similarly, the quantitative variation along a continuum is not a matter of indifference, but makes a qualitative difference, altering the determinate character of the underlying reality that is being measured.

Quantity, which started out being indifferent, becomes determining; and quality, which defines and determines, becomes something indifferent. This inversion of the principles of measurement takes place because both shifts, from determining to indifferent, and from indifferent to determining, presuppose a continuing unity – a persistent substratum in which the same components continue to function.[5]

We have, then, a single unity that persists through all the minor changes in quantity and all the transformations of quality. The two interacting moments are 'measuring' something that maintains itself through all the shifting – a continuing persistence. It is what Aristotle would have called independent matter; in more contemporary language, we could describe it as the 'real' thing. We now need to work out the logic of this new term.

There are three aspects to what we are now considering. In the first place, the 'real' thing is one and the same reality that not only underlies all the different qualities that emerge, but also is qualitatively determined by minor quantitative adjustments. When Hegel made the logical move from quality to quantity, he began to draw a distinction between what a thing is and how it is determined. With regard to a thing's basic being, magnitude is a matter of indifference. In the discussion of measure, in which quantity was used to specify a quality, we referred to something real that was being measured. In due course we had to talk of a persisting substratum that allowed for variations in proportion. All of this anticipates in an imprecise way the fully fleshed out definition we now have, in which the qualities that are to determine are indifferent, and the quantities that are indifferent nonetheless determine. Quantity and quality are now no longer contraries, but are integrated within a single concept. Their differences are complementary aspects of a single infinite reality.

This leads us into the second aspect of this new concept. The fact that the 'real' thing remains the same is not a mere assumption. It is required and established by the fact that each independent qualitative state emerges only from a quantitative variation. Those qualitative transformations require this basic unity, for it alone can explain why a simple change in ratio specifies a new distinctive quality and why a transformation in quality does not represent a change in being. This kind of measureless shift implies that a substratum continues through all of the various differences.

Finally, and in the third place, we can now understand how, in the infinite regress of the series of proportions, one quality continues through a quantitative alteration and is indifferent to it, yet at some point undergoes its own demise and is transformed into another quality. And we can understand as well how a continuous change in quantity can nonetheless result in quite distinct qualities. It is because of this underlying 'real' thing that the gradual quantitative move from one number to another along a continuum is disrupted when a new measured ratio produces a different kind of quality. At the same time this basic matter undergirds the qualitative transition into something quite different when there has been only a minor change in quantitative ratio. The measureless qualitative transformations in the nodal line, in which both the indifference of quantity and the determining power of quality are cancelled, is grounded in this underlying basic unity.

So we have the underlying unity, we have the way in which it is logically required by the surface transformation of qualities, and we have the way it logically supports the process by which a gradual quantitative alteration introduces a qualitative break, while a qualitative difference reflects only a minor quantitative change. The concept of the 'real' thing incoporates all of these moments within a single, complex meaning.[6]

Using comparison to clarify the stage we have reached, Hegel refers back to the point where one series of measured ratios stood opposite another series, so that the combination of a member from one side with one from the other would result in a neutral product. There the original things as well as their product were thought as independent and self-contained things – totalities indifferent to each other. Each of these things generated an exclusive measured ratio. In contrast, the new sense of measuring takes the ratios to be nothing but modes of the same substratum. Those measurements do not now define something as qualitatively distinct, but only spell out a particular state the 'real' thing has assumed. Alteration, which previously involved becoming something completely other, has now become only a change of state; and what passes over from one quality to another nonetheless remains identical throughout the process. Qualitative transformations within a quantitative continuum specify, or 'measure,' the distinctive character of an underlying substratum: what we have called the 'real' thing.

9

A Systematic Review

Hegel concludes the chapter 'Real Measure' with a brief review of the whole section on measure.[1] Discussing it offers an opportunity to reflect on the logical process he has followed and discern something of its systematic character.

Measuring uses a quantity to specify a quality. That definition sets the logical task. All of the complications that ensue throughout the chapter stem ultimately from trying to meet that standard.

Through them all, however, there is a basic pattern. First, an attempt to spell out what measuring means, using the resources so far available, turns out to be incomplete: a quantity does not completely specify, for possibilities emerge that have not been satisfactorily covered. Exploring these possibilities then leads to such problems and complexities that thought has to call a halt and reconsider. So it reflects on all the diversity that has emerged in light of the primary purposes of measuring. Such reflection identifies an essential core that becomes the basis of a new form of measurement. The pattern then recurs, but at a more sophisticated level.

Here we have the interplay of understanding, dialectical and speculative reason to which I referred in the first chapter. Now we can begin to see how it works in practice.

At the most basic level, measuring is understood as simply applying a quantity to a quality. When this fails to specify anything, some standard is required. This dialectical shift turns out to be unsatisfactory, however, for any rule is arbitrary. So speculative reflection attempts to overcome the problem by using one quantified quality, such as time, to measure another, such as space. In the ratios that result, it does not matter which units one uses, as long as they are used consistently.

Even measurement by ratios is affected by contingency. To remedy this the two quantified qualities need to be integrated so that both are aspects of the same thing. This qualitative bond justifies using one to measure another. In this way understanding spells out what is required to integrate the various moments speculative reflection has brought together and leads us into the discussion of real measure.

Understanding soon identifies the imprecisions of such a measurement, since it does not discriminate effectively between things. So we are led into a whole series of dialectical possibilities, which become ever more complex until speculative reason calls a halt and reflects on the total picture. Since at this stage the whole purpose of measuring is to specify the distinguishing quality of a real thing, thought should be interested, not in a diverse range of possible comparisons, but in those which the original thing really prefers: its elective affinity.

Yet, subjected to understanding's critical analysis, this achievement of speculative reason turns out to be unsatisfactory as well. Even though a thing might prefer to combine with a specific other, it can do so in a number of ratios, and there are no reasons why some of those ratios might not produce something qualitatively different from the original compound. So the nodal line develops dialectical complications, in that subtle variations in quantitative ratios generate qualitative leaps. Speculative reflection on this produces the conception of the measureless, which can only be integrated by considering the various moments of quantitative and qualitative change to be changing features of a single, underlying 'real' thing.[2]

When we reflect on the total pathway followed by logical thought in working out the concept of measure, we find that it, too, has gone through a kind of dialectic. What started out as measure has ended up with the measureless; using ratios to measure reals has resulted in a 'real' that cannot be measured at all. These paradoxes too need to be explored reflectively; and so thought is led to the distinction between being's superficial show and what is essential: the initial stages of the *Logic*'s second book on *The Doctrine of Essence*.

Were we to approach this discussion relying on representation and refer to Hegel's examples of specific weight, chemical affinity, and harmonics to make sense of it, we should find it difficult, if not impossible, to see any systematic 'argument' leading from one stage to the next. Conceptual thought, however, concentrates on the logical principles involved. From the type of reflection that scientists use to explore new and different forms of measuring, it teases out the reasoning that is its core, and sets aside the concrete instances. In this way it discovers an implicit rationale that all too often is overlooked because our attention is cluttered by the application.

Scientific reflection is inherently logical, says Hegel; it has its own systematic character. When exploring undeveloped possibilities, when becoming dissatisfied with a diverse multiplicity, when integrating a set of mutual implications with rigorous precision, thought is following its own self-imposed path. So scientific advances are not simply the result of new experiences. They are more likely to stem from the demands of strict conceptual thinking.

Few people are adept at abstracting from all representations to focus on the pure logical principles that underlie the scientific development of measurements. Because of this, not only has the philosophy of science become positivist – regarding scientific 'progress' as a matter of given, irrational leaps; but the systematic nature of Hegel's logical analysis has been missed as well. And those general features that apply to all measuring whatsoever have not been identified.

For the logic is more general than any particular application. The discussion of real measure, for example, is not restricted in its application to physics or chemistry but refers as well to the social sciences, which measure human phenomena by means of statistics. More important for our purposes, though, is the fact that 'measuring' can be used to describe a particular way of talking about thought itself.[3] For each move in the logical development of this chapter happens because the analysis achieved is measured against the basic purpose of 'measuring' and found wanting. So, for example, a simple ratio (between volume and weight) does *not* specify a thing with reference to other things; and the leap from quality to quality in the nodal line is measured only superficially by the quantitative progression. In other words the concept of measuring is being used to measure its own definitions.

Yet just as measuring falls prey to an unmeasurable shift in quality, so too the concept of measuring collapses, and is replaced by the concept of the 'real' thing, the substrate underlying the dynamic of qualitative change. At this point conceptual patterns more appropriate to Spinoza's philosophy of substance and mode or Kant's unity of apperception come into play.[4] So a careful logical analysis uncovers more intricate connections between concepts than we are wont to suspect. And the logic has led us into worlds that had seemed far removed from the simple task of measuring.

10

From 1812 to 1831

If any part of Hegel's system is to be immune to the ravages of time it should be the *Science of Logic*. Pure thought abstracts from the contingencies of experience and works out its dialectic in the a priori realm of rational concepts. Yet on comparing the revised edition of the chapter on real measure, just expounded, with the first edition of 1812, we find that Hegel had made extensive revisions that range from editorial adjustments to rewriting whole sections and radically altering the order of concepts.

In part this may have stemmed from Hegel's sense that the logical analysis was too difficult and convoluted. In 1831 he confessed that 'the development of measure that is attempted in the following is some of the most difficult material.'[1] Since the concrete forms of measuring belong to particular sciences, the logic works only with the abstract application of quantity to quality. Leaving aside the concrete examples that are so inextricably tied up with this concept in our imagination makes it hard to grasp what is going on.

Indeed, it must have been the intrinsic difficulty of this set of logical concepts that led Hegel to omit the discussion of real measure entirely from the various editions of the *Encyclopaedia*.[2] In 1830, for example, he moved directly from specific quantity and the use of a rule or standard (§108) to the measureless (§109). Apparently the digested version of the *Logic* that he used for his lectures did not need to go into the detail of his more theoretical work.

We shall see, however, that the concern to simplify will not explain all the changes that Hegel introduced. To be sure, he omitted whole paragraphs of the earlier text, and relied more extensively on illustrations from the natural sciences. But he also revised his use of terms to suggest that the earlier discussion was not logical enough, amending his use of 'neutralization' to describe the combination of entities, reworking his analysis of the nodal line, and radically transforming not only the location but also the significance of the 'real' thing, or *Sache selbst*. A review of such revisions will offer some clue to his systematic reasons for introducing them. Such a study should throw a different light on his project as a whole.[3]

For all the alterations, the basic sense of the argument was not affected. In both editions Hegel started with measuring a thing by means of an internal ratio; the same complications emerged from the need to compare; and the reaction to this complexity led to elective affinity, the nodal line, and the measureless. Apart from the emergence of the 'real' thing at the end, the categories and their order did not vary significantly.[4]

Hegel did change some of his titles. Originally 'Ratio of Independent Measurements' labelled not only the first three-part section (as in 1831) but also the chapter as a whole. Within this first section the first subsection was titled 'Neutrality' rather than 'Combination of Two Measures,' and the second was 'Specification of Neutrality' rather than the awkward 'Measure as a Series of Measured Ratios.' By 1831 neutralization is no longer used to describe the combinations used for comparison and is introduced only in a subsidiary way later on.[5]

This shift in focus required a complete rewriting of the first sub-section and a major revision of the second. These changes are of two sorts.

1 / In discussing the way something could be measured by an internal ratio, Hegel introduced in parentheses references to the way volume and weight are used to measure specific weight, and pointed out how volume was superficial and could be used as the unit measurement, while weight was substantive and could be counted. While in the first edition Hegel had suggested that he had specific weight in mind, in the second he specifically used this application to illustrate each stage in the argument.

In a similar way, the sub-section on elective affinity was rewritten to include a long paragraph that discussed how this concept applied not only in chemistry but also in musical harmonies. As these examples show, Hegel was more prepared to use representations in 1831 than in 1812.[6]

2 / In the second sub-section, an elaborate discussion of how 'determination' and 'constitution'[7] interact in measuring is replaced by a much simpler one, using 'something' and 'other.' Hegel could introduce this change because in 1831 he had already discussed the distinction between how a being is *determinate* in itself and how it is *constituted* by its being for another within the earlier section on 'finitude' where it was an implication of the relation between 'something' and 'other.'[8] So when Hegel came to the chapter 'Real Measure' he could dispense with the more complex terms

and simply refer to the logic of something. The latter language is much easier to grasp conceptually, yet maintains the comparison, not only with a set of opposites, but with others that share the same set of opposites. With this simplification Hegel could drop whole paragraphs from his text and reduce the length of the sub-section by a sixth.

In a similar vein, a difficult analysis towards the end of this sub-section, in which Hegel tried to show how, in the complex of opposing series, the qualitative passes over into the quantitative and vice versa, was scrapped entirely, to reappear in a much neater version in the section on the measureless. He was able to achieve the same results by referring in its place to an earlier discussion about how intensity and degree convert into extension and number, and by pointing out that here the direction is reversed.[9]

In these two ways – using more examples and simplifying the argument – Hegel strove to make the analysis more manageable. Two other changes later in the chapter, however, are not so straightforward.

3 / On first glance, his revisions to the first three paragraphs of 'Nodal Line' would appear to be another example of conceptual simplification. An obscure dialectical exploration of the quantitative and qualitative was abandoned. In its place Hegel made more explicit how an elective affinity, qualitatively defined by the preference two things have for each other, could be measured through their combination, where the components are moments related according to a single ratio. As we have seen, he had the determinate proportions that govern the chemical union of two elements in mind.

Already in 1812 the remark to this section cited the various products that could emerge from uniting nitrogen and oxygen: nitric and nitrous oxide to name two. In the interim, work on measuring the definite proportions according to which chemicals unite had advanced considerably.[10] In the second edition's new wording we see how those advances in chemistry had influenced Hegel's understanding of the logical argument. It offered a more effective way of moving from elective affinity to the measureless.

It was not that he now appealed to the chemical example to make his point, in the way he had used specific weight earlier. The illustrations remain in the remark, and the language remains abstract.[11] But by talking of moments of a combination and of measuring their ratio he described the procedures followed by chemistry in conceptual terms; and this made the logical analysis more effective than the earlier, more speculative discussion of the quantitative and qualitative. In other words, advances in science had made him aware of logical distinctions and possibilities for logical transitions not previously noticed. The greater precision opened the way to a neater systematic development.[12]

Once we start thinking about how developments in the sciences might have exposed new dimensions of systematic logical thought, we realize that there are other places in this chapter on real measure where scientific investigation has had its influence on the logical development. The use of ratios not only to measure specific weight but also to compare one specific weight with another would have been unthinkable, for example, before Archimedes found how to decide whether the tyrant's crown was solid gold or an amalgam with silver. The ordering of substances according to the way they unite with members of an opposite series could not have been detailed before Bergman had developed his tables of affinity in the eighteenth century. And even the name for the concept of elective affinity presupposed chemical experiments in which two salts, combined in a solution, exchanged radicals. For all that the *Logic* develops these concepts in abstract terms, its distinctions and transitions reflect insights that first emerged in the empirical sciences. So developments in chemistry open up logical possibilities that previously were not available to reflective thought.[13]

4 / We now turn to the most radical change Hegel made in this chapter. In the first edition of the *Science of Logic* of 1813, the concept, *Sache*, emerged well into the second book, *The Doctrine of Essence*. There the analysis of the logic of grounding or justifying led to the concept of something absolutely unconditioned, within which things relatively condition each other. This was the 'real' thing or heart of the matter – in German, *die Sache selbst*.[14]

Most editions of the *Science of Logic* combine the second edition of book one with the first edition of books two and three. So it appears that Hegel had two discussions of this concept. Yet when we look at the way in which Hegel reworked the order of the categories in the various editions of the *Encyclopaedia* between 1817 and 1830 we cannot be confident that he intended to leave *die Sache* in its original location when he came to revise the second book. For this term disappears completely in 1817, to reemerge in 1827, not in connection with 'ground,' but under the discussion of real possibility as a set of conditions leading to necessity.[15]

It was subsequent to publishing the third edition of the *Encyclopaedia* in 1830 that Hegel revised the *Science of Logic*. The 'real' thing, which had (in the *Encyclopaedia*) moved from 'Ground' to 'Necessity,' is transported back into the discussion of measure, a section that had been quite emasculated in the shorter version. Apparently, the reworking of this discussion in the longer text opened up a new place where *die Sache*, as underlying substrate, had a role to play. Hegel may have intended to return to it again in the *Doctrine of Essence*, but for the first time its initial appearance is in the *Doctrine of Being*.[16] So there is here a more radical reworking of the logical order than anything seen before.

The change in location of this category from the *Doctrine of Essence* to the end of the chapter on measure alters its sense. What, in the first edition, was a detailed and intricate network of meanings in which conditions ground and are grounded in a mutual dynamic, has become an indeterminate substratum, presupposed by, and explaining, the qualitative transformations that occur in a quantitative continuum. The 'real' thing is no longer the developed essence that emerges into existence, but rather an underlying being that only anticipates whatever might be meant by 'essence.'[17]

This major reworking of the order of the *Science of Logic* can be explained once we recall the changes already discussed in 'Nodal Line.' By making more explicit that the moments or components of the nodal line remain the same while their proportions vary, Hegel found that he was preparing the ground for a primitive sense of substratum. The concept 'substance' had to be reserved for later, when he came to the 'absolute' relations of substance, cause, and reciprocity. *Die Sache*, being more imprecise, satisfied the demands required by the logic at this point. In addition, it would expedite the transition from the logic of being to the logic of essence. It did not evoke the essential/inessential distinction, but was more immediate and indeterminate, closer to the sense of what simply is. So the persistence of the same components throughout the qualitative transformations of the nodal line allowed for the introduction of this term much earlier than Hegel had originally envisioned.

Hegel had then to rethink the logic of the measureless. Once again he could abandon the language of determination and constitution, for he no longer needed to have them reciprocally work on each other to produce a unity – a unity that could convert what start out as independent entities into states. Instead he could explore the way in which the quantitative infinite cancels and inverts the qualitative infinite and vice versa. The dialectic of quality and quantity, which had been removed both from 'Series of Measures' and from 'Nodal Line,' now received its unique and full articulation in the way the measureless defines itself as the 'real' thing.

In the chapter on real measure, then, Hegel made a number of significant and not so significant revisions. He simplified and illustrated with examples; he became more cautious with the language of neutrality; he revised the logic of nodal line; and he relocated the concept of the 'real' thing. What do these changes tell us about Hegel's systematic project in the *Logic*?

Allow me to propose three explanations for these changes, all of which have implications for Hegel's understanding of the logic. First, logical operations can be applied to their own products. Second, the distinction between representations and concepts is not a rigid either/or, even with regard to the logic; they can mutually affect each other. Third, over time new logical distinctions, logical transitions, and logical solutions emerge that can alter the systematic structure. It is worth considering each of these in more detail.

1 / Logical operations can be applied to their own products. In the last chapter I mentioned three distinct logical operations: thought understands by determining its concepts more precisely; thought moves or passes over dialectically from one concept to another that lies implicit as a possibility in the first; thought speculatively considers the two terms together in a synthesis, finds they are inconsistent or even contradictory, and investigates the ground that allows them to be integrated within a single concept. Hegel calls these understanding, dialectical reason, and speculative reason.

In the changes made between 1812 and 1831, Hegel on the one hand simplified arguments, dropping lengthy discussions of determination and constitution; and on the other hand elaborated the concept of the measureless by introducing more detail on the interaction of the quantitative and the qualitative. These two moves go in contrary directions. The first reflects on a complex process and reduces it to its simple ground or essence; the second elaborates distinctions that show more precisely what a concept involves. In other words, they are applications of the third and first logical operations – of speculative reason and understanding. So the moments of the logical method are not only used to develop the argument from measurement as a simple internal ratio to the nodal line and the measureless; they can also be used self-reflexively to refine and 'perfect' any analysis that has previously been developed. The logic functions recursively to correct and improve itself.[18]

2 / Representations and concepts mutually affect each other. In the course of my exposition I drew a distinction between the ways in which a particular way of measuring is instantiated in specific weight or in chemical affinity and the inherent logic of the concept of measuring itself. Yet Hegel, in his revisions, modified an originally abstract analysis by introducing a number of such concrete applications.

The problem with illustrations, I argued, was that they could not explain the transitions from one mode of measuring to the next. These followed for conceptual reasons alone. Examples do, however, make it easier to grasp the structure of a particular mode of measuring; they convert the abstract into the concrete. Underlying Hegel's decision to use them more exten-sively, then, lay a recognition that both operations – representing and thinking – are functions of the same intellect, and that they can affect and influence each other.

We say that pure concepts are abstract; they have been isolated from the concrete data of experience. But on their own they have an inherent dynamic: they are affected by determinate possibilities within their own meanings. Some of those possibilities are the criteria and conditions to be satisfied when the concept is applied. To use it correctly in a particular sit-uation we refer not only to details of that situation, but also to schematic features within the concept that allow it to mesh with them. The two must fit. Because of these schematic features the concept 'elective affinity' can apply to both sounds and chemicals; and 'combinations' can be both chem-ical unions and simple amalgams. While the characteristics peculiar to each application will condition how the category is used, the schema both invites such an application and sets limits for it. Any concept contains within its meaning the schema by which it represents things in the world.

At the same time, representations and applications are not totally devoid of thought. They are already understood as a form of measuring, as a pro-portion, as numbers that specify a quality. While this understanding is inte-grated with the concrete details of the particular case (weight and volume, for example, or numbers as primes and powers), analogies (such as compar-ing chemical affinity with harmonics) can unveil schematic features that are of more general significance. By focusing on these, the intellect can refine a representation until it approaches the abstractness of pure thought.

In other words, the capacity of thought to determine its concepts more specifically, and the analogies that can be recognized between representa-tions allow the two intellectual operations of conceiving and representing to influence each other and provide a bridge between them.[19]

3 / Developments in the history of science can introduce new moments to the systematic pattern. Scientists apply concepts they already have; in experiencing the consequences of that application, they notice determinate details that raise possibilities never before noticed. Or in attempting to explain certain puzzling facts, they recognize for the first time a parallel with other, quite remote, phenomena; the analogy turns out to be fruitful and leads to a new general principle. Some of these developments may be peculiar to the specifics of nature; but others throw light as well on social and political relations, and even on the way ideas are organized. So the advent of the machine led to a general concept of mechanism, which

Hobbes could apply both to society and to the workings of the mind; and investigation of the determinate proportions that hold between chemicals in a union pointed to a kind of measuring that had its own distinctive logic.

The concepts of mechanism, then, and of a fully articulated nodal line would not have been part of the logical arsenal before their significance had emerged in experience. But this does not mean that they are a posteriori and conditional. It was, after all, conceptual considerations that led scientists to initiate their investigations in the first place and pointed them to new possibilities. Experience only made them aware of limitations within those concepts and indicated ways of overcoming them. Experienced fact was thus the occasion for discovering the logical necessity, but not the condition that made it logically appropriate.

So developments in science can lead to rethinking the logic, not only by identifying new concrete details, but also by showing how conceptual structures themselves need to be reworked. These new approaches are fitted into a larger, logical context that organizes and directs intentional human action.

At times the readjustments might be minor – a new distinction between combination and neutralization, for example. At other times, however, it could involve a major reshuffle, so that the 'real' thing ceases to be a fully articulated ground and becomes simply an underlying being. None of these reworkings, however, take us beyond the operations of pure thought. They are the product of trying to understand, of dialectical transitions to new possibilities, and of speculative quests for governing principles.

Systematic thought, then, is not fixed once and for all. It is a function of the intellectual community and the product of reflection on its representations and applications. Over time the contingencies of particular circumstances are abstracted away, and the inherent dynamic of pure thought becomes more explicit, articulated in logical arguments and systematic texts.[20]

Time generates new contingencies, in part because thought continues to act on, and react to, both the world of experience and its own earlier results. So the systematic patterns of thought continue to be rethought. At times this is a function of thought reflecting more carefully on its own operations; but at times it discovers new logical patterns by reflecting on the unexpected results of applying its concepts to the world. Through it all thought continues to understand more precisely its own operations, discover dialectical transitions to opposite, as yet unexplored, possibilities, and discern new principles through speculative reflection on the total pattern.[21]

'How could I maintain,' wrote Hegel in the introduction to the *Science of Logic*, 'that the method I follow in this system of logic – or rather which this system follows on its own – is not susceptible of still greater perfection, of a more thorough working out in detail; at the same time I know it to be the only true method.'[22]

11

The Remarks

In the *exposition de texte* I deliberately passed over the two rather lengthy remarks that Hegel included in this chapter. Since these remarks are not part of the logical development, they are not couched in its abstract prose and are thus much more accessible to the general reader. There is, then, no need to present a full analysis. They do, however, tell us how the concept of measure applied to the chemistry (and other sciences) of Hegel's day. So I shall offer an outline of their content, and then explore some questions that arise concerning Hegel's relation to natural science.[1]

The first remark, appended to the subsection on 'Elective Affinity,' begins by citing the chemical realm of acids and bases as an example not only of two opposing series in which a member from one can neutralize a member from the other, but also of an acid preferring one base over another. Hegel then referred to the work of Richter and Fischer in calculating the determinate proportions within saturated compounds. (In 1831, he did not find it necessary to do more than mention the detailed elaboration of those calculations by Berzelius subsequent to 1812.) Another paragraph cited Berthollet's research showing that the 'so-called' elective affinity in chemistry was a function of cohesion and solubility and could be affected by changes in temperature.

Then in 1831 Hegel introduced a long polemic against the theories propounded by the Swedish chemist Berzelius on two counts: his atomism and his electro-chemical theory. This added little to what had already been written in the remark to §330 in the *Encyclopaedia*.

In both editions Hegel went on to note the distinction between a saturated chemical union and a simple amalgam (in which proportions could vary along a continuum); and he concluded by suggesting that science should be able in due course to find the logical principle or rule that would organize the specific weight of substances into a systematic order.

The second remark is appended to 'Nodal Line,' and is largely a discussion of examples from mathematics and the natural sciences and from the moral and social sphere. Between the two sets of examples Hegel pointed out how the conventional wisdom that there are no leaps in nature is controverted by the examples from harmonics and chemistry: not only the various unions of nitrogen and oxygen, but also the transformation of water from solid to liquid to gaseous state.

In the previous section, I considered how material from the second remark likely influenced the revisions made to 'Nodal Line.' Several interesting questions on the relation between logic and the sciences are raised, however, by the first remark. I shall group these under five heads: neutralization, elective affinity, atomism, the periodic table, and electrochemistry.

1 / Neutralization. I have already noted that Hegel, in his revision, dropped the term 'neutralization' from the titles of the first two subsections. It emerged only within the second sub-section to name the possibilities a thing has of combining with several alternatives rather than one. Hegel no longer used the term for the case where the appropriate example is specific weight.

This change in use reflected a distinction that Hegel had already noted in the remark in the first edition, and explicitly developed in the paragraphs on 'Chemical Process' from the *Philosophy of Nature*.[2] The German chemist Winterl had proposed the verb 'synsomatize' for the process of amalgamation where two bodies (metals or liquids) combined such that they retained their distinctive characteristics in the mixture (such as tin and copper in bronze).[3] This was to be distinguished from a chemical union in which a new kind of entity emerged (such as the salt produced when sulphuric acid and lime interact). In the former, the combination could be effected in varying proportions. In the latter, a saturated union reflected a single ratio; other proportions would leave part of one or other component unappropriated. Only the latter could be strictly called a neutralization; and Hegel's revision of the logical text in 1831 took this into account.

It thus became clear that in moving from the first sub-section to the second we are changing the modes of measuring, and not simply expanding the range of possibilities. Measuring in the first sub-section (as Hegel stressed in his 1831 version) can apply to specific weight and combinations of specific weights. Such forms of measuring can be used for both amalgams and chemical unions. In the second sub-section, however, measuring involves chemical unions between substances in contrary series, the best example (as he noted in the remark) being acids and bases. While such chemical unions could also serve as examples in the first sub-section, the logic there need not be restricted to them.

When we reflect on Hegel's logical analysis in these terms we find complications. Amalgams can be combined in varying proportions. This means that there is no single figure for the specific weight of the combination; it has no single specifying measurement. In the first edition, Hegel explicitly stated that different quantities could be used, and so the ratios are variable. In the second, he retreated to more abstract language: the quantities used are not inherent, but external to the things being measured. In either case, to measure the combination as a way of specifying the original thing can only be effective where the unit quantities of the two substances are arbitrarily set. There is no single neutral state.

When the argument moves on to the second sub-section it at first appears that the shift is simply a variation in range. The first sub-section had talked about a comparison of one thing with some other substances by means of their combination; the second introduces a comparison with others that do not combine with the first. Hegel had distinguished between some comparable alternatives and others in terms of the possibility or impossibility of combination. On first contact this shift does not seem to offer a logical justification for the abrupt shift from simple amalgams to saturated unions or neutralizations. Can we reconstruct an argument to fill this lacuna?

The move has, in fact, not involved just an extension of range. It has introduced an exclusive moment. A particular thing combines with some things but *not* with others. Not only that, but the others with which it cannot combine can nonetheless be compared with it. They are not simply diverse in an indifferent way, else they would be useless for purposes of measuring.

The fact that a combination with one kind of thing is possible and combinations with other kinds of things are not possible has already moved beyond a simple amalgam, where entities are simply mixed. It does not by itself imply that the possible combinations have a point of saturation, where the differentiated qualities of the two components are fully neutralized. That moment will become fully explicit when we move on to elective affinity and the nodal line. It is, nonetheless, implicit. For the kind of combination involved is distinctive; the two things are oriented towards each other; and the way they are differentiated is in some sense overcome in their combination.

All of these features characterize a chemical object, the concept with which we shall begin the chapter on 'Chemism.' At this point, much earlier in the *Logic*, Hegel could not appeal to that more complicated category to explain the shift. The reasons for it were left undeveloped, to be articulated later when thought explored more sophisticated concepts.

What we do see, however, is that, once again, the transition from one kind of measuring to the next, effected in strictly logical terms, does not take along with it particular applications. Measuring specific weights satisfies the first kind of measuring, but it does not involve discriminating between possible and impossible combinations. Once that distinction is taken into account, we have shifted to syntheses that can more accurately be called neutralizations, and we have moved into the proper sphere of chemistry, as Hegel himself points out in the first sentence of 'Elective Affinity.'

2 / Elective Affinity. Hegel justified the logical move to elective affinity by reacting to the complexity of the total set of measurements involved when things from two opposite series combine. The original purpose had been to measure the specific quality of a thing, but this had developed into an indefinite range so extensive that anything distinctive was lost. Only by noticing the preferences a particular thing had for combination could one begin to get at its specific quality. These preferences offer something definitive.

Yet Hegel went on to cite the work of Berthollet, who had shown that affinity is not as exclusive and as preferential as it seems. Cohesion and solubility are the key conditions, and can be altered with changes in temperature and pressure. Therefore under certain circumstances a 'weaker' affinity can take precedence over a 'stronger' one. The exclusive character of this phenomenon appears illusory.[4]

It was probably Berthollet's evidence that led Hegel to add the adjective 'so-called' in most references to elective affinity. But his acceptance of these results raises some questions about the logical analysis. For if there is really no such thing, chemically, as elective affinity, why should this concept be taken up in the *Logic*?

In his remark Hegel tried to regain the initiative from Berthollet (and Berzelius). In 1831 he wrote: 'Here, with regard to the nature of the *qualitative* that lies in elective affinity, it makes no difference whether it appears and is grasped in the form of those circumstances as its conditions. With the qualitative as such a new order begins, whose specification is no longer a merely quantitative difference.'[5]

It was important for Hegel that, under any particular set of circumstances, a thing prefers one combination to another. This was the distinctive quality that specified its inherent determination. That circumstances alter cases only contributed more detail to the measurement.

In other words, when it comes to *measuring* elective affinity, one includes in the calculation the range of temperature within which the preference is for one substance rather than another and, if need be, some calculation of the cohesiveness and solubility. It is the distinctive quality as evidenced by a thing's preferences that one wants to measure, and that includes its qualitative conditions.

So, despite what A. Doz suggests,[6] Hegel accepted Berthollet's attack on elective affinity, while claiming that it is irrelevant to the logical question.

He did not accept, however, Berthollet's second charge, against the theory of determinate proportions. The French chemist had claimed (presumably because volumes could be affected by temperature and pressure and Gay-Lussac's investigations of determinate proportions had been in terms of volume rather than of specific weight) that chemical substances could be united along a continuous range of ratios (paralleling the possibilities for amalgamated metals).[7] As we have seen, in accepting the distinction between a simple combination and a union, Hegel adopted instead the conclusions of Fischer and Berzelius that chemical unions were not so plastic.

3 / Atomism. The atomic theory, central to Newton's physics, had been applied to chemistry by John Dalton. In adopting this hypothesis as a way of explaining the regularities of chemical proportions, Berzelius attacked the more speculative approach taken by the Germans in their philosophies of nature. It is worth citing his polemic in full:

The speculative philosophy of certain German schools, having started to extend its application to theories of the exact sciences, has created (not without some presentiment of the truth) a new system which is called *dynamic* because it establishes that matter is the result of the opposed tendencies of two forces, of which one is contractive and the other expansive, and of which the former, if it succeed in totally subjugating the other, would reduce the matter of the whole universe to a mathematical point. This theory supposes that, at the moment of their chemical combination, the elements mutually penetrate each other and that the neutralization of their chemical properties, which most often is the result of this union, consists of their mutual penetration. It is precisely because of this way of envisaging chemical combination that the phenomena of determinate proportions has never been so unanticipated by philosophy than in the very time when one has begun to notice and verify them. They would have even remained for ever unknown under the aegis of this philosophy and in particular by the direction it has taken in these last fifteen years; but the less one has anticipated [the phenomena of determinate proportions], the more they ought to lead necessarily to ways of seeing and explaining chemical facts quite different from those given by dynamic philosophy; that is what has happened.[8]

In his remark Hegel took exception to this charge:

When it is claimed that the phenomena of determinate proportions would have been completely unanticipated by the dynamic point of view, this would be only an external historical condition, quite apart from the fact that Richter's stoechiometric series in Fischer's compilation was already known to Berthollet and developed in the first edition of this *Logic*, which proved the vacuity of the categories on which rested the ancient corpuscular theory, as well as the one that wants to be modern.[9]

The reference to Richter is significant, for this chemist had studied at Königsberg and apparently heard Kant's lectures.[10] Possibly stimulated by Kant's claim that chemistry would never be a science since it could not be set out in mathematical terms, Richter investigated the proportions of the elements involved when two salts in a solution exchanged their radicals. He then set these out in a mathematical equation.[11] Berzelius extended this theory of proportions to all chemical relations.

In the first edition, Hegel's discussion of measuring had explored determinate proportions as measurable ratios. What was implicit in the discussion of the opposing series became explicit in the subsection on elective affinity and in the section and remark on the nodal line. He even cited the different proportions of nitrogen and oxygen that enter into nitrous and nitric acid.

Hegel's defence, then, has some merit.

There is a way, however, in which Berzelius's charge was justified. In 1831, Hegel commented about the developments that had taken place since 1812: 'To want to review the information about the ratios of the mixture of chemical elements which has been so extensively developed in all sides since these lines were first written, would be a digression, since this empirical (and in part only hypothetical) elaboration remains enclosed within the same conceptual determinations.'[12] In other words, he specifically set aside any discussion concerning the specific numbers involved.

But Berzelius, basing his investigations on Dalton's theories, had established experimentally that the proportions were not only determinate, but followed a simple progression: 1:1, 2:1, 4:1 or 3:2. It was this limited range of possibilities that drew Dalton's and Berzelius's attention. If it were simply a question of definite proportions in the manner Hegel (or Berthollet) spoke of them, then one would expect complex ratios, such as 17:25 or 31:100. It was the basic regularity, found in data of various sorts, that pointed towards a theory of chemical units, which could be called corpuscles, molecules, or atoms. 'According to this system,' wrote Berzelius, 'bodies are compounds of atoms, and one atom of one element can combine with 1, 2, 3, etc. atoms of another element, but not with indeterminate degrees or fractions of atoms. In the same way, an atom of one composite body could combine with 1, 2, 3, etc. atoms of another composite body.'[13]

Hegel was well aware that the determinate proportions according to which chemicals combined followed simple progressions. In his lectures of 1819–20 he expanded on this point in some detail: 'One major law concerns the diverse levels of oxidation of a base; when two bodies combine in several ratios, these quantities are in a very simple progression of 1, 1½, 2, 4, 8, etc.' Similarly when an acid unites with an oxide 'these two quantities have a simple ratio of oxygen, a multiple of a whole number.'[14]

When Hegel, in the *Logic*, dismissed these figures as a digression, he set aside the puzzling regularity that the atomic theory was designed to explain. The simple arithmetical progression in the empirical ratios offered evidence that the units by which chemical substances combined with each other were not divisible into fractions.

Hegel rejected the atomic theory on conceptual grounds. The conjunction of primitive spheres and empty space could not satisfactorily explain how and why substances combined. Berzelius, with his supposition that atoms were spheres and could thus have direct contact with a maximum of twelve other spheres, had adopted without question the metaphysical conceptions of Newton and Democritus.

That conception would ultimately prove unworkable, to be replaced by one where the basic chemical units are minute fields of energy. With that change of focus, however, they ceased to be atoms in the traditional sense of indivisible spheres of matter, and fitted more closely to the Hegelian perspective in which relations are as important as distinctions.

His conceptual problem with atomism, however, blinded Hegel to the way the simple progression of determinate proportions justified the belief in basic chemical units. In a sense, then, Berzelius was right. The philosophy of nature did not anticipate the direction chemistry was to take throughout the nineteenth century; its achievements would have remained forever unknown under its aegis.[15]

4 / The periodic table. For all that Hegel overlooked the evidence for chemical atomism, there is another way in which he anticipated future developments. When talking about specific weights he wrote:

They are a ratio of weight to volume within a body; the exponent of the ratio which expresses the determination of a specific weight as different from others, is a determinate quantum only of comparison, an alien ratio for external reflection, that is not grounded on a proper qualitative relation to an opposing existence. One could take up the task of recognizing in the exponents of the series of specific weights a system based on a rule that specifies a merely arithmetic multiplicity as a series of harmonic nodes.[16]

In due course it was Mendeleev who found a way of transforming the multiplicity of specific weights into a periodic table, establishing a rule that became the basis for searching out new chemical substances.

Here, then, Hegel recognized that empirical data had to be taken seriously if one was to find the principle or rule that governed them. What is of interest, however, is that he drew a parallel between this search and the quest for a rule to explain the measured distance of the planets from the sun.

This had been the focus of Hegel's dissertation, and it has led to one of the caricatures which subsequent philosophy has used to dismiss his philosophy of nature.[17] Hegel, they say, tried to prove that there could be no planet between Mars and Jupiter. But in this remark Hegel suggests that he was not there deducing natural phenomena from a priori axioms; he was rather investigating principles that would explain why the planets are spaced the way they are. His goal, then, was no different from that of Mendeleev in constructing the periodic table of the elements. He was not practising deduction, but rather discerning the rational principles that would explain why things are the way they are.

Such explanatory proposals are not a function of the *Science of Logic*, however. As we have seen, that discipline works with pure concepts. In the cases Hegel mentions it is the empirical data of specific weights, of chemical affinities, and of distance from the sun that need to be organized and ordered.[18] While thought is involved, it cannot follow its own a priori path in reaching a solution. That is why Hegel says that these are tasks to be faced, and science has a long way to go to achieve them.

Thought's search for the principles that govern a diversity is the process Hegel called speculative reason. In the *Logic* thought considers only its own products and recognizes their implicit conceptual structure. Having turned to nature it is confronted with a multitude of contingencies and has to find some order. But it uses the same logical process of discovering the inherent rationality in apparent confusion and contradiction, now rendered more difficult because the essential pattern lies hidden in a surfeit of diversity.

Because Hegel was aware that science advanced as it found underlying principles that govern apparently random measurements, he could anticipate that something like the periodic table would be discovered. This confidence reflected his conviction that nature, for all of its diversity, is inherently rational.

5 / The electrochemical theory. Hegel's attack on Berzelius's electrochemical theory added little to what he had already written in the remark to §330 in the 1830 *Encyclopaedia*.[19] He left aside the claim of the physical identity of electricity and chemistry, and discussed only those aspects that concern the process of measuring. Berzelius could explain the phenomena of elective affinity only by transforming electrical polarity from an opposition of positive and negative into two independent qualities, each of which can vary in degree, so that one substance (oxygen) has a greater intensity of negative polarity than another (sulphur). Hegel pointed out that the only evidence for both of these claims – unipolarity and degree of intensity – was the varied phenomena of elective affinity itself. There was no independent confirmation. When we consider in addition that electricity could not explain either the permanent characteristics of an acid, nor the transformation that takes place in bodies when they are chemically united, we have no strong justification for Berzelius's bold hypothesis.[20]

This means that when Berzelius sought to define the quality of a substance by measuring the intensity of its positive or negative charge, the only data he could use was the strength of the bond that a substance has in a chemical union. The act of measuring involved nothing more, and nothing less, than the measurements used in determining elective affinity. His hypothesis offered nothing of value for Hegel's logical argument.[21]

I

SCIENCE OF LOGIC

B / CHEMISM

12

Mechanism

A second chapter in Hegel's *Logic* that has a direct bearing on chemistry is the one titled 'Chemism.' It is found between 'Mechanism' and 'Teleology' in the third book of the *Logic*, under the general heading of 'Doctrine of the Concept.' Here, instead of focusing on basic categories and their interrelation, Hegel discusses the act of focusing itself. It is conceiving, not just concepts, that is in question.[1]

Conceiving is the process of getting our thoughts worked out in detail. We normally call it: understanding.[2] Once understanding fully comprehends its own operations in judging and inferring, however, it recognizes not only that it is itself subjective, but also that it can be used to understand objects – that realm which is conceivable, yet not subjective.[3]

The act of understanding the objective realm involves the subjective dynamic of conceiving, judging, and inferring; at the same time it considers the object to be independent of this dynamic – at first thoroughly independent, then oriented towards another object, and finally as allowing itself to be organized by concepts into a mediated process. In other words, we understand the objective world to be mechanical, chemical, or amenable to purposes. The categories that name these modes of understanding are called mechanism, chemism, and teleology.[4]

The kind of concept being investigated is complex. We are not simply thinking objective terms like 'being,' 'thing,' 'quantity,' 'actual,' or 'cause.' At this point the categories name *how we conceive objects*. They involve the distinction between the object as such and what it is to be. Both moments must be included: what is to be understood and the understanding; that double aspect controls and determines the logical development.

In discussing these general concepts of mechanism, chemism, and teleology, then, I shall distinguish the understanding from the object understood. Unfortunately, we also call the act of understanding 'conceiving,' and its product a 'concept.' So the same term functions at two levels: to describe the total pattern of mechanism or chemism, and to describe a particular way of thinking about an object. Although, in general, I am not happy with the use of 'notion' to translate the German *Begriff*, I shall use it in this context to name the general, inclusive category, and the words 'concept' and 'understanding' where I want to distinguish them from the conceived and the understood.

Since the notion of mechanism sets the stage for Hegel's discussion of chemism, a brief review of its logic will prepare the way for the main exposition:

When we think of the objective realm *mechanically*, we understand it to be made up of independent objects which, if they are altered at all, do not move themselves, but are acted upon. Since this realm is to be quite other than thought, any such movement must come from other objects. So we have a diversity of mechanical entities, each one moved only by the movement of others; each responds and in turn acts on the others. There is, then, a reciprocity of action and reaction. When these movements balance each other, we have an equilibrium.

We can now think of the balanced system of action and reaction as a single object, equally mechanical. But when we use this new concept of a mechanical object, we find that an important difference has emerged. In the first stage, each object was basically the same as every other. Therefore the action of one is just as strong as the reaction of the other and an equilibrium ensues. At this second stage, we can think of balanced systems as involving more or fewer first-order objects, so that any movement they impart would be stronger or weaker. Hence, a balance is not so easy to achieve. Were the differential between these objects too great, there would be no mechanical interaction at all; the weaker would simply give way. So a real mechanical relationship develops when the weaker resists the action of the stronger, while yet being influenced by it.

The mechanical perspective of independent objects can be maintained as a permanent way of viewing the objective realm if the weaker objects revolve around the stronger object as their centre; at the same time, each of the weaker objects, as itself an equilibrium, becomes a secondary centre. A mechanical system of this sort has a persistent pattern, the principles of which can be conceptually identified, and understood as laws.

The laws that emerge from mechanism spell out the way mechanical objects are related to each other. Each is no longer defined as strictly independent, simply responding to external forces, but rather as oriented towards an other. Such a way of conceiving the objective realm, however, is no longer strictly mechanical, for it presupposes an attraction between opposing objects. To view objects not as independent, but as oriented towards each other in this way, is to conceive them not mechanically but chemically. So at this point Hegel can leave the notion of mechanism and move on to that of chemism.

13

The Chemical Object

To get at what is distinctive about an object that is conceived to be chemical we compare it with the kind just considered.[1] A mechanical object is complete in itself and indifferent to whatever happens to it. Any movement or change intervenes from outside. In contrast, a chemical object is to be oriented towards another. Since this is essential to its nature, the kind of orientation it has makes a difference to the kind of thing it is.

Chemical objects, then, are not all the same. They are differentiated from each other as particulars within a more comprehensive genus. But we need to be cautious. They are not simply diverse, each having a distinctive quality. Rather, one object is oriented towards another and vice versa. What differentiates them is also what they share – a principle by which they are determined as direct complements. This determination is common to both and thus a universal.[2]

So it is not simply an act of understanding – a concept – that thinks of chemical objects as parts of a system, as was the case in the logic of mechanism. The object itself refers to something more general. What defines it as chemical is the mutual determination it shares with another object. The two together make up a complete picture.

At the same time, each object exists as something singular – external to, and in some sense independent of, the other.

In other words, the chemical object has within itself all the components of the whole notion of chemism. It exists as a singular object that can be referred to, but it is also tied in with other chemical objects in a larger pattern.

When we refer these two descriptions to the same object, however, we have a problem. For singularity sits uneasily with universality, especially when, as singular, the object is separate from its counterpart and when, as universal, it is to be identified with it. The former is the way it exists; the latter is its determining principle or concept – what it is to be. These two descriptions can be held together in the same definition only if the object is in process of overcoming the singularity of its existence and realizing its principle. What corresponds to its implicit concept is, in fact, this drive to overcome its one-sided antithetical status and make itself into a real whole.[3]

We can only understand the nature of this drive and what results from it if we spend some time fixing the two conflicting moments in the concept of a chemical object. We need to think about each one of them independently to get at the contradiction involved.

On the one hand the object is an independent whole, complete in itself. We distinguish this fact that it refers only to itself from the complementary fact that it refers as well to something else. Were we to allow its independence to slip, we could not do justice to its peculiar character as a chemical *object*.[4]

On the other hand, we have an immanent determination that differentiates the object from another that is its direct counterpart or opposite. Abstracted from its context, this determination is just a formal universal, under which the object is subsumed; so this orientation to something external characterizes as well the way the object immediately exists. Were this side ignored, we would not have a *chemical* object.

This means, however, that the object is in no way an integrated whole that need refer only to itself. Its unity is not positive, but rather negative, defined by its differentiation from its complementary opposite. The object is a unit because it contains both moments of this opposition: the unity and the differentiation. Since it is a separate singular, its full character can only find expression if there is not one, but two particularized objects involved, differentiated by the external orientation each has for the other. So we never do conceive a chemical object on its own terms. We must refer not only to what it is, but also to what some other is as well.

To this point we have been thinking about what differentiates an object only as it applies to that object. But we should also consider this principle of differentiation on its own.[5] From this perspective the differentiation defines the way we specifically conceive the whole; it is the way we individuate this pair of chemical objects from other pairs. We use this differentiating determination to define the general essence or real genus of the object – that which inherently qualifies it.

Having already suggested that the chemical object is the drive to overcome its one-sided existence, we can now characterize this drive more precisely. The object is an immediate object of thought, directly referred to, but it is also inherently characterized as a particular, opposed to another particular under a general concept. We have not developed this description simply for our subjective purposes; rather, we understand this to be part of its objective make-up as chemical. However, as involving both immediacy and mediation this description of the object is contradictory, since antithetical moments are necessary to define it as something chemical.

Finding such a contradiction is no excuse for abandoning this exercise altogether, but rather a reason for searching out a context whereby the concept can become coherent. Any such solution cannot be achieved simply by reworking our way of thinking, however, for the contradiction stems from the way the chemical object is defined. Therefore the object itself is nothing but a striving to overcome the limited determination of its being, and to translate into existence the whole concept of what it is to be. For all that it was originally supposed to be complete in itself and independent, the conceived chemical object is unstable and transient. It has been brought to this pass neither by outside forces nor by external considerations, but by its own inherent nature. So the object itself initiates the process towards a more adequate notion of chemism.

14

Process

1 / The presupposition for any chemical process is not only that the concept of a particular chemical object has an internal incoherence, but that the tension finds explicit existence in two objects that stand over against each other. They are directed towards each other in a relation that could be called affinity.[1]

We have already come across this term when looking at the logic of measuring. There, however, it represented nothing more than how an object can generate measurable combinations with some things but not with others. At this point we are not concerned with measuring, but with the basic determinations of an object by which it is inherently directed towards something else. 'Affinity' carries both of these levels of meaning, and they become explicit in quite different parts of the logic, since the former sense is simple and abstract, whereas the second sense is more complicated and involved.[2]

As we have seen, each of the chemical objects involves a contradiction between the determinate way it must be conceived and the one-sided nature of its existence; each exists as nothing else but the striving to secure release from this internal tension. By complementing each other in some kind of combination, they would make reality conform to the concept that governs both of them.

This pressure towards combination is so strong (since it stems from the contradiction noted in the previous chapter) that the two objects can only retain their separate existence by some kind of external force: the concept of chemical object requires that the existing particulars not be allowed simply to dissolve into each other. In other words, the presupposition for any thought of a chemical process must contain not only the basic affinity of these two objects, but also their independent existence. Held apart as extremes, they can achieve their union only through the addition of some kind of mediating, or middle term.

To be sure, the basic concept of chemical object, which defines both extremes, is a kind of middle, for it considers both objects together under the same principle. But that is only something subjective; it has nothing directly to do with the existing objects that are being understood. Their separated existence stands opposed to, and cannot be identified with, the shared concept.

The point of the process is to alter this existence, so that the two objects are simply united, without reference to anything else. The resulting unified existence would be quite different from their initial status as separate. This difference between what goes into the process and what comes out is important. For it, too, must in some sense be grounded or justified; it cannot simply appear out of nowhere. To make the process work, then, we need a third term that can be added to the two objects already there and that will introduce the formal element of unity.[3] It will provide a common basis whereby the two independent objects will be able to communicate with each other.

Because any element of real difference has been left to the two opposing extremes, this third or mediating term contributes nothing more than an indifferent neutrality to the tension that divides them. And it does so, not because the objects themselves create it, but because thought, in its attempt to make coherent the concept of a chemical object, has required it. Whenever reflection tries to explore how one thing can ground another whose content is different (in this case the independent existence of each and their common principle), it finds that it must posit a middle term that will introduce that different feature. So for all that this middle term will have to exist, it offers nothing more than the moment of the objects' unity, as abstracted by thought. It is not a full-fledged chemical object; it is only an existing element.

Nevertheless, it serves three functions: it reaffirms the separate existence of the two objects, since unity comes from somewhere else; it enables the process to happen by bringing them together; and it contributes its own bit – the unity – towards the final result. For these reasons, conceptual thought requires this middle term to resolve the contradiction it has discovered in the independent objects it refers to.[4]

When the two objects are brought together in this common element, two things happen. First, the tension is dissolved and they achieve some kind of peaceful co-existence. This achievement is, however, not only positive, but also negative. For, second, the concrete concept that governs the whole process has thereby been realized; and this has reduced the real differences of the objects to a unity. They have lost that differentiated character that initially defined them as chemical; the opposition and tension that separated them has been muffled now that the striving has arrived at a peaceful, mutually complementary neutrality. But this means that the objects have become something different from what the notion of chemism says they are supposed to be.

What was to resolve the basic incoherence in the notion of chemism has done too much. For the neutral product lacks any chemical characteristics whatsoever; the process has exhausted any orientation towards another, and so the process itself is extinguished. In escaping from the contradiction between the concept as a totality and independent objects referred to, the two objects lose their differentiated character. They are no longer extremes standing against each other and separate from the mediating middle term.

The language of extremes being brought together by a middle is the language of Aristotle's syllogisms. Conceptual thought, when understanding objectivity in a chemical way, recognizes that this process (by which chemical objects become a neutral product) embodies the pattern of inference. The latter, taken on its own, is purely formal. Chemical process provides some content for that form.[5]

For Hegel, using the structure of syllogistic thought to make sense of the objective world enables understanding to achieve satisfaction. For the language of mediation by which terms are both distinguished and connected is the language of explanation. In this way we show not only why things are the way they are, but also how. Thereby we resolve the anomalies and paradoxes we find in objects immediately offered to thought. So it is worth while pausing for a few moments to investigate how Hegel's analysis of syllogism applies in this context.

The differentiated objects are particulars that are combined by means of an abstract element into a neutral product that realizes the general concept. Since the mediating element has no determinate characteristics of its own, it can simply be indicated, as a singular. So we have a 'syllogism' in which particulars become something universal by means of a singular. We can represent it as P-S-U.

As singulars are naturally the subject of judgments, this would reflect Aristotle's third figure: M-S, M-P, so S-P.[6] The problem is that judgments in Aristotle's syllogisms are simple predications, and the conclusion in this figure is a particular judgment. In the process we have been discussing, however, neither the particular objects nor the final product can be *predicated* of the mediating entity. In the major premise, both the middle term and the final product are neutral; so there is something common, for all that one is abstract neutrality and the other is concrete. But in the minor premise, the middle term brings to the particular objects something they do not already have – a sharing, or communication. The strict syllogistic pattern does not seem to apply.

The inference is more like an induction, in which a number of particular things are gathered into a single community so that one can determine what is general or universal about them. Induction employs reflection, presupposing immediate and external givens and positing their essential character. Similarly in this case, it is the conceptual thought, reflecting on the contradiction implicit in the chemical object, that has come up with the analysis of this process.[7]

Now the major premise affirms that formal neutrality can be abstractly identified with real neutrality; in the minor premise formal neutrality allows the particulars to communicate with each other; and the conclusion says that the particulars are subsumed into a universal product. Unlike simple induction, however, the mediating singular is not the activity of reflecting itself, but an existing abstract element. Induction is here embodied in an objective realm.

The language of syllogism will return as we proceed through this chapter of Hegel's *Logic* and into its application within the philosophy of nature. For the moment, Hegel goes on to consider how we can understand, not the process, but its product. The product is something neutral like the mediating term, but this time we have a real and concrete neutrality, not an abstract and formal one. What formerly were particular objects have become ingredients; they have lost the properties that could maintain their independent differentiation. The tension, which was their productive capacity, has disappeared.

I mentioned earlier that the neutral product is a unity that has negative force because it has cancelled the original differentiation of the object. This cancellation is an inherent part of its definition, for it must presuppose that differentiation if it is to be a *chemical* product. Yet the differentiation has disappeared in the process; there has been no mediating agent to maintain its significance. So the new 'chemical' object is just a formal unity. It is supposed to be the unity of two differentiated objects, but it cannot, on its own terms, show how or why they had to be differentiated. That is simply an assumption of conceptual thought. So we have an object that, on its own terms, is not really chemical, yet thought assumes it to be so because it was derived from a differentiation. Once again we have a notion of chemism that is not fully coherent.

2 / Not only has the presupposed tension between opposites been dis-solved into a neutral product, but the negative unity that makes the process happen has disappeared as well. The result has turned out to be an object that has no chemical characteristics whatsoever.

But essential to the concept of a chemical product is the assumption that it had been differentiated. Conceptual thought reflects on this new kind of chemical object and identifies what must be added to make it genuinely chemical. In contrast to the quiescent neutrality, one needs a singular, dynamic activity. Since that negative unity is essential to the concept of the product as chemical object, it has to be included in the total picture. But now it is distinguished from the object and external to it. The product is one thing; the process, another. At this stage both moments are part of what is meant when we think of products in a chemical way. There is no clear way, though, of showing how the two of them are connected. The process cannot simply be rekindled; for that to happen some differentiation must be presupposed, but any difference has vanished in the original pro-cess. A chemical tension together with its resolution cannot be generated out of nothing; and the object we have is nothing but a peaceful neutrality.

We now focus on the moment of pure chemical activity to understand its distinctive characteristics. As something separate from, and outside of, the object, it is independent; yet it is essentially negative, turning against what-ever it presupposes. It is abstractly singular, referred to as something with-out any content whatsover; yet at the same time it is understood to exist. Since whatever is abstract is intrinsically related to its concrete comple-ment, whatever reality it has on its own account involves some reference to an object to be acted on. Indeed, we only came to this concept and isolated it as distinct because of the chemical inadequacies of the neutral product.

This means that the negative unity of pure chemical activity has its own inherent tension: it is to be separate and distinct, yet essentially directed towards something else. In other words, it has acquired the characteristics of a chemical object, even though it is not an object; for its very abstract-ness has turned against itself. So this concept too becomes internally inco-herent when taken on its own. To resolve the tension, this moment of pure process becomes restless activity, turning anywhere to find something that it can consume – something that will give it concrete content.

Within the general notion of chemism at this stage, the only thing we have that could serve as content for this activity is the chemical product. Its peace-ful neutrality was the condition, not only necessary but also sufficient, for postulating the independence of the activity. Without any further justifica-tion, then, the 'negative unity' of pure process can turn on this object.

Adopting a role similar to that played by the earlier formal neutrality, the neutral product can enable pure activity to overcome its internal tension. Unlike that initial middle term, it is not formal and abstract, but concrete and determinate. For all its quiescent neutrality, then, the product offers the content required by the activity's abstractness.

We next turn to look more closely at the process involved when chemical activity as negative unity is directly applied to the neutral object. We have the first stages of another syllogism, where the abstract singular of the pure process is one extreme, and the neutral product is the middle term. Their unmediated association is one premise. To get the syllogism fully worked out, however, we need to identify the other extreme. This is a task of understanding.[8]

Since the activity as negative attacks whatever is already there, this process will break up the simple neutrality of the product. At first, we might expect that this break up of the product would reestablish the opposition of objects in tension with which this whole discussion of chemism began. But that need not follow. For the pure negative activity lacks any content of its own, and so contains no principle that would generate any specific differentiation between objects. Since the middle term or product already is the realized unity of the differentiated objects, they need not reappear to serve as the second extreme of the syllogism we are now trying to construct.

They do have a role to play, however. In the first syllogism, the neutral product was the universal term; it is the general that combines particulars. If that product has the same character in this syllogism, it would be the universal that, as mediator, divides itself into the pure activity and the broken up pieces. That would represent a disjunctive syllogism, in which a comprehensive operation mediates by both distinguishing a concept into disjuncts and recognizing that they exhaust its full description.

As it enters this syllogism, however, the product is not universal in that sense.[9] The original objects were differentiated in a particular and distinctive way. Their product, for all of its universality, reflects that particularity. And it continues to be particular even after the differentiation has disappeared. In other words, the initial differentiation influences this analysis by specifying that the product, while universal, is nonetheless a particular universal.

In the present syllogism, then, the product, as middle term, really serves as a particular. The restless activity is, as we have seen, a singular object of reference, a unity that excludes and divides rather than generalizes. So the remaining term of the syllogism will be a universal.

We identified the previous syllogism as something reflective: it was understanding that required the middle term. Here, however, the movement is much more direct. The pure process acts negatively on the neutral product, and out of the neutral product comes something universal. This reflects the formal pattern of the Barbara syllogism, where the major premise spells out the universal nature of the particular (product), in a kind of subsumption; and the minor uses the particular (product) to give content to a singular (activity); the conclusion, then, shows how pure activity can generate something strictly universal.

We can now determine what this universal will be like. In the first place, the activity is strictly negative; it works against the content that it presupposes. So it breaks up the neutral product. The second extreme, then, is a number of things; to be genuinely universal these must be quite indifferent to each other. They cannot be particulars within something more general; nor can they incorporate anything particular about the middle term. Such indifferent universals are abstract, since any concrete content would specify their differences. This abstractness fits with another aspect of the picture we are developing, for, as we have seen, the activity lacks any content; it too is abstract. Once again the pattern fits the framework of the Barbara syllogism: a purely abstract singular is mediately connected with an equally abstract universal by means of an abstract, although perforce more determinate,[10] particular.

We can infer, then, that the second extreme of this syllogism is simply a collection of undifferentiated universals – what would be common to any neutral product whatsoever.

Such universal components of the neutral product would be, in the first place, the abstract, indifferent basis of its composition. But conceptual thought can recognize that having simple, abstract bases would not be enough to make up its particular character; some principle is required. So in the second place, another component is needed that has the capacity to stimulate. This second sort of abstract universal, while distinct from the original sort, is just as much something indifferent, yet common to all kinds of things.

So we have a syllogism. One extreme is the independent activity as a negative unity; the middle is the neutral product as a real unity; the other extreme is what makes this reality something chemical dispersed into its abstract moments. The pure process, which works against the character of whatever it affects, attacks the particular object that serves as a mediating moment to break it up into abstract components.

We have talked of the process as a syllogism of the first figure, in which a particular mediates. But in fact we did not simply move from singular to particular to universal. The whole analysis was driven by the notion of chemism; that is, by the need to spell out the character of objects when considered chemically. Because that general concept governs the whole analysis, we cannot rest content with the neutral product, but have to isolate negative activity as its abstract counterpart. Nor can we leave those two in uneasy partnership, but have to identify what happens when the activity turns on the quiescent object. Further, the demands of a full conceptual explication insists that within the overall picture we distinguish the various moments into singular, universal, and particular as well as show how they fit together in a syllogistic pattern. Once we acknowledge the governing role of the overall notion, however, we discover that a different kind of syllogism has been playing a role behind the scenes.

In this new inference, the notion of chemism is a universal that has spelled out its own internal components; these have been distinguished from each other as particulars; and they exhaust all that is needed for a single, complete, and coherent concept. This pattern represents what Hegel calls the third syllogistic form: a universal mediates between a particular and a singular; but in such a way that it takes the initiative and by particularizing constructs a full, concrete totality. We now have a legitimate disjunctive inference.

Describing it this way, however, does not complete our task of understanding objectivity in a chemical way. While we have derived the concept of an abstract component, we have not yet focused our attention on those components to determine what they involve. So we turn from our general reflection on the process to look again at the second extreme: the diverse universals that result from the break up of a neutral product.

We have seen that they are indifferent to each other. What makes one distinctive has nothing to do with any of the others. Unlike the neutral product (which had to presuppose the differentiated objects incorporated into it), they do not need to explain their existence with reference to anything else. They are rather quite abstract, each one a bare universal whose specific character is something that pertains to it alone. They can be called elements, for this term describes whatever is determinate without reference to anything else. Any distinctive character each one might have is original with it.

3 / The term 'chemical object' started out referring to an object that had an inherent orientation to something else. We then used it to describe the neutral product of a chemical process. Now we have a third kind: elements that are freed from any basic tension whatsoever. Though they can barely be called chemical, they serve as the underlying base upon which concep-

tual understanding can establish the presuppositions necessary for the objective realm to be considered chemical at all. This foundation of basic elements has emerged from a thorough understanding of a chemical process whose product is really different from its starting point. As yet, however, we cannot understand how these abstract elements could be used to ground or justify our reference to chemical objects inherently oriented towards each other. We need to reflect further.

The elements on the one hand persist as simple and indifferent to anything else; on the other hand, they are determinate – each distinct from the other. These two descriptions are contradictory, for if they are determinate, they are not simple, and if they are distinct from others, they are not indifferent to them.

We can resolve this contradiction in the basic description of chemical elements only by considering what role they play. Inherent in being elements is the necessity to divide themselves between one object and another in such a way that a tension is created. In this way, their indifferent determinations become the basis for making distinctions, and their simplicity introduces complexity into the picture. Once we include this dynamic role in the concept of a chemical element, we can explain how one object can be differentiated from an other, be neutralized by it, and yet make its simple determinacy into a persisting and independent reality. Only on this understanding can we make sense of the paradox that emerged when we derived the elements as simple yet inherently determinate.

We have now completed the picture of chemism, for the final result of the disjunctive syllogism is to return back to the beginning where the notion all began. The elements imply and require the objects in tension that, though they seek each other, are so independent that they can only be combined into a neutral product by means of a formal third term, external to both of them yet providing a shared basis for communication. We have come full circle. By distinguishing the various moments of that circle we have progressively resolved each of the incoherent concepts that has emerged.

To consider the circle as a whole, however, is to move beyond chemism. For we no longer have independent objects in tension; they have become components organized into a pattern. So we are on the verge of passing over to a more comprehensive sense of objectivity. Hegel, as we have seen, never makes such a move directly. Only when it is justified by a thorough and careful analysis will we have any clear conception of what the next stage specifically entails.

15

Chemism's Demise

Hegel paused to make a remark.[1] It might seem as if the complex circle we have just developed is some abstract and irrelevant construction of thought having nothing to do with the real world; objects, even chemical ones, just do not behave this way. Nonetheless, he said, one can find instances of such a process in normal chemistry. A body will adjust the oxygen in its composition, making one part more strongly oxidized than another; the less oxidized bit can then combine with another body in a neutral product. Such a neutralization would not be possible were the proportion of oxygen higher.[2]

Here we do not have one object immediately directed towards another, but intermediate steps are taken with an eye to the whole picture. The totality of the initial ratio (or concept) generates the conditions it needs to establish a real connection with something else, thereby bringing its 'concept' to reality. This illustration shows that the complete notion of chemism is not an abstraction, but covers certain natural and social phenomena.

We are, however, at the limits of this particular concept. Chemism is the term to use when thinking about objects that remain indifferent and external to each other, even though this externality has been cancelled in a first and preliminary way. While oriented towards something else, they are yet distinct and separate. So even when we conceive of objects using the fully developed notion of chemism, we cannot say that all external relations have disappeared; there remains a residue of independence.

Although we have a circle, then, chemism does not describe a totality that is self-determining – both generating its distinctive and opposing moments and reconciling them again. At each point chemism starts with some given presupposition, shows that this presupposition contradicts the concept of what chemism is to be, and thereby initiates a process. The product may itself turn out on reflection to be the condition for another process; but that second process does not follow directly from the first. Rather, once again, the neutral and self-contained product is assessed against the concept of chemism.

To be sure, we have discovered in chemism a totality of three syllogisms. The first one has the formal neutrality of an independent object for its middle, which enables the two objects in tension – its extremes – to communicate with each other.[3] It is the syllogism of chemical combination. The second syllogism takes the product of the first (the real neutrality of the original differences) as the middle term, which then bridges the transition from a pure negative activity on the one side to indifferent elements on the other. This is the syllogism of chemical analysis or separation. The third syllogism is the move from dispersed elements to the objects in tension with which we began.

What mediates that final process is nothing but the conceptual framework that governs the whole logical analysis. It takes the abstract tension between the indifference of the elements and their determinate character, and shows it to be the necessary condition for that concrete tension in which two objects are oriented towards each other. This final move functions only because it is driven by the general notion of chemism. It is designed to explain how the objects with which we began come to be differentiated.

In the third syllogism, then, it is clear that the inference does not follow from the inherent determinations of the chemical object – in this case the elements – but from the governing demands of the concept under which they are understood and described. Once we identify this distinction between the governing role of the concept and the process which the object undergoes, we find that it has functioned earlier in the analysis as well.

The neutral product that results from the first process is self-contained in itself. If it turns out to be differentiated from other objects, and subject to other combinations, that would not follow from the first process on its own. Nor does it require that a consuming activity break it up into its elements. Further, that activity could work on all kinds of things other than this neutral object. So it is only the subjective concept as implicit principle that both establishes the connection between the first two processes and points out that a neutral product would not be a chemical object, were it not considered in conjunction with some kind of negative activity.

In other words, none of the mediating processes generates or requires the one that follows. The neutral product, the indifferent elements, and the objects in tension, which are their results, simply emerge as independent entities. The result of one process does not on its own lead to the next. It is the 'subjective' way of thinking about them that requires the connection, while the 'objective' side of chemism is nothing but a set of independent processes. The fact that the product of one becomes the presupposition for another is not inherent, but brought to it from outside. It is the governing notion of chemism that both develops each syllogism and connects the syllogisms into a circle.

Were we to remove this overarching conceptual framework, however, we would still have two distinct and independent processes that have their own internal logic: the combination of independent objects into a neutral product and the reduction of a compound into its elements. One starts from chemical objects; the other from pure chemical activity. Given these assumptions, the processes are inevitable.

Whatever was introduced conceptually is now left aside: the requirements that led from one process to another, and the theory that showed how elements can become the conditions for chemical objects. What remains is the essential core of what is objective in chemism. One process describes combination; the other involves separation. To be sure, we can only separate something that is already combined; and we can only combine things that are initially separate. Yet for all this formal reference of the two processes to each other, they remain quite independent and distinct. The elements that are separated out by the second need not be the same things that started out in tension in the first. And if in fact some elements turn out to be differentiated opposites, the kind of opposition they have, as defined by their particular properties, will be quite different from that which triggered the first process.

In other words, these two mediated processes can be described in the same terms we originally used to characterize chemical objects. For all that they are directed towards each other as complements, they are nonetheless independent of each other.

Yet when we review our analysis more closely we discover that these 'chemical objects' (that is, the two chemical processes) nonetheless lose their independence and merge into something else.

For in each process, some element of externality and simple immediacy is objectively overcome. There are three progressive stages. In the first, the independence of the differentiated extremes is dissolved; the sharp distinction between objects as one-sided and the concept as totality is broken down as well. In the second, the unity and independence of the product is cancelled; it ceases to be strictly neutral and disappears into fixed, undifferentiated elements. In the third, the elements lose their abstract universality and establish determinate differences. The externality and independence that was supposed to characterize chemical objects is nothing but a condition that passes away in a process, thereby generating some other object. Each one we have identified – differentiated particular, neutral product, and abstract element – functions as both the result of, as well as the condition for, one of the processes. Together they make up a kind of circular pattern.

In other words, chemical objects on their own are not as independent and external as they appeared. For they have shown themselves to be amenable to the kind of systematic pattern that the subjective concept imposed. When the concept points out that a product is but the condition for another process, it is not introducing something alien, but exploiting characteristics of the objects themselves.

Once this is recognized, we are no longer thinking about objects as simply chemical. They are not independent givens, alien to the conceptual framework attempting to understand them. Rather, what is objective allows itself to be overreached by conceptual thought and incorporated into its purposes. Such a purposive understanding of objectivity we call teleology. With this new general notion, Hegel leaves the chapter on chemism behind and moves on to discuss how a subjective purpose can use the objective realm as a means to accomplish its ends.[4]

16

From 1807 to 1830

The chapter on 'Chemism,' as part of the third book of the *Science of Logic*, was never submitted to a thorough revision. So the *exposition de texte* just offered has been based on the (at times confusing) discussion of the first edition of 1816. Unlike real measure, however, this concept did find a place in the *Encyclopaedia Logic*.[1]

The basic structure of the 1817 text is familiar to anyone who has worked carefully through the chapter in the larger *Logic*. The first paragraph identifies the chemical object as something differentiated, whose determinate existence contradicts its concept. The second paragraph looks at the chemical process that results in a neutral product. In the third paragraph the product fails to satisfy the concept, because the differentiating and animating principle has been lost. The fourth paragraph spells out the process of separating a neutral product into its extremes. The fifth and final paragraph effects the transition to purpose, as the objects show themselves to be amenable to the concept. The same pattern is found in 1827, although the third and fourth paragraph are collapsed into one.

Yet in 1817 Hegel introduced changes that suggested a fundamental rethinking of one part of the argument; he amended the text again when he came to the revisions of 1827. These alterations provide further evidence for the way he modified his thinking over time.

1817

1 / We come upon new material in the second paragraph, which discusses the combination of differentiated objects into a neutral product. In 1816, Hegel had pointed out that – as a *real* process – there needed to be mediation, and he mentioned two alternative middle terms. The first was the

implicit nature or concept that is the ground of the differentiation. The second had an independent existence, to match the independence of the original objects; it was an abstractly neutral entity, such as water or speech. But he nonetheless talked about this process as a first syllogism. The second and third syllogisms applied to separation and differentiation respectively; they were not versions of combination or uniting.[2]

The syllogistic structure of combination has been quite transformed by 1817. The reference to an abstractly neutral middle term that had independent existence has disappeared entirely. And while the mediating power of the concept remains, it is mentioned only later on. Instead the 'syllogism' of combination moves from the concept as universal, by way of the differentiation of the chemical objects (which is particularity) to the product as singular. Mediation by a particular is a pattern that fits the abstract Barbara syllogism.

It is not easy to identify the two 'premises' and the inferential 'movement' that leads to the conclusion. In one premise, it appears that the different objects particularize the universal concept. It is a relation of *subsumption*. In the second premise, a single difference seems to *inhere* in the two objects. By way of the two objects the single difference passes over into a single neutral product that actualizes the universal.

But Hegel does not stop there. He completes a cycle of three syllogisms within the same paragraph on combination. For, he says, this process could be understood in terms of the other two forms as well. On the one hand, a singular activity transforms the particularized objects into a product that embodies the universal. This synthesizing dynamic fits the description of induction. On the other hand, the universal – the essence implicit in both the particular objects and their differentiation – comes to be something objective. As in the disjunctive syllogism of the ontological argument, the concept determines itself as existing.

Although Hegel is still using the language of syllogism in discussing chemical combination, he has nonetheless drastically altered its application. Instead of three distinct processes of combination, separation, and differentiation (each of which provides the condition for its successor), the one process of combination is understood in three different ways.[3]

What motivated this major revision to the argument within less than a year? There are three possible answers to this question. First, the syllogistic structure had been quite obscure in 1816. Second, in thinking about chemical process in the *Philosophy of Nature* Hegel noticed logical distinctions he had previously missed. Third, he realized that he had to separate more effectively the moves that a concept logically requires from those that reflect the contingencies of natural existence. I shall consider each of these in turn.

i / In my exposition of the 1816 text, it was difficult to establish with any certainty the logical structure of the process of combination. Hegel mentioned two candidates for the middle term, both of which posed problems when we tried to distribute the conceptual determinations of universal, particular, and singular among the three components in the process. This obscurity suggests that Hegel did not have time to sort out all the details. The *Science of Logic*, he complained, was written in the spare moments he had as a recently married father, teacher, and headmaster of a secondary school.[4] Second thoughts a year later showed that this section was more cumbersome than necessary; so in reworking it for the *Encyclopaedia*, he allowed the structure to be more explicitly syllogistic.[5]

This kind of rethinking employed the two contrary operations I mentioned when talking about the development in real measure: on the one hand reflection focusing on the essential core; on the other hand, understanding individuating new distinct moments.

ii / In the *Philosophy of Nature* of 1817, Hegel divided chemical processes into four. The first two were (a) the oxidation of metals and (b) the production of acids by fire. (Hegel grouped them in the same paragraph because both produce differentiated objects.) The third was the union of acids and bases in a neutral salt. The fourth was the exchange of radicals when two salts are combined in a solution.[6]

When we look at these, we find three different operations: one in which water divides (or particularizes itself) to oxidize metals; one in which fire, as a (singular) restless activity, combines a combustible body with the oxygen from air; one in which the polar opposition of two bodies (or the universal they share) brings about a neutral salt. The fourth includes the essential features of the first three – differentiation and neutralization – within a single totality, and so does not introduce anything distinctively new. As I suggested in parentheses, the mediating agents in these forms of combination correspond to the middle terms of the three syllogisms introduced into the *Encyclopaedia Logic*.

The fact that there is in nature no one form of chemical union may have made Hegel aware that the language of a single process mediated by an abstractly neutral middle term was not the only logical alternative. Further, the processes that chemists did talk about easily fitted the three-fold syllogistic structure. So he rethought the *logic* of chemical combination to see whether such a pattern could be derived a priori. In other words, science made him aware of logical possibilities he had previously missed.[7]

iii / In 1816 the middle term was given independent existence as an abstract neutrality. At the same time the differentiated bodies had to be kept apart by force. Both comments introduced precisely that aspect of externality and contingency that one associates with the realm of nature. They introduce a jarring note into the inherent transitions of pure logical thought. In his rethinking this material, then, Hegel may have recognized that he was here relying on representations drawn from the natural order, inappropriate to the realm of pure thought. They could be abandoned until he came to the philosophy of nature. So he developed the move from differentiated object to neutral product in more abstract and theoretical terms.

2 / When we move from the three syllogisms of combination to the rest of the discussion of chemical process in 1817 we find a simplification. In 1816, the moves to separate out the elements and to animate the elements into differentiated objects provided a second and third syllogism for the analysis. In 1817, the third process has disappeared altogether.[8] Combination and separation thus become two complementary processes. Although external to each other, the product of one disappears into the process of the other.[9] The move to teleology is simplified thereby: since that reciprocal pattern conforms with the concept of chemism, there is no longer an alien object to constrain the concept's freedom.

Most likely Hegel here abandoned the more detailed argument of the longer text because he did not want to complicate the skeleton of the *Encyclopaedia* with a recursive structure in which the pattern of three syllogisms would work at two different levels. In contrast to the earlier elaboration of chemical combination, then, these latter changes provide no evidence that he had fundamentally altered his conception of the logic of chemism.

1827 AND 1830

The key for the changes Hegel introduced ten years later may be found in a new sentence that introduces the third paragraph. Chemism is now called the relation of reflection with respect to objectivity. Reflection is a way of thinking analysed in the larger *Logic* under the 'Doctrine of Essence.' It is the intellectual activity that presupposes and posits an alien or external immediacy to determine what is essential therein.[10]

By appealing to the language of reflection, Hegel can justify several important motifs: chemical objects are presupposed to be external, not only to the act of conceiving, but also to each other;[11] and they are presupposed as immediate.[12] The independence that characterizes the content of the notion of chemism is also a function of the way it is thought to be.

Further, in the initial stages, reflection *posits* a totality; that is, it considers the object as a whole.[13] And at the end, when the supposed immediacy of the objects turns out to be vacuous (since each is the product of a process), the concept becomes free and self-contained, now able to determine itself, rather than adapt (as reflection had) to a presupposed externality.[14] This triggers the move to teleology.

What we have here is a more self-conscious use of the language of thinking. Free, self-determining conceptual thought is different from reflection, which responds to a presupposed and alien immediacy. Not only are these two modes of thinking distinct when applied to objects, but reflection, when fully applied to chemical objectivity, generates the conditions for a more self-contained conceiving.

Hegel has, then, become more sophisticated in his understanding of the way pure thought functions in the *Logic*. The distinction between reflecting and conceiving, already elaborated in principle in the first edition of the *Science of Logic*, is now used to explain the way chemism differs from mechanism and teleology.[15]

As an additional bonus, this distinction clarifies how conceptual thought moves from simply thinking about an alien mechanical or chemical object to being a subjective intention that can use objective means to accomplish its ends. Using another vocabulary, thought moves from speculative reason, still affected by what it wants to explain, to understanding, able to determine itself.[16]

One other change is worth noting briefly. In 1830 Hegel added a gloss to the final paragraph that spelt out the two processes that together make up the concept of chemism. They are, he said, 'the reduction of the differentiated to the neutral, and the differentiation of the undifferentiated or neutral.' This expressly collapses the third move in the larger *Logic* – from elements to differentiated objects – into the second process of separation. But at the same time it uses the phrases that had already become the motif for chemical process in the *Philosophy of Nature*. There, in the §326 of 1827 he had pointed out that the natural process corresponds to the concept in that it posits the different as identical (it undifferentiates, he adds in 1830) and differentiates, animates, and separates the identical. In other words Hegel was making explicit the role played by the logical concept of chemical process within the philosophy of nature.

1807–8

While the *Encyclopaedia* versions trace later developments in the concept of chemism from the version in the larger *Logic*, we also have a text that suggests some of its pre-history. Volume 12 of the critical edition contains a manuscript, entitled 'On Mechanism, Chemism, Organism and Cognition,' that the editors tentatively date to Hegel's stint in Bamberg as newspaper publisher (1807–8).[17] Despite the title, provided by the editors, the second section is not called 'Chemism' by Hegel, but 'Chemical Process,' a term Hegel carefully avoids in the *Logic* of 1816. In addition, the entities involved are not called 'objects,' but 'things' (*Dinge*).

Despite this more concrete vocabulary, the text does not discuss actual chemical processes (as did the texts from the Jena period), but works entirely with conceptual terms such as 'syllogism,' 'extreme,' 'middle,' 'element,' 'singularity,' and 'universality.' Even 'thing' is not a term restricted to nature and spirit, but serves as a more general concept.[18]

In this discussion each thing is itself a syllogism, in which its singularity mediates between the universal essence that it shares with its differentiated opposite and the particular ways in which the two are contraries. At the same time, the two opposites function as the extremes of a mediating pattern, one universal and passive, the other singular and active; these two independent beings are then brought in contact by way of a third thing, or element.[19] In due course this middle term (as particular) is shown to be transient, needing to be balanced by another kind of middle that is active and singular. In other words, Hegel moved from a syllogism 'of being' to a syllogism 'of essence.'[20] The two together, however, are one syllogism, in which the implicit universal essence becomes explicit as a being. This product of its process is the realization of the concept.

In common with the Jena philosophy of nature, this discussion moves directly on to organism and living process. The language of 'thing' does not allow, it appears, for the intermediate stage where a subjective concept appropriates an object as means.

When we take this early draft together with the two versions of the logic of chemism of 1816 and 1817, we can see Hegel continually working with the fit between the chemical process of combination and the conceptual language of syllogism. An inference involves using a middle term to establish a conclusion. Hegel's task was to discern which precise logical language was appropriate for describing the mediated combination of differentiated objects into a neutral product. In 1816, by talking of 'objects' rather than 'things,' he was able to remove one level of complexity. In addition, he separated the syllogism of separation from that of combination. But as we have seen, even then he was not satisfied. Because he never got to the third volume in his revision of the *Science of Logic*, we will never know what his considered view of chemism would finally be.

17

How Chemism Is Systematic

As we have just seen, some of Hegel's revisions to the *Encyclopaedia* in 1817 and 1827 highlighted similarities between chemism in the *Logic* and chemical process in the *Philosophy of Nature*. Before exploring how far that likeness extends, we need to reflect on the logical process and ask how it is systematic. If we do not answer that question, we cannot identify what are the distinctive features of the *Philosophy of Nature*.

The logic of chemism is more sophisticated than the logic of real measure. There, a measurement was to specify a quality in quantitative terms. The quest for a full specification led first to complications, and then to a reaction against that complexity. The overall concept of measuring, however, remained only implicit in the background; it was not part of the definition at each stage.

In chemism, the concept has a more explicit role to play. The object is thought as something immediate and external to any act of conceiving; it is to exist. Yet it is not to be simply inert and mechanical, but chemical. This distance between the concept of what the object is to be and how it exists as conceived reproduces the pattern of reflection within the notion itself (as Hegel came to recognize). Thought responds to something presupposed and does not determine itself in the way comprehensive thought does.[1]

This discrepancy between the conceiving and the conceived – between what the object is to be and what it in fact is – generates the key systematic advances. A chemical object exists as something immediate, yet is oriented intrinsically towards something else. Analysis of the components of that double definition shows how they are contradictory, a contradiction that can only be resolved if the object is not fixed but dynamic. Its chemical character becomes objective when it combines with its complement. That process in the conceived object enables it to correspond to the initial conception of what it is to be.

Yet the neutral product of the first process does not satisfy the concept of chemism either, since it is now separated from chemical activity. These satisfy the concept of chemism only when the activity decomposes the product into its elements; once again a process brings the object into conformity with its concept.

Similarly, in the third syllogism, the elements can be considered chemical objects only if they so distribute themselves among objects that a chemical differentiation is produced.

In this development, paradoxically enough, the object conceived becomes more and more inert: from a differentated object to a neutral product to an abstract element. At the same time, what the concept requires becomes more and more abstract: from a simple mutual reference to a singular activity to a pure conception of chemism.

That paradox emerges because the chemical object is supposed to be immediate, yet at the same time satisfy the concept of chemism. To bridge that gap the concept introduces a further object: the third term of a mediating process. So the language of syllogism comes to express the interaction between the concept of what the object is to be and that object as it exists. As the process becomes more rigorously defined, the terms become more abstract.

So when thought steps back and considers the full pattern of chemical processes, it notices that, for all of the supposed immediacy and externality in the objective realm of chemism, there is nonetheless a structure of mediation. The mediated product of one process is the immediate object of the next. Nothing is absolutely presupposed; nothing is completely alien to the demands of the concept. The supposedly independent objects show themselves to be chemical only when they are the conditions for a process.

In the logic of chemism, thought distinguishes between what its concept requires and what it refers to, and it explores what that object of reference would need to be like to match the concept. All of this is built into its comprehensive notion.

How, then, does Hegel's three-part schema of understanding, dialectical reason and speculative reason fit this logical analysis?

Understanding's task is to define its terms. It focuses on the components of a concept's meaning. So it first recognizes that a chemical object involves both immediate externality and differentiation, and it specifies just what each of those moments involves. Then it identifies what is missing from the concept of a neutral product that needs to be included to make it chemical.

Finally it shows what is the necessary counterpart to the elements' abstractness. In other words, understanding is the moment of conceiving; it is the concept that explores what a chemical object is to be.

Dialectical reason is the moment of transition. It is, in fact, what happens when the understanding does its job thoroughly. In each case, as we have seen, the result turns out to be an incoherence, a contradiction that needs to be resolved.

Speculation, or reflection, suggests a resolution, not by imposing something conceptual on the object, but by investigating how the object itself adapts to the conceptual demands. A process, or structure, of mediation resolves the contradiction.

The three logical operations do not only function in the moves from process to process. They also determine the structure of the chapter as a whole. The chemical object is an understood singular. The processes are dialectical transitions whereby objects become something else: differences are neutralized, products are decomposed, abstract elements are differentiated. Finally, speculation considers the total picture, and recognizes that the three syllogisms make a circle, in which the processes and the products are independent and external to each other, yet each is mediated as well as immediate. When this total picture is thoroughly understood, thought discovers that the conceived object is not just alien to, and presupposed by, the act of conceiving; but that it is amenable to conceptual manipulation. So the objective realm poses no limit to the concept's freedom of self-determination.

This whole development follows from the demands of pure thought. Getting concepts precisely defined generates inconsistencies; resolving the incoherence in a way appropriate to the conceptual requirements generates new problems; eventually the set of solutions falls into a pattern, whose characteristics, once thoroughly understood, reveal a different concept of objectivity. There is no need to refer, in any of this, to actual chemical bodies or to discrete historical persons. Hegel's discussion of chemism involves a systematic development that is logical on its own account.

II

PHILOSOPHY OF NATURE

CHEMICAL PROCESS

We now turn to the eleven paragraphs in Hegel's *Philosophy of Nature* devoted to chemistry. As noted in the introduction, my approach changes from an *exposition de texte* in which we try to think through the logical steps that lead from concept to concept to a more straightforward commentary. I have provided a fairly literal translation to parallel the German original, notes with background for specific terms, and a discussion of how the data of chemistry are being integrated with Hegel's systematic principles.

18

§326

Die Individualität in ihrer entwickelten Totalität ist, daß ihre Momente so bestimmt sind, selbst individuelle Totalitäten, ganze besondere Körper zu seyn, die zugleich nur als gegen einander differente Momente in Beziehung sind. Diese Beziehung, als die Identität nicht identischer, selbständiger Körper ist der Widerspruch, – somit wesentlicher *Proceß*, der dem Begriffe gemäß die Bestimmung hat, das Unterschiedene identisch zu setzen, es zu indifferenziren, und das Identische zu differenziren, es zu begeisten und zu scheiden.

Once developed as a totality, individuation has its moments so determined that they are themselves individual totalities: complete and particular bodies that are nonetheless connected as moments differentiated from each other. This connection, as the identity of non-identical, independent bodies, is a contradiction, and thus essentially a process that, in accordance with the concept, has the characteristic of positing the different as identical, so that it becomes undifferentiated, and of differentiating the identical, so that it is animated and divided.

NOTES

Individuality The English reader of this term needs to be careful. For 'individual' is frequently used to translate *Einzelne* and *Einzelheit*, as well as *Individuum* and *Individualität*. *Das Einzelne* is a logical term for the singular object of reference and stands in relation to concepts, both universal and particular. In Hegel's usual order, it comes third in any analysis. *Individuum* appears in the *Logic* only within the concept of life and captures the way life is a subjective totality confronting an objective realm. Life individuates itself.

Within the *Philosophy of Nature*, *Individualität* is used for all three chapters of the second section, which has the general title 'Physics.' The first section covers mechanics and described characteristics that apply to nature in general: space and time, matter and motion, and the system of absolute mechanics, in which subsidiary centres revolve around a primary centre. The third and final section, called 'Organic Physics,'[1] looks at geology, botany, and zoology; where earth, plants, and animals function as units, complete in themselves. In contrast to the *Logic*, *Individualität* here precedes, and prepares the way for, the discussion of living organisms.

So the middle section on physics stands between nature considered abstractly or universally and nature considered as integrated, singular organisms. The characteristics described are ways of differentiating among natural entities. Physics is nature particularized. When, therefore, Hegel titles the three chapters of this middle section universal individuality, particular individuality, and total individuality, he is not using individuality as a simple synonym for singular objects of reference. The term is functioning as a gerund ('individuating') rather than as an abstract noun. Hegel is interested in those natural characteristics by which bodies are individuated and so distinguished from each other. He makes this clear in his lectures of 1819–20, when he says that 'the highest point of particularizing is individuality.'[2]

To indicate this technical use of *Individualität* for the way entities are particularized, I have relied on the English word 'individual' and its cognates. 'Single' and 'singular' are consistently used for the logical object of reference, *das Einzelne*.

In this distinction between 'individual' and 'singular' Hegel appears to be differentiating the discourse of the *Philosophy of Nature* from that of pure logic. The way a thing is individuated cannot be established by pure thought, but must be derived from its own determinations.[3] By contrast, logic itself can recognize the partiality of its own act of conceiving and overcome it through an act of pure reference, whose focus is a singular. Therefore Hegel prefers *Individualität*, with its Latin root, for this part of his system, and leaves the German *Einzelnheit* for the more theoretical part.[4]

The two terms, however, are near synonyms. So, when Hegel places the section on individuality in the middle of the *Philosophy of Nature* he is not simply reproducing the conceptual pattern of particular concepts between universal concepts and singulars. Something like singularity is also being introduced at the second stage.⁵ This apparent anomaly is resolved when we appeal, not to his logic of the concept, but to that of the syllogism, which has a different order. The syllogism mediated by particularity is first; the syllogism mediated by singularity is second; and the syllogism mediated by universality is third.

The use of the term 'individuality' at the second stage, then, suggests that inferential thought and not simple conceiving is behind the systematic structure; at this stage the *Philosophy of Nature* is exploring how individuating can mediate. Similarly, mechanics talks about how movement particularizes matter. And geology and biology explore how the earth and organisms as wholes (or universals) organize themselves and their environment into determinate parts that yet interact.

In other words it is the mediating activities of moving, individuating, and organizing and the way they parallel the three syllogisms, more than the simpler triad of universal, particular, and singular, that determine the overall structure of the *Philosophy of Nature*.

Totality Hegel uses this term for the third chapter of the section on physics. We have already noticed that this section is governed by the concept 'Individuality,' which is then divided into three: the act of individuating is either universal, particular, or total. The physics that individuates in universal or general ways relies on light; the fundamental divisions of the natural order into air, fire, water, and earth; and the meteorological process. The physics that individuates in particular ways builds on specific weight, cohesion, sound, and heat. When we turn to the physics that individuates things 'totally' we are talking about the way bodies as a whole are involved in generating their individuality. By using this term to complete the triad with universal and particular, Hegel signals that 'totality' is standing in for the logical term 'singular.' So an individuated whole can be taken as a singular object of reference.

Even in this third chapter of the section, however, there are stages. Whole bodies are involved in all the phenomena described. But magnetism regards only their most general arrangement; colour, smell, and taste particularize whole bodies by the way they influence others; electrical polarization shows how they influence each other. In the final section, on chemical process, the totality covers both bodies and their relationships. While total bodies are differentiated from each other, that differentiation is itself a totality.⁶

In the *Logic*, totality is a function of the act of grounding. When all of its conditions are present, something emerges into existence; the totality reconstitutes the immediacy of being.[7] So, when a body is considered as a totality, it is neither simply subsumed under a universal, nor is it differentiated from another particular; it is an object referred to. A totality is the way a singular would appear in the philosophy of nature.

From another perspective, however, this stage incorporates features of the third syllogism – the one in which the universal mediates and determines how it is individuated and particularized. The object as a whole establishes its magnetic field; controls its colour, smell, and sound; responds to friction by generating an electrical polarity; and determines chemical processes. The totality, then, is also something universal, incorporating all the entity's particular features. As a concrete universal it individuates bodies at this stage in the philosophy of nature.

Body The term 'Body' appears only in the philosophy of nature. 'Entity,' 'thing,' 'actual,' 'real,' even 'object' are all logical terms. They are used to describe concepts and thoughts, as well as entities that are quite other than thought. 'Body,' however, is a way of thinking about matter.

Matter is a function of movement and place, of space and time, of external relations. While it is the most general way of talking about natural reality, it can also be broken up quantitatively into a number of discrete bits of matter, each one of which becomes a unit. Bodies are these units of matter.[8]

Contradiction We have already come across this term in the logical discussions. A contradiction emerged when we found that we needed contradictory categories to characterize a chemical object. Its resolution came by way of a process in which the tension was neutralized.

The need to overcome inconsistencies appears to be a requirement of thought. Hegel suggested, however, that this dynamic is inherent in the natural order as well. Natural bodies are finite. To characterize these bodies accurately we need to spell out their basic positive quality as well as the conditions under which they would cease to be what they are. The limit marks the point at which a body becomes something else – where the positive quality ceases to be.

Looking more closely we see that the limit works to destroy the positive feature just as that quality endeavours to maintain itself and cancel any barrier that restricts it. The two aspects of a finite thing contradict each other. So, when a positive quality ignores its limit it brings about its own demise. One body ceases to be and another comes into being.

Begeisten When used with respect to people, this German term can be translated as 'become enthusiastic or delighted.' An analogous stimulation happens to chemical bodies. For this verb and its cognates appear in all but three of the eleven paragraphs of this section.[9] Hegel also used the adjective when talking about elements in the logic of chemism to distinguish between the animating principle and the indifferent basis.

The fact that the root of this word is *Geist* or spirit – the term Hegel used for the all-encompassing reality that overreaches both nature and history – can lead the unwary and the romantic into supposing that, for Hegel, the realm of nature is spiritualized. That reads too much into a word that has the more conventional sense of animating – of stimulating something so that an activity occurs.[10]

COMMENTARY

'Body' is a concept that appears in the context of natural space and time. While 'individuality' and 'totality' occur in the Logic, they become important for Hegel's systematic purposes only in the section on physics. So the language of this paragraph situates it squarely within the philosophy of nature.

At the same time there is no reference to anything empirical, or to any discoveries made by the natural sciences. Hegel is concentrating on analysing concepts. He is preparing the philosophical ground for introducing chemical phenomena.

This focus on conceptual analysis is indicated by the adjective 'developed.' It is a term from the logical language of conceiving: a concept develops.[11] So this stage in the philosophy of nature has developed conceptually from what has preceded. There is no natural evolution.

In chapter 31 we shall discuss the paragraph that leads into this discussion of chemical process and show how thought reflects on the empirical information provided by density, colours, smells, taste, and electricity. The result of that reflection is a new way of looking at nature, one in which whole bodies separate into a tensed relation of differentiation and in which that tension is overcome to produce an integrated entity.

This new approach is conceptual, the product of thought; it is not a given of experience. And so the first step that one takes at this level is a reflective one. The specific characteristics of this concept need to be spelt out. It involves, Hegel says, an 'individuality whose moments are determined to be individual totalities, quite particular bodies, which yet at the same time stand in relation to each other as differentiated moments.'[12] This is the theoretical framework that will determine the whole discussion of chemical process. It has developed from the conceptual demands that thought raised in the previous stages.

Further reflection, however, shows that this kind of structure has its problems. While the moments are independent bodies, different from each other, they are yet identified within a total individuality as directly related to each other. To say that bodies are both identified and not identified is contradictory; the contradiction can be overcome only if the two moments are not fixed, but are the terms of a process from identity to difference and from difference to identity.

The phrases used in developing this argument are familiar. They are almost the same as those he introduced in 1827 to §203 of the *Logic*; so Hegel is preparing the ground for the first explicit reference to chemistry, in §328.

But these words have a wider application; for this kind of process corresponds to the structure of conceiving in general, not just to chemical process. Hegel made the same point when developing the logic of magnetism: 'The activity of the form is none other than that of conceiving in general: positing the identical as differentiated and the differentiated as identical.'[13]

To identify conceiving with this double process might appear strange to anyone who believes that conceiving is simply thinking unalterable thoughts. But for Hegel conceiving involves understanding what we are thinking about; understanding not only fixes the determinate differences between the components of a concept, but also shows how and why they are connected the way they are. In other words, understanding something involves grasping its explanation, and any adequate explanation shows how determinate moments are to be differentiated out of a basic identity and how those different moments nonetheless are identified within a single pattern.[14] In other words, the demands of the philosophy of nature have turned up a network of meanings that, although supposed to be something we might find in nature, is inherently logical.

We have, then, an image of the *logic* of chemical process. Differentiated objects combine into something undifferentiated; an identity is differentiated into its moments. How does the reasoning that has led to this conclusion differ from what went on in the *Logic*?

It is the transience of electrical phenomena that leaves conceptual thought dissatisfied and triggers the move to the next stage. This is something we can only learn from experience. In contrast, the *Logic* arrived at chemism by way of the simple thought of objects oriented towards each other, a concept implicit in the laws that govern a mechanical object.

Much takes place in Hegel's *Philosophy of Nature* between his discussions of mechanics and chemistry. Mechanics is not just thoughts about objects (as mechanism was), but concerns gravity and the way weight affects matter in motion. That organization of nature in general does not explain how and why bodies are individuated, however, so it is necessary to turn to physics. There, the physical elements, specific weight, magnetism, smell and taste each contribute another mode of natural individuation; and electricity shows that whole bodies, not simple properties, are involved. Because at each stage one should never move further than necessary, the pathway is long.[15]

In the *Logic* we are working with the whole realm of objectivity, whether as mechanism or as chemism, and thought focuses on how the individual objects are related to the total conceptual picture. In the *Philosophy of Nature*, on the other hand, we need to show in detail how bits of matter come to be distinguished from each other, and then connected together into individuated wholes. Totality must be established, not presupposed.

The *Logic* moves in the realm of pure thought. It explores *possibilities*. In contrast, the *Philosophy of Nature* must investigate the way conceptual demands are in fact *actualized*. Each actualization reveals to conceptual thought features and aspects that have not yet been handled and need to be explored. So this more laborious task transforms the simple transition from mechanism to chemism into the long and detailed journey from mechanics through physics to chemistry.

19

§327

Zunächst ist der *formale* Proceß zu beseitigen, der eine Verbindung bloß *Verschiedener*, nicht Entgegengesetzter ist; sie bedürfen keines existierenden Dritten, in welchem sie, als ihrer Mitte, *an sich* Eines wären. Das Gemeinschaftliche oder ihre Gattung macht schon die Bestimmung ihrer Existenz zu einander aus; ihre Verbindung oder Scheidung hat die Weise der Unmittelbarkeit, und Eigenschaften ihrer Existenz erhalten sich. Solche Verbindungen chemisch gegen einander unbegeisteter Körper sind die Amalgamation und sonstiges Zusammenschmelzen von Metallen, Vermischung von Säuren mit einander, und derselben, des Alkohols u.s.f. mit Wasser und dergleichen mehr.

First we have to set aside the formal process, which is a combining of things that are simply diverse, not opposed to each other. These require no existing third term, a middle, in which they would be implicitly one. What is common to them (in other words their genus) already constitutes the way their existence is directed towards each other. Their combination or separation has the character of immediacy, and the properties of their initial existence are retained. Such combinations of bodies that do not chemically excite each other are amalgamation and other alloys of metals; mixtures of acids with each other; and of acids, alcohol, and so on with water, and others of the same sort.

NOTES

Formal/real Hegel distinguishes between a *formal* process (here) and a *real* one (§328), underlining the terms in both places. This distinction goes back to the logic of essence, where Hegel has explored the various forms of grounding or justification.[1]

In the *Logic* the concept of ground emerges as the way of resolving an inescapable contradiction. In a similar way, the language of process here responds to the contradiction involved when bodies are both identical and not identical.

The shift in language from ground to process is not inappropriate. A process moves from one state to another. The first state is the ground of the dynamic – the reason for the product. So Hegel is justified in using the logic of a grounding relation when exploring the kinds of processes that might be involved.

In a formal ground, there is no difference in content between the ground and what is grounded by it. Any distinction is simply formal, a matter of superficial structure. So the move from difference to identity or vice versa would not affect the basic characteristics of the things being joined or separated.

By contrast, in a real ground the process of grounding introduces a real change or transformation in the content. The result is not simply the sum of its constituents, but something qualitatively different. So the shift is not reversible.

That change in content poses a problem, however, for what initiates the process, or ground, can only explain what is the same in the result. Any qualitative change is not covered by it. Either that is left as an unexplained surd, or a second condition (or ground) is required for a full explanation. This separate condition mediates the grounding process, providing a bridge between the original ground and the really distinct product. This is why Hegel moves so easily from talking about a real process to talking about a middle term, or mediator, whereas the formal process can be unmediated or direct.

Diverse/opposed These two terms are also analysed within the logic of essence.[2] They are some of the criteria reflection uses to determine what is essential. Both diversity and opposition involve identifying and differentiating, the two moments of the contradiction in the §326.

Pure identity is quite other than difference, and pure difference is quite other than identity. But this absolute otherness cannot be maintained, since each implicitly assumes the other. Differences are drawn between identical things and different things are identified. The real question is how identity and difference are related to each other.

What identifies the different things in a diversity is irrelevant to whatever differentiates them, and vice versa. Considering them all together under the same perspective need take no account of their distinctive features. We have a simple collection. Similarly, examining how they are different from each other tells us nothing about how they can be classified or identified. The two characterizations are indifferent to each other.

Diversity is appropriate for the kind of process examined in this paragraph; since the content remains the same both before and after, any *differences* between the bodies being combined (or *identified*) is irrelevant to the process. The bodies need only come from the same general category or genus. In Hegel's examples, the genera are metals and liquids, and amalgamation ignores how the metals or liquids are differentiated from each other.

In an opposition, however, two things are explicitly antithetical to each other within a single framework (as blue and red under the category of colour). Their difference is subordinate to, and governed by, their identity; it explicitly breaks up the general picture into incompatible particulars. So whatever opposes one body to another assumes some basic identity that they share. Only the general perspective recognizes that they are complements.

This is the logical relation traditionally called 'contrary': two predications cannot both be true, but they would both be false, were the general concept they both assume inappropriate.

Opposition was a feature in the logical concept of a chemical object, since the two differentiated objects were opposed to each other as complementary instances of a general concept.

Opposed bodies, then, are different from each other; but their differences particularize the way they are identified. Their identity sets them against each other as particulars or contraries. Coming from the other direction, the distinctions that separate them are mutually complementary, so that their differences require their identity. One can move either way.[3]

Contradiction is the concept that follows these two in the strictly logical sequence. In a contradiction, the opposition is not relative to, and established by, a more general or inclusive identity, or vice versa. Rather things are identified and differentiated in the same way and from the same perspective. It is this application of opposite categories to the same reality that cannot be maintained and requires the search for a ground or explanation.

There are, then, three ways by which identity and difference can be combined in a single concept: as diversity (where they are indifferent to each other), as opposition (where one is defined relative to the other), and as contradiction (where both apply in exactly the same respect). In none of them can the concept be fully integrated into a unity. Thought shifts from one of the terms to the other. When that is no longer possible – in a contradiction – we have something that cannot coherently be thought at all, and we have to find some way of grasping the horns of the dilemma.

Immediacy As with all negative terms, it is frequently difficult to get a positive sense of what this concept involves. Probably the best way is to rely on the negative moment: what is immediate is something that is not mediated; it happens directly. In this paragraph, it refers to a mixture that does not require any intermediary or third term to make it come about.

This term also occurs in the logic where the role it plays is more complicated. Hegel says that a concept can be considered immediately – as it simply is in thought – without any reference to the mediation (or reflection) that brought thought to that point. In other words, immediacy can emerge from mediation. That is a paradox that can only be resolved if we realize that thinking has the ability to cancel and dismiss its own mediating activity. It can say: All this took place, but it is not really necessary or significant to the meaning of the term; we can just take the concept as it is.

That self-cancelling capacity is not a feature of nature. When we turn to reflect on, or understand, nature we find that it is simply there as immediate. Nonetheless, to take it as it is, does require that thought explicitly refuse to allow its own mediating dynamic to function. Pure reference, after all, is not a simple intellectual act, but a highly complex one.

To be sure, experience may show that there are natural processes that have in fact mediated these givens. What at first appears to be naturally immediate will show itself to be mediated.[4]

Amalgamation etc. Since chemistry studies the transformation of bodies when they are combined and separated, it was necessary for chemical textbooks to distinguish a chemical union from one that was only mechanical – a simple amalgam or mixture. Thus Trommsdorff, in his *Systematisches Handbuch* (§58), defines the former as follows: 'When two heterogeneous bodies combine with each other so that together they constitute a completely homogeneous mass, in which we can no more distinguish one from the other, that is, in which no part is found where there is not a part of each of the united bodies, we call this in general a chemical combination [*chemische Verbindung*].' A simple union [*Vereinigung*] leaves the parts of the two bodies separate, even though they may be so fine and dispersed that it is hard to isolate them. When liquids are mixed, a simple union is called a solution, while a combination is called a dissolution.

Hegel does not adopt Trommsdorff's terminology. *Verbindung* (combination) is used only in this paragraph as the general term for amalgamations, alloys, and mixtures. When a chemical change occurs, he uses the term *Vereinung* (union) and its cognates. Note, however, the difference in spelling between this latter term and the one Trommsdorff used for amalgamations. The two initial bodies do not 'agree' but are 'made one.'

In 1800, J.J. Winterl, a teacher in Budapest, proposed a new term for this non-chemical union: 'May I be allowed to distinguish this most diverse species of solution from that which combines acids and bases, which is opposed to it in other respects as well, by its own name: synsomacy.'[5] The examples he goes on to cite are those listed by Hegel in this paragraph. In the 1827 edition Hegel introduced Winterl's name for the process parenthetically, and he used the term as a verb, co-ordinate with 'amalgamate' in his remark on elective affinity in both the 1812 and the 1831 *Logic*. The term never did catch on, however, so Hegel dropped it from the 1830 edition of the *Philosophy of Nature*.

The distinction between the two types of process, however, continued to be important. In his *Lehrbuch der Chemie* Berzelius calls the simple amalgamations by which metals produce alloys (he uses *Zusammenschmel zungen*) *Legirungen*, and he compares them with the simple mixtures of alcohol and water.[6] He attributes the difference between a solution and a dissolution to Lavoisier: 'The one can take place in all proportions while the other, changing the nature of the body dissolved, admits only fixed and invariable proportions.'[7]

COMMENTARY

For all that Hegel exploits the logical distinctions between formal and real, or between diversity and opposition in this paragraph, there is nothing in the previous paragraph that requires the discussion here. The direct move would have been to turn to actual processes in which differences were really neutralized and identities were really differentiated. And that was what Hegel had done in 1817. Indeed, Hegel himself marked this paragraph as a detour with his initial suggestion, added in 1830, that this kind of process is to be shunted into a siding.

To be sure, the logical points are consistent with, and offer one way of elaborating, what has already emerged. We have identified conceptually a kind of process, and the next task is to see how this process actually occurs in nature. Since the process is to bridge the contradiction between identity and difference, diversity arises as one possible alternative for combining the two; and one can imagine a process in which the form of difference is changed for the form of identity (or vice versa) leaving the content unaffected.

But this is a possible move, not a necessary one. We could have drawn on lots of other logical categories to introduce complicating distinctions into the systematic stage we have now reached. So the question is: why does Hegel choose to explore the particular option of formal ground at this point?

The answer can be found in the chemical textbooks. Chemists like Trommsdorff used the contrast between combination and union to define the distinctive characteristic of the chemical realm.

It was not, then, the strict demands of logic that required this paragraph, but the conclusions of chemists themselves. For all that Winterl's technical term, *synsomacy*, did not catch on in chemical circles, the distinction between a simple mixture or amalgam and a genuine combination was so basic that it should not be omitted from the philosophy of nature.

Once he admitted the need to discuss this alternative kind of process, Hegel found that the empirical description of amalgamation fitted with the language of formal grounding: there is no change in the nature of the substance involved, but only a difference in the spatial form. Its counterpart, real ground, is appropriate for the chemical kind of union. So the natural phenomena allow, indeed invite, the language of formal and real process, diversity and opposition, immediate and mediated.[8]

The text of the paragraph hides this systematic development. For it starts out by describing the process in the most abstract logical terms, and it turns to concrete cases as examples only at the end. Such a move from definition to examples was also characteristic of the chemical textbooks, but there it was clear that the author was taking a distinction found in nature and trying to give it a theoretical description. Given the systematic claims of the *Encyclopaedia*, Hegel's text suggests a more inferential and sequential argument than is justified.

A simple amalgamation does, however, presuppose that the two things being mixed are of the same genus; they have something in common. Metals can be amalgamated with metals, acids mixed with acids; but there is no such union when metals and liquids are brought together. Their differences are too great to make any genuine mixture possible. So this process does not involve a *mere* diversity, despite what Hegel says. Some general principle or genus is required to 'mediate' the process. This is perhaps why Hegel, unlike Trommsdorff, calls this process a *combination* of diverse things. Some kind of relevant identity governs what happens. It is only that the differences do not involve an explicit opposition; nor is the result qualitatively different from what went before. The entities are simply diverse.[9]

20

§328

Der *reale* Proceß bezieht sich zugleich auf die chemische Differenz (§200ff.), indem zugleich die ganze concrete Totalität des Körpers in ihn eingeht (§325). Die Körper, die in den realen Proceß eintreten, sind in einem Dritten, von ihnen Verschiedenen, vermittelt, welches die *abstracte*, nur erst *an sich* seyende Einheit jener Extreme ist, die durch den Proceß in die Existenz gesetzt wird. Dieses Dritte sind daher nur *Elemente*, und zwar selbst verschieden, als theils des Vereinens, die abstracte Neutralität überhaupt, das *Wasser*, – theils des Differenzirens und Scheidens, die *Luft*. Indem in der Natur die unterschiedenen Begriffsmomente auch in besonderen Existenz sich herausstellen, so ist auch das Scheiden und Neutralisiren des Processes jedes an ihm ebenso ein Gedoppeltes, nach der concreten und nach der abstracten Seite. Das *Scheiden* ist einmal Zerlegen der neutralen Körperlichkeit in körperliche Bestandtheile, das andere Mal Differenziren der abstracten physischen Elemente, in

The *real* process is connected directly with chemical differentiation (§200ff.), since the whole concrete totality of the body enters directly into it (§325). The bodies that enter into the real process are mediated in a third, which is simply diverse from them. This third is the abstract, initially only implicit, unity of those extremes, which is to be established through the process. So only *elements* can serve as this third, and do so in diverse ways: in part as the element of uniting, abstract neutrality in general or *water*; in part as the element of differentiating and separation, or *air*. Since in nature the different moments of conceiving set themselves out in particular existence as well, the separating and neutralizing in the process are also each doubled with respect to it: on the concrete, and on the abstract side. *Separating* involves on the one hand the breaking apart of the neutral corporeality into components that are bodies, on the other hand the differentiating of the abstract physical elements into the four even more

die vier hiermit noch abstracteren chemischen Momente des Stickstoffs, Sauerstoffs, Wasserstoffs und Kohlenstoffs, welche zusammen die Totalität des Begriffs ausmachen und nach dessen Momenten bestimmt sind. Hiernach haben wir als die chemischen Elemente: 1) die Abstraction der Indifferenz, den *Stickstoff*; 2) die beiden des Gegensatzes, das Element der für sich seyenden Differenz, den *Sauerstoff*, das Brennende, und das Element der dem Gegensatze angehörigen Indifferenz, den *Wasserstoff*, das Brennbare; 3) die Abstraction ihres *individuellen* Elements, den *Kohlenstoff*.

Ebenso ist das Vereinen das eine Mal Neutralisiren concreter Körperlichkeiten, das andere Mal jener abstracten chemischen Elemente. So sehr ferner die concrete und die abstracte Bestimmung des Processes verschieden ist, so sehr sind beide zugleich vereinigt; denn die physischen Elemente sind, als die Mitte der Extreme, das, aus dessen Differenzen die gleichgültigen concreten Körperlichkeiten begeistet werden, d.i. die Existenz ihrer chemischen Differenz erlangen, die zur Neutralisirung dringt und in sie übergeht.

abstract chemical moments of nitrogen, oxygen, hydrogen and carbon, which together make up the totality of the concept and are determined according to its moments. Thus we have as the chemical elements: (1) the abstraction of indifferentiation: *nitrogen*; (2) the two elements of opposition, the element of differentiation on its own account: *oxygen*, or what burns; and the element of indifferentiation as an opposite: *hydrogen*, or the combustible; (3) the abstraction of their (i.e. the physical elements') *individuated* element: *carbon*.

Similarly, uniting involves neutralizing concrete corporealities on the one hand, and, on the other, those abstract chemical elements. In addition, for all that the concrete and the abstract determining of the process is diverse, both are also, at the same time, united; for the physical elements, as the middle of the extremes, are that out of whose differentiation the indifferent concrete corporealities are stimulated; that is, they evoke the existence of that chemical differentiation that yearns to be neutralized and passes over into it.

[§200ff. refers to the paragraphs on chemism from the *Encyclopaedia Logic*. §325 covers the transition from electricity to chemistry; it is discussed in Chapter 31.]

NOTES

Moments of the concept Conceiving, or the most disciplined form of thinking, involves three distinct operations. First it generalizes, categorizing under the most universal features. Second it specifies this generality, introducing distinctions, separating this particular form of the universal from others, determining it more precisely.[1] Third it indicates that which cannot be captured by either the general or the specific difference – the singular, which may be subsumed under particular categories, but cannot be captured by them. In abstract terms we have universal concepts, particular concepts, and singulars.

In nature, bodies are a dispersed diversity. The task of thought is, first of all, to abstract some general and universal features or categories from that diversity. Then we check whether this generalization can be particularized – whether the things within the genus can be understood as different from, and contrary to, each other. In abstract terms, we can say that these particulars cancel or negate each other, since one species excludes the others; and that they yet, as determinations of the universal, share a common base or structure. These two moments, both essential in determining what are particulars, fall apart in nature and acquire independent existence.

So when Hegel considers nature conceptually, he finds that it is organized in a fourfold pattern, where one moment is universality, a second is singularity, and the other two are the complementary parts of particularity: negative separation and neutral community.[2]

The act of conceiving can think about itself as well. It can focus on its own activities and particularize them, isolating them from each other, until each becomes something singular and radically distinct. This is the process of abstraction, and is used both in universalizing – when the general term is fixed as a static collection of its instantiations – and in individualizing – when the singular term is not amenable to any categorial description at all, but can only be referred to.

In the *Logic*, the abstract universal and the abstract singular, as radical opposites, have to be coupled together. That happens in a judgment – at first in an affirmative, singular judgment. Then, as each form of judgment cannot express completely the kind of connection it requires, it is revised through a logical sequence that eventually ends up with syllogisms and inference. In this way what starts out as abstract develops towards concrete completeness.

In the *Philosophy of Nature*, the distinction between abstract and concrete is also important. In the first place, natural bodies are experienced as concrete. At the same time they make up a whole world, a universe that is all inclusive. The task of thought is to find ways of organizing that totality – of discovering how it can be individuated according to certain categories, what elements make it up, and how they interact. At one level this involves noticing differences that are already there in experience, and finding the right ways of classifying them. The task of philosophy is to control that act of observation, so that each difference categorized does not presuppose too much, but builds on differences already noticed. It is this careful control that enables the philosophy of nature to be systematic. This classification of differences responds to the concrete determinations of bodies as they are found existing in nature.

But thought can push further. It not only controls how it observes; it can, in the second place, take the initiative and analyse, using experiment to determine what are the universal and the particular features that lie below the surface and are really essential. This controlled investigation involves a conceptual abstracting – separating out aspects and fixing them as independent. Rather than grouping under categories, it analyses elements. Such a procedure does not just take up what experience offers. It *uses* thought's capacity to particularize. It is the thoroughgoing use of this strictly conceptual operation that produces the abstract results of scientific analysis. In other words, analysis is nothing less than the abstractive capacity of conceptual thought applied to nature.

When Hegel talks about the moments of conceiving, then, at one level he is distinguishing between universal, particular, and singular. But at another, he is referring to what happens when particularizing is applied self-reflexively to generate the abstract from the concrete. So throughout this section, when he refers to abstract processes or abstract entities, he is identifying the results of thought's analytic initiative.

Element This concept emerged in the logic of chemism's process, discussed in chapter 14. Elements are produced when an independent critical activity breaks up a neutral object into its abstract components. There the process was part of chemism, but in fact it is characteristic of much thinking that focuses on compound objects. Elements are the product of analysis.

A long tradition that reaches back to the Greeks identified the basic elements of the world as earth, air, fire, and water. Traces of this vocabulary could still be found in chemical textbooks in Hegel's day. Thus J.B. Richter, while identifying elements as the simplest indestructible substances, or matter which cannot be broken up artificially, pointed out that there seem to be more than just the traditional four, and mentioned phosphoric acid.[3] Vegetable alkalis and metallic acids, he said, are as different from each other as earth and water. He also distinguished between physical elements (and he listed water, magnetic matter, electricity, and light) that, while not analysable into dissimilar parts, do not lose their peculiar appearance when mixed with other material, and chemical elements (alkali salts, earths, and sulphur) that, while not analysable into dissimilar parts, *do* lose their peculiar appearance when mixed with other material and generate other appearances. A chemical element is immediate (vitriol, salt, phosphorus) when it can no longer be broken up artificially into dissimilar parts, mediate (vinegar) when art can do so.

Just about the time that Richter was writing Cavendish showed water to be a compound, and the study of gases identified air as a mixture of azote (or nitrogen) and two other gases we now call oxygen and carbon dioxide. More and more the term 'element' came to be used exclusively for the results of chemical analysis and the traditional vocabulary was abandoned. In his *Lehrbuch der Chemie* of 1825 (original edition 1811), Berzelius started out by distinguishing simple bodies, bodies not yet decomposed, and bodies that are the conjunction of simple bodies, and he pointed out that earth, air, fire, and water had all been shown to be compounds.[4]

Hegel considered the limitation of the term 'element' to chemical entities rather arbitrary.[5] He maintained the traditional division and distinguished the four 'physical elements,' which are the most general features of the terrestrial realm, from 'chemical elements,' which enable chemical processes to function.[6] These two types of elements merit separate notes.

Physical elements Hegel treated the physical elements early in his discussion of physics. The first chapter of this section handles the universal ways in which bodies are individuated. The most general is the distinction between light and darkness: the sun and stars that produce light are distinguished both from the moon and comets that reflect it and from the earth that receives light from both.

The next step is to handle the terrestrial elements. They are the most general components of the planet earth identified by reflective thought. It can be broken up into the atmosphere, the oceans and seas, and the dry land; fire transforms and destroys the other elements.

It is tempting to draw a parallel between this fourfold division and the more abstract one of gas, liquid, solid, and energy.[7] The physical elements are not abstract, however, but the basic components of bodies; they incorporate much of the qualitative characteristics of our everyday experience of the world. We respond in different ways to each of them; and the distinctions among them provide a foundation for our further analysis of the natural order.

So we should not read too much into the four physical elements. Water is not here contrasted with acids and alcohol; earth is not a kind of body distinct from metals or salts; nor does atmospheric air exclude sulphur dioxide and methane (or marsh gas as it was called in the early nineteenth century).

These general categories are not exclusive, but inclusive. The distinctive bodies mentioned in the previous paragraph (which Hegel would include in chemistry rather than among the general divisions of the terrestrial sphere) are found in nature once one uses a more refined method of analysis. But in the larger scale of nature, these secondary substances are absorbed and disappear, not simply from our purview, but from the environment as well.[8] Distinct gases are dispersed within the atmosphere, acids and alcohol are diluted into the seas and oceans, and the various solids are mixed and combined in the great land masses. Through it all combustion and heat plays a role: in melting the core of the earth (volcanoes), in evaporating water, in producing the meteorological phenomena of winds and storms. This fourth function cannot be reduced to any of the other elements, but has its own independent place among them.

I have set out this context for Hegel's discussion of physical elements to suggest that in analysing the universal forms of individuating he was not talking about science, but about the most general characteristics of our *experience* of the world. These characteristics provide the presupposition for all subsequent scientific analysis. Indeed some sciences, like the study of seasons and climate and the investigation of drought and natural plenty, still presuppose the general categories of heat, earth, water, and air.[9]

Hegel organized the four elements along conceptual lines. There will be a universal, a singular, and two particulars: division and neutrality.

The most general will not contain any internal divisions, but be elastic and fluid, penetrating everywhere.[10] Air, however, is not simply universal and simple. It has a destructive capacity as well. It is a factor in everything else that might be individuated, wearing away earth surfaces, absorbing water, extinguishing fire, as well as generating fresh water (through rain), feeding flames, and depositing wind-blown sediment; air not only maintains life, but also threatens it.[11]

At the other extreme, of singularity, we have the element characterized by difference and individuation. It provides a solid core that holds the other elements together into a single totality. It is, in other words, the earth as element, which maintains the integrity of the earth as planet.

In between lies the moment of particularity – which falls apart into that which negates and that which is shared. On the one hand there is the element that functions on its own account, half-way between the simple, general negativity of air, and the self-contained independence of earth. Fire, however, is transient and so devours itself, leaving bare neutrality as its counterpart. On the other hand, water is neutrality that is not at all self-contained, but quite fluid and plastic, amenable to being both destroyed and generated by fire.[12] As something singular that nonetheless does not exist on its own account, it lies half-way between the indeterminate universality of air, and the resistance and fixity of earth. Fire and water, then, function as the two sides of particularity: divisive activity and neutral community, completing the 'natural' pattern of four.

Chemical elements One can trace the development of this concept through the chemistry texts in Hegel's library. J.B. Richter, who accepted phlogiston and so took what we now call metallic oxides as simple substances,[13] divided chemical elements into salts, earths, and others. Among salts he listed mineral, vegetable, and animal acids, along with alkalis; earths included metallic, alkaline, and 'pebble' earth.[14]

J.B. Trommsdorff, in his textbook of 1800, accepted the revolution instituted by Lavoisier. But he did not bind himself to the vocabulary of elements. 'In our investigations we come finally to parts that we cannot break up further into other dissimilar parts, and these are called elements, primary principles, primitive stuff, or even simply stuff. It would be better to call them "undecomposed substances."' Caution prevented him from calling them 'undecomposable.'[15] His list started with caloric, added oxygen, hydrogen, nitrogen, and carbon; then went on to sulphur and phosphorus. The rest of the 'elements' were divided into metals, alkalis (he listed potash, lime, soda, strontion, and baryte), earths (silica, magnesia, aluminum, glycerine, etc.) and finally three acids that do not fit anywhere else: muriatic, boracic, and fluoric.

Trommsdorff's caution was justified. In the year his first volume was published, Volta announced the successful construction of an electric pile that would produce a spark; before very long Berzelius and Humphrey Davy were using this instrument to decompose not only water, but also the alkalis, earths, and the halogenic acids that Trommsdorff had listed as elements.

In his *Lehrbuch der Chemie*, Berzelius provided the list of simple substances that emerged from these investigations.[16] The language of 'earths' was no longer appropriate, since it had covered what were now known to be compounds, almost all of which were oxides. In its place, metals were distinguished from metalloids. 'The universal characteristic of these latter bodies, whereby they are differentiated from metals, are in general the incapacity to conduct electricity and heat combined with a lower specific weight, which is no more than three times that of water' (166). Berzelius' list of metalloids includes oxygen, hydrogen, nitrogen,[17] sulphur, phosphorus, chlorine, iodine, fluorine, carbon, boron, and silica.[18]

The discovery that alkalis and earths are compounds altered the conception of metals, since they exposed chemical materials that were clearly of the same class. These 'new' metals included potassium, sodium, lithium, ammonium, barium, strontium, calcium, aluminium, beryllium, and zirconium. Metals are 'burnable, non-transparent bodies that conduct heat and electricity and, when polished, take on a peculiar, so-called metallic, shine' (661). Berzelius allowed that some of them might still be analysable into more elementary components: 'The circumstances that make the simplicity of the other metals questionable are their supposed emergence in organic nature out of materials in which, as far as we have yet been able to determine, they are not contained' (729).[19] It is likely that Hegel had not read Berzelius' full text when he revised the *Encyclopaedia* in 1830.[20] By this time, however, he did know that earths were oxidized forms of radicals, which he called metalloids, and from Berzelius' shorter text he had learned that potash could be decomposed by a galvanic process, in which its radical formed an amalgam with mercury.[21] So in the main text he abandoned the language of 'earths' that he had used in 1827 and in certain circumstances substituted 'metalloids.' In 1817, he referred to the hydrogen acids in a remark (later dropped), so he did know about the discovery of the halogens: chlorine, iodine, fluorine. He simply refers to metals in general.

For all that he was aware of these developments, Hegel was not prepared to call the newly isolated basic chemical substances 'elements.' He reserved that term for the constituents of air and water. That this is the basis for his restriction is clear from the 1817 version of this section. In the discussion of oxidation, oxygen and hydrogen are identified as the components of water, and oxygen and nitrogen are identified as the constituents of air in the paragraph on combustion. Subsequent to this, Hegel had a short paragraph, reproduced by and large in the one we are now discussing, that says that these three elements 'have the abstraction of their individual (individuated?) element in carbon.'[22]

In his remark to §334 he made disparaging comments about the way empirical chemistry lumped different things – metals, the gases (oxygen and hydrogen), the metalloids, sulphur, and phosphorus – into a single disordered whole. He stressed that they are different kinds of things, classified by the kinds of processes that produced them. Elements like hydrogen and oxygen are derived from abstract, analytic experiments; metals are refined in a more concrete process; while the metalloids (or, as they had previously been called, earths) are isolated in other ways. To call them all elements is a misnomer, for an element is of necessity the result of a process driven by conceptual thought, and so it does not describe a concrete body, but rather something abstract, considered on its own.[23]

The evidence suggests that Hegel was still working within the framework of Trommsdorff's textbook. Yet Davy's and Berzelius' analytic experiments had used equally abstractive processes to isolate metals like sodium and aluminium, and halogens like fluorine; these substances also do not exist in a pure state in nature. While Hegel was aware of these developments, they did not lead him to reconsider his classification of the elements.

So we must look further for his restriction of the term to nitrogen, oxygen, hydrogen, and carbon. In the logic of chemism elements are defined, not only by the fact that they are produced by decomposing compound products, but also by the fact that they can then divide themselves among substances to generate differentiated objects. Oxygen and hydrogen in water and oxygen in air (which then leaves nitrogen as a residue) function in this way. Along with carbon, they are basic to almost all processes by which chemically differentiated substances are generated. And for Hegel chemistry was essentially process, not components. So it is not only the processes by which they are isolated, but also the processes they initiate, that determine which four are to be the sole elements.[24]

One further comment is necessary. Trommsdorff cites caloric as a basic imponderable (or weightless) element, taking this over from Lavoisier. By the time Hegel was writing, no one took this position seriously, since such an element had never been isolated. He has discussed heat and caloric earlier in the context of 'particular individuality,' along with specific weight, cohesion, and sound.[25]

COMMENTARY

For all that we have been thinking of the previous discussion in terms of the natural science called chemistry, Hegel introduces the term 'chemical' only at this point. §326 was purely reflective. It brought together the various logical requirements that had to be met at this stage, without referring to what kind of natural phenomena would actually satisfy those demands. §327 set to one side a natural process that bore some analogy, but lacked certain defining characteristics. Even the chemical textbooks distinguished a mixture or amalgam from a union that is strictly chemical.

However, Hegel is not yet turning to the science of chemistry. We have already discovered that chemism is a logical concept – a distinctive way of conceiving what is objective. So he is not referring to the textbooks of

chemistry when he writes 'chemical differentiation,' but back to the logic –
to the paragraphs earlier in the *Encyclopaedia* and to the chapter in the
larger *Logic* devoted to chemism.

He justifies this appeal to the *logic* of chemical object and process not in
any ad hoc way, but by recalling one of the defining characteristics of the
stage now reached in the philosophy of nature: what are to be differentiated and identified are not isolated aspects or features of bodies, but bodies
as a whole; 'concrete totalities' is his word. The move from part to whole
had been the theoretical response to the partiality and transience of electrical phenomena, developed in the paragraph that immediately precedes the
sub-section on chemical process.

In §327 Hegel had already shown that the process appropriate to this
stage of the philosophical development must be real and not formal. Now
his appeal to the logic of chemism is justified by the fact that the bodies
involved are concrete totalities. His argument is a priori, building on conceptions already established and needing no reference to new experiential
data.[26]

He is now ready for his next move. We noted in the last chapter that a
real ground is different from what it grounds. The ground certainly carries
over into the product, but something new is introduced that alters the original content. So we are posed with the need to explain the differences that
have occurred.[27] We require a third term that mediates the grounding relation by introducing whatever will differentiate the grounded from the
ground.

At this stage of the philosophy of nature, there is an identity to be differentiated and a difference to be identified. The third term, or middle, has to
ground the difference in the first case and the identity in the second. Yet it
will embody neither the full differentiation of content nor the full identity,
since that will include the content supplied by the real ground. This middle
term is only difference in the abstract in one case, implicit identity in the
other; it is either pure differentiation or pure identification. Concrete difference or identity results when this abstract contribution combines with the
content contained in the real ground to make the process actually happen.

Because it is abstract and isolated in this way, the middle term is neither
differentiated from, nor opposed to, the things that are the real ground. It is
not, strictly speaking, a 'chemical object.' Instead it divides itself among the
components of the real ground either to differentiate them or to neutralize
them. This, as we have seen from the *Logic*, is the role played by elements.

At this stage, the only elements in the *Philosophy of Nature* are the physical ones: earth, air, fire, and water. Which of these can serve as mediating

agents of a real process? Even to answer this question we are not reduced to observation. For we have enough information from the description of the various elements to be able to anticipate experience. Water functions as abstract[28] neutrality, an identity that bridges differences, and so would best serve as the catalyst for uniting opposed bodies. Air, as we have seen, has a destructive capacity but, unlike fire, is not transient and fleeting. Therefore it would be the catalyst for the process of differentiating or separating.

In 1817 Hegel showed, in relation to particular chemical processes, not only that water and air were the middle terms, but also how they were composed of oxygen, hydrogen, and nitrogen. In the revisions made in 1827, however, Hegel worked strictly reflectively to this point, without reference to actual phenomena. In 1830 he extended these reflections further, for he introduces the next sentence with a conditional clause: 'Since in nature the different moments of the concept are also set out in particular existence ...' The shift from the previous sentence was too abrupt in 1827; some justification that was logical and not empirical was required. This clause is so dense, however, that at first glance it offers little help. Only gradually does its significance come clear.

First note that, in the logic of chemism, chemical object and neutral product were described as existing. That, then, is a logical requirement already contained in the earlier reference to chemical difference; it is not some new premise introduced at this stage. The same applies to the comment that the different moments of the concept are involved. The logical analysis of chemical process advanced by appealing to the differences between universal, particular, and singular and their roles in syllogisms. What is distinctive about this clause – what nature adds to the picture – is the fact that the existence is *particularized* – discriminated into differentiated moments.

Recognizing this helps us understand how this conditional clause can serve to justify Hegel's conclusion that the real process is doubled into a concrete and an abstract process. Particularizing, thoroughly carried through, involves abstracting, isolating things away from their concrete context. This act of conceiving, once applied to nature, 'sets itself out' in *particular* existence. That this is not the *only* way nature appears is indicated by Hegel's use of the particle *auch*, 'as well.' When nature is submitted to conceptual analysis, it will be broken up into particular abstract elements. But this type of process is quite different from the concrete processes of differentiation and identification, where total, individuated bodies are involved. The abstract process is artificial and not natural. It is governed throughout by conceptual intention; it does not simply happen.

So we are still functioning in the theoretical realm. Because nature allows itself to be particularized by conceptual thought, we can anticipate that the two processes of identifying and differentiating can be found, both in concrete phenomena, and in the more analytical context of the laboratory, with its rigorously controlled experiments that ensure the separation of abstract entities.

In this way Hegel opens up the prospect not only for the traditional 'concrete' chemical experiments with acids, bases, and salts; with combustion and rust; with decomposition and refining; but also for the kind of 'abstract' chemical research that had occupied the previous sixty years. He can now turn to the evidence of science.

Scientists had isolated and identified the distinctive elements, not found as such in the natural order, that explain chemical differentiation and chemical process: oxygen, hydrogen, nitrogen, and carbon. They had also effected artificial combinations – taking the elements thus isolated and reuniting them in unprecedented proportions.

We can now see how Hegel's a priori logical principles govern his argument, for the elements isolated by the chemists provide 'particular existence' for the diverse moments of the concept, and so have the fourfold pattern of universal, opposed particulars, and singular. Inert nitrogen is abstract indifference; solid carbon is abstract individuality; oxygen, necessary for combustion, is the one pole of the opposition, differentiation on its own account; hydrogen as basically inert, but susceptible to being burnt in the presence of oxygen, is the other. So they provide an exact parallel to the four physical elements: nitrogen is the major constituent of air, oxygen is necessary for fire, hydrogen (as its name suggests) is basic to water, and carbon is solid, like earth. Together they make up the totality of the concept, so that there is no need to look beyond them to see if there are other elements of the same order.[29]

While all of this has been structured logically, Hegel does not pretend that he could deduce the four chemical elements a priori. He accepts the results of chemical investigation for the content. But he could not accept an indefinite diversity and an unordered mixture of different kinds of things. The task of philosophy is to comprehend – to organize the data of science into a coherent pattern. That determines what is to be considered significant in scientific investigation, and how it fits into a philosophic framework.

Hegel concludes the paragraph by bringing its various constituents together into a single perspective. He had started by talking about the basic structure of a real process. Then he showed that an internal distinction –

between concrete processes and abstract ones – was required. The discussion of the elements documents what he means by abstract. But he can not leave matters thus. Concrete and abstract are not simply diverse; they are opposites and complement each other. In the concrete process the physical elements are to serve as the catalysts, or middle terms. They are to take bodies that are basically indifferent to each other and stimulate them, first, to a chemical differentiation and, then, to a chemical combination. But on their own these physical elements are simply there, something given. Analytic chemistry had shown how the chemical elements make up the middle terms of air and water that trigger the processes. The physical elements were now known to be internally differentiated, so that they became, not inert media, but agents in the processes of bringing chemical differences to existence and of neutralizing them once they have emerged. The abstract and the concrete are integrated in a complete explication of the real process.

So Hegel structures this whole paragraph §328 according to the moments of conceiving. Within an initial, general characterization taken from the *Logic*, he introduces several distinctions among particulars (abstract and concrete, the four elements) and then reintegrates them into a single complete picture.

21

§329

Der Proceß ist zwar *abstract* dieß, die Identität des Urtheilens und des In-Eins-Setzens der durchs Urtheil Unterschiedenen zu seyn; und als Verlauf ist er in sich zurückkehrende Totalität. Aber seine *Endlichkeit* ist, daß seinen Momenten auch die körperliche Selbstständigkeit zukommt; sie enthält damit dieß, daß er *unmittelbare* Körperlichkeiten zu seiner *Voraussetzung* hat, welche jedoch eben so sehr nur seine Producte sind. Nach dieser Unmittelbarkeit erscheinen sie als außerhalb des Processes bestehend, und dieser als an sie tretend. Ferner fallen deßwegen die *Momente* des *Verlaufs* des Processes selbst als unmittelbar und verschieden aus einander; und der Verlauf als reale Totalität wird ein Kreis *besonderer Processe*, deren jeder den anderen zur Voraussetzung hat, aber für sich seinen Anfang von Außen nimmt und in seinem besondern Product erlischt, ohne sich aus sich in den Proceß, der das weitere Moment der Totalität ist, fortzusetzen und immanent darein überzugehen.

To be sure, the process is *abstractly* to be the identity of both the judging and the setting-in-one of what are, through the judgment, different; as a circuit, it is a totality that returns into itself. But its *finitude* lies in the fact that corporeal independence also applies to its moments; finitude implies that the process has for its *presupposition immediate* corporealities, and its products turn out to be no different. As immediate in this way, they appear as persisting outside of the process, and this latter appears as added to them. For this reason as well, the *moments* of the process's *circuit* themselves fall apart as immediate and diverse; and the circuit, as a real totality, becomes a circle of *particular processes*. Each of these has the other as its presupposition, but, on its own, receives its beginning from outside, and is extinguished in its particular product; it does not proceed on its own into the process that is the next moment of the totality, nor does it pass over into it in an immanent way. A body emerges in one of these processes

Der Körper kommt in einem dieser Processe als Bedingung, in einem andern als Product vor; und in welchem besondern Processe er diese Stellung hat, macht seine chemische Eigenthümlichkeit aus. Auf diese Stellungen in den besondern Processen kann sich allein eine Eintheilung der Körper gründen.

Die zwei Seiten des Verlaufs sind: 1) vom indifferenten Körper aus, durch seine Begeistung, zur Neutralität; und 2) von dieser Vereinung zurück zur Scheidung in indifferente Körper.

as condition, in another as product; and its distinctive chemical character depends on the place it has in a particular process. So a classification of bodies can only be justified by the roles they play in particular processes.

The two sides of the circuit are: (1) from the undifferentiated body, by way of its being animated, to neutrality; and (2) from this union back to the separation into undifferentiated bodies.

NOTES

Judging and judgment Judging involves a discrimination, a separation into parts that are then coupled back together. This double character is captured in the German term *Urteil*, which, etymologically, means 'primordial division' and, in the infinitive form, 'primordial parting.' In Hegel's systematic argument, a judgment always breaks a concept apart into its components, and then reconnects them in an abstract and formal way: through predication, negation, membership, condition, or disjunction; as possible, actual, or necessary. Judging lies midway between the simple identity of conceiving on the one hand, and the mediated unity of an inference on the other.[1]

Circuit This expression translates the German *Verlauf*, which plays an important part in this paragraph, although it is not discussed directly either in the *Logic* or earlier in the *Philosophy of Nature*. It is mentioned in §212 on teleology, where Hegel pointed out that mechanical and chemical processes follow their own *circuit*, but under the governance of a controlling purpose. The term suggests the actual operation of a process as it moves from its beginning to its end.

Finite A finite being has a limit. Whenever it goes beyond that limit it ceases to be and something else comes into being. Yet a finite being is not simply transient; it also has a distinctive character that defines what it is to be. Since that positive quality is at the same time the limit that marks its negation, a finite being is understood to be contradictory once its various moments become fixed: what makes it finite both defines and destroys it. As inherently contradictory, the concept also is finite, always pointing beyond its own limits to something else that can only be the infinite.[2]

Finitude – referring to entities that have absolute limits – is the appropriate term to characterize natural things and the roles they play. They do not have, within themselves, the capacity of becoming infinite. Whenever they go beyond their limit they cease to be.

Presupposition When Hegel used the expressions 'presupposition' and 'immediate' in this paragraph, he was showing the close parallel between the logic of reflection and the structure of a natural chemical process. Chemical processes are finite, they have limits beyond which they cannot go. These are the bodies, which are not just oriented towards each other, but are also independent, totalities in their own right. The process, then, is external to the entities that enter into it or emerge from it. In a similar way, the intellectual act of reflection starts from something that is immediately given, which thus serves as a presupposition, and looks below the surface to discover what is essential, which it can then posit. Any such mediation is external (and so inessential) to the terms being mediated.[3]

Particular processes In the larger *Logic*, chemical process involves three processes: neutralization, separation into elements, and animation of elements so that they differentiate objects. In the *Encyclopaedia*, only the first two are mentioned, and it is these two that are specified at the end of this paragraph. However, as we have seen, the logic of chemical combination (or neutralization) has a different structure in the shorter version. The one process is variously described as three syllogisms (rather than one), where particular differences, singular activity, and self-determining universal each serves as the middle term.

In the *Philosophy of Nature*, conditioned as it is by finitude, not only does neutralization function independently of separation, but the three forms of combination fall apart into particular processes, each cut off from the others. Divisible water mediates the first (§330), singular fire mediates the second (§331), the universal bond between acids and bases mediates the third (§332). The fourth (§333) is a process that in principle contains all three. It is the particular embodiment of their unity.

Classification of bodies At this point in his lectures on the *Philosophy of Nature*, Hegel drew a distinction between its task and that of empirical

chemistry: 'The particular behaviour of the body and its peculiarly qualified process is, to be sure, the subject matter of chemistry. In contrast, we
have to consider the process in its totality, and how it separates off the
classes of bodies and identifies them as stages of its passage, which become
fixed.'[4] What is important philosophically is finding the right *classification*
of phenomena, and showing how that makes it possible to organize their
diversity into a totality. So in the third edition Hegel introduced the two
sentences beginning 'A body emerges ...' to this paragraph, as well as
amendments to the subsequent paragraphs, to highlight the philosophically
appropriate type of chemical classification.

This systematized a remark he had included even in the first edition.[5] In
objecting to the way chemists assembled diverse sets of chemical substances under the category of 'elements,' he argued that, since chemistry is
defined by the chemical processes in which substances are transformed into
other substances, the proper mode of classification would build from the
processes by which substances are produced, as well as those in which they
are presupposed as given. Chemicals, then, are defined by their functions
and powers, not by their simple qualities, whether primary or secondary.[6]

In this he was adopting an approach taken by Berthollet. In his *Essai de
Statique Chimique* of 1803, the French chemist had said that 'since every
reciprocal action produces a combination, all the chemical properties that
distinguish a substance are derived from their affinities, or from their tendency to combine with other substances; and all the phenomena to which it
contributes depend on the combinations into which it enters or from which
it is eliminated ... There are in substances, dominant affinities that are the
source of their characteristic properties; there are others that give way to
these, but which nonetheless give birth to several remarkable phenomena.
The first in particular ought to serve for classifying substances and to
explain the principal effects that result from their action; but the others
should not be ignored.'[7]

This was, in fact, the route followed by earlier textbooks. In 1800, for
example, Trommsdorff distinguished metals, which can form oxides, from
what were then called earths (a classification that included metallic oxides,
alkalis, and 'pebble' earths). Each kind of earth is defined functionally:
alkalis are soluble in water and turn litmus paper blue, pebble earths do not
dissolve in water, are resistant to fire, do not melt, and have no smell or
taste. Similarly, salts are 'bodies that emerge from the combination of acids
with alkalis, earths, and metallic oxides.'[8]

As we shall see, Hegel classifies the four kinds of corporeality as metals,
oxides (or earths), combustibles, and salts. This classification of bodies is

taken over from earlier science. Indeed, in his lectures of 1803–4 he said: 'We thus understand what it is when the ancients have said that bodies are composed of mercury, salt, sulphur and earth'; and he identifies mercury with the metallic, sulphur with the combustible.[9] In contrast to that early discussion, where the classification comes first, and the discussion of actual chemical processes comes later, in 1830 Hegel classifies bodies in terms of their functions within chemical processes.

COMMENTARY

The paragraph starts with a contrast between the abstract and the finite process. (Notice the terms Hegel stresses in the first two sentences.) Abstraction is always the work of thought, and up to this point the pure theoretical principles of the process have been considered. In §326 these were first mentioned as making differences identical and differentiating identities; then in §328 they were defined more precisely as uniting or neutralizing and separating or making different. As complementary, these two operations reflect the double character of judgment, identifying discriminated moments and discriminating within identities. Because all of this happens in thought, the various moments can be considered together as aspects of a single circuit: what start out different are united, but then the resulting identity is separated into the original differentiated things. The dynamic movement ends up where it begins; the course run makes a complete circle – a totality.

This, however, does not tell us how the world of nature functions; for thought cannot anticipate. Yet it need not wait for experience to learn that its abstract conclusions will not be embodied concretely. That recognition is implicit in the basic characteristics of nature as other than thought, as finite and contingent.

By this stage in the philosophy of nature we do not need to talk theoretically about finitude. We already have bodies that are independent; though they are oriented towards each other, each is itself a totality, with its own determinate quality. That quality not only defines it positively, but also marks its limit. What emerges once that limit is passed will be some other body, with its own distinctive quality. However, thought cannot anticipate what that other will be. To determine that we need to turn to chemical observation and experiment.

The rest of the paragraph logically works out the implications that follow from this finitude of the chemical bodies.

1 / We start with bodies just as they are. They are immediately given as

complete bodies. Reflective thought presupposes them as the necessary conditions for any chemical change. Since they are unmediated, any process that occurs will be added to these things from outside. Thus the process will resemble reflection, always external to what it acts upon. And just as reflection's task is to prescind from its own functioning when positing what is really essential, any result of the process will have its own character, quite apart from the process. It, too, will be a simple given, an unmediated corporeality. As a result of the process, it simply acquires another quality, different from the one that limited and defined the original thing.

So the unmediated independence of a body is basic. Any *chemical* property is distinct from its immediate, qualitative being and emerges only when an alien process intervenes to push it beyond its limit.

2 / Because each body is finite and independent, the processes are as well. Whatever transforms a given body is itself unmediated; it simply happens. So, with a diversity of bodies, there will be a diversity of processes. Instead of a circuit that returns to its beginning, there will be a number of particular processes, each one defined by the immediately given body that serves as its condition, and by the immediately qualified body that turns out to be its product. It may well be that the product of one process is the condition for another; but since those bodies are independent and immediate, a product does not initiate any further process on its own. Again that would have to be introduced from outside.

While it may be possible, then, to organize the processes into a circle, in which chemicals (which are on the one side product and on the other condition) provide the connection, any natural chemical process will not of itself move through the whole cycle. It stops once its product comes to be. The total picture, with the double functioning (product and condition) of each body, would be recognized only by reflective thought.

3 / Nonetheless, while the bodies are unmediated and independent, they can be considered as chemical only to the extent that they function within processes where differentiated bodies are united and identities are differentiated. Therefore if we are going to define substances in chemical terms, we must refer to the processes they are amenable to and the processes they result from. They need to be defined functionally. Each substance has its own particular defining capacities.

It is the task of empirical chemistry to investigate the particular connections between substances and processes. The philosophy of nature, however, is concerned with the general pattern, with classifications. It will follow chemistry in classifying bodies in terms of the *kind* of processes they condition or result from. In a similar way, the processes will be classified according to the *kind* of bodies that they presuppose and produce.

This poses a challenge for the philosophy of nature. On the one hand, the particular processes and substances are those that are given in nature. On the other hand, they are to be grouped and organized into classes. Classification involves using thought to group and order the diversity of experience into kinds or types.

Reflection here prejudges empirical data in the following manner. Because we are interested in chemical phenomena, there will be processes that move from different independent bodies to some kind of unity; and there will be processes that take united, or neutral bodies, and break them up into independent bodies. Because the finite independence of bodies must itself be broken down before a full chemical union is possible, the first process will need to differentiate and 'animate' them before it can neutralize the differences. The two abstract sides of the conceptual circuit thus provide a general framework for classifying the diversity of chemical processes and substances.

Hegel concludes the paragraph with a summary that both integrates the abstract and the finite moments of the preceding discussion and prepares the ground for the next five paragraphs on particular processes. Abstractly we have an identity of two operations: a judging and a setting-in-one. Concretely, we have immediate bodies and particular processes. Combining the two, we have undifferentiated bodies that are animated and then neutralized, and united bodies separated into undifferentiated bodies.

Once again Hegel's paragraph starts from a general characterization, moves into particular details, and then reintegrates the two features in a concrete proposal for what is to follow.

22

1 / Vereinung

1 / Union

§330

a / Galvanismus

a / Galvanism

Den *Anfang* des Processes und damit den *ersten* besonderen Proceß macht die der Form nach *unmittelbare* indifferente Körperlichkeit, welche die unterschiedenen Eigenschaften noch unentwickelt in die *einfache* Bestimmung der spezifischen Schwere zusammengeeint hält, die *Metallität*. Die Metalle – die *erste* Art von Körpern – nur *verschieden*, nicht begeistet gegen einander, sind Erreger des Processes, dadurch daß sie, durch jene gediegene Einheit (*an sich* seyende Flüssigkeit, Wärme-und Elektricitäts-Leitungsfähigkeit), ihre immanente Bestimmtheit und Differenz einander mittheilen; als selbstständig zugleich, treten sie damit in Spannung gegen einander, welche so noch *elektrisch* ist. Aber an dem neutralen, somit trennbaren Medium des Wassers, in Verbindung mit der Luft, kann die Differenz sich realisiren. Durch die Neutralität, somit

What constitutes the *beginning* of the process, and hence the *first* particular process, is a corporeality that is, according to its form, *immediate* and undifferentiated. It holds the different properties, as yet undeveloped, united together in the *simple* determination of specific weight: metallity. Metals – the *first* kind of bodies – are only *diverse*, not animated vis-à-vis each other; they initiate the process in that, through their solid unity (implicit fluidity, the capacity to conduct heat and electricity), they share an immanent determinacy and differentiation with each other. At the same time, as independent, they develop a mutual tension, that is as yet simply *electrical*. But, with the neutral yet divisible medium of water, in combination with air, the differentiation can be realized. Through the neutrality, indeed the now exposed differentiability, of water

aufgeschlossene Differenzirbarkeit des (reinen oder durch Salz u.s.f. zur concretern Wirkungsfähigkeit erhobenen) Wassers tritt eine reelle (nicht bloß elektrische) Thätigkeit des Metalles und seiner gespannten Differenz zum Wasser ein; damit geht der *elektrische* Proceß in den *chemischen* über. Seine Production ist Oxydirung überhaupt, und Desoxydirung oder Hydrogenation des Metalls (wenn sie so weitgeht), wenigstens Entwicklung von Hydrogengas, wie gleichfalls von Oxygengas, d.i. ein Setzen der Differenzen, in welche das Neutrale dirimirt worden, auch in abstracter Existenz für sich (§328), wie zugleich im *Oxyd* (oder *Hydrat*) ihre Vereinung mit der Base zur Existenz kommt; – die *zweite Art* der Körperlichkeit.

(either pure or raised to a more concrete effectiveness through salt, etc.) there comes on the scene a real (and not merely electrical) activity of the metal and of its tensed differentiation from water. In this way the *electrical* process passes over into the *chemical* one. Its production is oxidation in general and deoxidation or hydrogenation of the metal (if it reaches that stage), or at least the development of hydrogen gas as well as oxygen gas. That is, the differentiations, into which the neutral was broken up, are posited as abstract existences on their own account (§328), in that their union with the base comes into existence at the same time as *oxides* (or *hydrates*), which are the *second kind* of corporeality.

NOTES

Electricity As Hegel's remark to this paragraph makes clear, he draws a sharp distinction between electrical and chemical phenomena. Nonetheless, once the theoretical paragraphs and the aside about amalgams are bracketed, he has moved directly from electrical phenomena to those of galvanism, in which one can discern both electrical and chemical aspects, for electricity is discussed in §§323–5, immediately preceding the section on Chemical Process.[1]

Electricity he calls 'totality in particular individuality.' When decoded, this abstract language says that bodies are here individuated by the way they are differentiated from each other – they are particulars within a more general framework. In electricity, this differentiation does not simply reflect a diversity of colours, smells, or tastes, each of which relates one aspect or feature of a body to a sensing agent. Rather, two bodies are polar opposites: for all that they are independent and interact according to strictly mechanical principles, they are directly related as contraries and together make up a totality.

When we turn to the ways in which electricity actually occurs, we find that a physical difference is generated by mechanical friction. This tension does not affect the bodies as concrete wholes (since they continue to be independent and 'selfish'[2]); the difference between them, which defines their electrical individuality, is noticed only when something abstract, like light, moves from one body to another. That movement, however, cancels the differentiation, leaving the bodies as they were before because the undifferentiated light immediately disappears and the only mechanical effect is a momentary shock or vibration.

The transience of electrical phenomena requires the systematic move to chemical process. For Hegel, the peculiar value of galvanism is that it enables us to distinguish clearly the transience of electrical phenomena from the permanence of chemical phenomena. 'In comparison with chemical relations (for all that these are relative, for example, to temperature) the electrical are quite fleeting, transient, and amenable to reversal by the slightest circumstance.' Even were the electrical polarity maintained over time, it would not result in bodies with transformed qualities.[3]

Galvanism In 1791 an Italian doctor, Luigi Galvani, published an account of some amazing discoveries: '(1) When the thigh nerve of a dissected frog was touched with a scalpel or iron rod (but not with glass) whilst at the same time a spark was drawn from an adjacent electrical machine; (2) when lightning struck, or a thunder cloud passed, near a wire connected with the frog's leg; (3) when the muscles and nerves were simultaneously touched with a metallic arc, or better an arc composed of two metals (iron with copper or silver), then in all cases the frog's legs were convulsed by muscular contraction.'[4]

This announcement triggered a number of investigations of the phenomena. In 1798 Johann Wilhelm Ritter cited experiments, also mentioned by Volta and others, where silver-zinc arcs were used to produce sour or flat tastes on the tongue or sparks in the eye; he theorized that any pair of substances, one of which was more acidic than the other, would produce such an effect as long as they were connected by organic material. The ground of the phenomenon, he claimed, was zoological; indeed it revealed the essence of the animate life process.[5]

However, in a letter to Sir Joseph Banks, president of the Royal Society, dated March 20, 1800, Alessandro Volta reported that he had generated an electrical spark without any organic material at all, using an apparatus in which circular discs of copper (or silver) alternated with discs of tin (or zinc), each pair separated by pieces of card or leather soaked in water or other liquid.[6]

Scientists soon discovered that the voltaic pile[7] could produce a wide range of effects, and its action was stronger when water was replaced by certain acids. Indeed a similar process could be produced by using only one metal and two or three different fluids.

By May 1800 Carlisle and Nicholson had noticed that the zinc pole was oxidized, and hydrogen collected at the silver pole. Before very long the instrument was being used to decompose compounds. Particularly active in this enterprise were the Swedish team of Berzelius and Hisinger, and Humphrey Davy. Berzelius discovered ammonium and silenium. In 1803 with Hisinger, he showed that combustible bodies and salt bases collected at the negative pole, while oxygen and acids were drawn to the positive pole.[8] Davy first showed that distilled water produced pure oxygen and hydrogen, then analysed alkaline earths like potash and soda to identify their radicals: potassium and sodium. He also separated muriatic acid into chlorine and hydrogen, and subsequently identified other halogens, such as fluorine and iodine.

A debate developed concerning the nature of galvanism, as the process continued to be called. Volta suggested that it was the content of the two metals that generated the force – their electrical differentiation.[9] Others, including Davy at first, thought that the action was chemical: it was the oxidation of the metal at the positive pole that was the 'first mover' of the electricity.[10] This debate on whether the process was primarily chemical or electrical continued throughout the early years of the century.

Berzelius, citing an experiment of Humphrey Davy in 1806 where oxidation did not change the electrical charge on the positive pole, drew the conclusion that it was not the oxidation, but the simple contact and friction of the metals that was the true cause of the electrical circuit in the pile.[11] On this basis, he ventured a more elaborate hypothesis: the whole range of chemical affinities could ultimately be explained simply by the electrical charge innate to each substance. Electricity was thus a way of qualifying individual things, not a function of two bodies in polar tension.[12]

Berzelius, as we have seen, incorporated into this theory the view that chemicals combined in only certain specific proportions (suggested by Proust, Kirwan, and Richter), and adopted Dalton's explanation that chemical stuff was made up of atoms, so that an atom of one material combined with one, two, or four of another (or at times, two of one combined with three of another).[13] It was, then, the specific positive or negative charge defining each kind of atom that determined whether it was chemically attracted, or indifferent, to other atoms. On this basis, Berzelius ordered all the basic 'elements' into a series in terms of their relative positive or negative charge. In sum, galvanism was nothing but a sophisticated electrical process.

This bold theory was controversial in the scientific community. There was no evidence of a unipolar electrical quality. Opposite electrical charges may be a necessary condition of galvanism, but that by itself could not explain why the process could continue over time, since in other cases electrical charges were quickly neutralized by a transient spark. The persistence of the process seemed to depend on something else that could only be the chemical action of the pile: either the decomposition of the liquid or the oxidation of the metals.[14] The metals and the liquids were not just conductors of something that flowed between them. One or more had to be continuously active as agent.

Ritter, who earlier had identified galvanism with the animal vital powers, proposed another way of interpreting the hydrogen and oxygen that appeared when water was the liquid component. For Ritter electricity (like heat and light) was an element without weight; so water combined with positive electricity to create hydrogen at one pole and with negative electricity to produce oxygen at the other, leaving the respective poles with the opposite charge.[15]

A colleague of Hegel's, Georg Friedrich Pohl, adopted Ritter's hypothesis and used it as the basis for further experiments.[16] He was convinced that in the three-member galvanic chain, 'the relation between fluidity and metal was the peculiar soul of the activity, while the contact electricity of the differentiated metals provided only the means of stimulation that gave the activity life.'[17] In fact, the polarity the metals had in simple contact was reversed when a fluid medium was introduced.

In Pohl's view, the galvanic process was therefore chemical, for it had to take account of a circle of differentiated bodies that act on each other, and produce bodies of a different and distinctive nature. Chemists had talked of water as a second-class conductor (whereas metals were first-class), because electricity did not flow through it with as much ease. Pohl argued in opposition that the metals were simply passive conduits whereas the fluid was active, generating and maintaining the process. When the electrically differentiated metals stimulated the activity, the water became a dynamic alternation of positive and negative charges. It was this 'dialectical' alternation, not the charge as such, that constituted the living activity of the fluid, so that it could work on the oppositely charged extremes of the chain in opposite ways.[18] So, he concluded, 'it is not the contact electricity of the metals in themselves, but the electricity of the fluidity, heightened to the analytic effect of chemism, in contact with the metals, which conditions and establishes the genuine activity of the galvanic chain.'[19]

While Pohl poured scorn on the foreign chemists who did not have the advantage of the Germans' speculative awareness of the vitality of nature, Berzelius wryly dismissed the dynamism of the German philosophy of nature, which could not on its own have ever arrived at the theory of definite proportions. The debate was not simply about galvanism, but about the role of philosophy in chemical theory.[20] It is not surprising, then, that Hegel could not resist taking sides, not only in the remark on this paragraph, but also in his remark on elective affinity in the 1831 edition of the *Logic*.

Metals Hegel adopted the defining characteristics of metals from the chemical literature: their solidity, their specific weight (which is greater than that of the earths and metalloids), and their role as conductors of both heat and electricity, evidence of an inherent fluidity.[21] In the classification of bodies that Hegel develops, this is the only class that can clearly be identified with what we now call elements, or simple substances. He appears to have recognized that the simplicity of metals is immediate, and he used this as a reason for putting them first.

Berthollet pointed out that 'the dominant characteristic of metallic substances is their inflammability, or the affinity they have for oxygen. All other combinations they can form give way to this affinity, to the extent that the force of cohesion does not have sufficient energy to maintain them.' He went on to say, 'Metals dissolve in acids only when they are in an oxidized state.'[22]

The second kind of corporeality or oxides In 1827 Hegel called these earths, but by 1830 he recognized that the term had fallen out of favour. In the remark to §334, he replaced it with 'metalloids.' The two terms, however, are not synonyms. Metalloids named simple substances that are not metals (and in some classifications are also not gases). Earths referred to a number of substances most of which turned out to be oxides, whether metallic, alkaline, or neutral. In the edition of 1830, while introducing the classifying language of 'kind of corporeality,' Hegel dropped the term 'earth' and referred simply to oxides and hydrates.[23]

He knew that the product of this process was a compound and not a simple substance. Yet he argued that, from a chemical point of view, the bodies that result when oxygen or hydrogen combines with metals represent a distinctive chemical class that functions in a peculiar way. So he is not here referring to earths or oxides in general. Alkalis are explicitly mentioned in the next paragraph under the third kind of body. And 'pebble' earths like silicate and glycerine, being totally inert, do not have any chemical characteristics at all. Since the process he is describing has a metal as its starting point, its product must be a metallic oxide.

COMMENTARY

We are now ready to consider actual chemical processes. Logic prescribes that any beginning must be *simple* and *immediate*. So, of the variety of processes that are to be discussed, the first one should start from the kind of chemical body that can best be characterized in these terms. That is as far as pure thought can take us; we turn to experience for concrete content to fill in the schema.

Chemistry has shown that, of all the bodies that one encounters in experience, only metals are simple, unmediated and undifferentiated. They have not yet been decomposed, and for all of the differences among them, they nonetheless share the common features of being solid and having a greater specific weight than other substances. By these fairly basic characteristics they can be classed on their own, without reference to any process they may be involved in.

The immediate simplicity of metals is confirmed by the fact that they are indifferent to each other. They are simply diverse, neither stimulating nor reacting to each other. Nonetheless, experience has shown that they do serve as the presupposition for a chemical process. For their simplicity makes them good conductors of physical 'fluids'; so, when they come in contact, the different ways they conduct heat and electricity strain their relationship. At the same time, cohesion and specific weight ensure their continued independence. So the contact does not produce any substantial change in either, only an electrical tension between them.[24]

The differentiation that is only implicit in electrical polarization becomes a difference in real bodies once water and air come into play. We have already seen that Hegel argued in a seemingly a priori way for having these two physical elements as catalysts for chemical processes. In §328 he suggested that water is the means of combination, air of separation. Here both play a role, possibly because the water is separated into two kinds of air.[25]

Hegel's recognition that salt solutions heighten the activity of the voltaic cell showed that the water he said serves as catalyst is not to be considered a particular chemical substance, but rather the physical element, a more general classification that can include a variety of liquids. The only condition was that the liquid should be neutral. A salt could be added, but an acid or caustic alkali would trigger a different kind of process.

Galvanism does require at least one liquid component. Air, however, is not a factor in most galvanic processes (although the water, once decomposed, does become air). Including it within the catalyst makes sense only if Hegel was discussing not just galvanism, but oxidation in general (as he had done in 1817). For a metal can be transformed into an oxide just as easily when it is exposed to both air and water (as in rusting), or to air alone (as in tarnishing).

The catalyst of water (and air) transforms a simple electrical polarity into a chemical transformation. The results turn out to be different from the original conditions. So there is real transformation. Pohl had argued that simple conductors cannot explain the process, for conductors are passive, allowing a current to flow through them. To effect chemical change one has to have an agent that acts on the conditions and transforms them. This agency, according to both Pohl and Hegel, comes from the dynamic relationship between the water and the metals – a dynamic that can be increased when salts are dissolved in the water.

Water, as we have seen, is implicitly divisible. Once this divisibility is united with the diverse electrical charges of the metals in contact, what was implicit becomes explicit. The metals come to be differentiated from each other, not by way of a transient charge, but in their persisting constitution. In other words, the conjunction generates an activity that changes not just the form of things, but also their content.

Hegel, in distinguishing between an electrical tension and a real differentiation, drew on contemporary chemical debates. Davy, for example, had pointed out that contact electricity could not explain the permanent transformation of bodies in the galvanic process. In the remark to this paragraph, Hegel entered into the polemics, citing from Berzelius's *Essai* a number of admissions that the electrical theory could not explain the full chemical process. Further, the fact that a voltaic cell lost its power once the chemical changes had reached a point of saturation also tied the ongoing process to chemistry. The electrical circuit remained active only as long as the liquid necessary for the chain to function (whether water or salt solution) continued to be decomposed.[26]

Having discussed the initial conditions and the mediating dynamics of the process, Hegel now turned to its products. In both 1817 and 1827, he was primarily interested in oxidation, and the resulting oxides. In 1830 he recognized that more was involved. Galvanism had isolated the radicals of alkalis and earths, not by oxidizing them, but by removing oxygen from an oxide. Combined with certain metals, the hydrogen liberated from the water forms hydrates. And the water is broken up into its 'abstract' components, hydrogen and oxygen.[27]

We have, then, a diverse set of processes. It includes, on the one hand, the distinction between concrete and abstract – between the generation of new kinds of bodies (oxides and hydrates) on the one hand, and the isolation of the abstract elements of hydrogen and oxygen on the other. But it also covers both combination and separation: differentiated oxides are compounds, but deoxydized potassium or dehydrogenized chlorine are simple substances, separated out from compounds like potash or muriatic acid. Hegel appears to have all of these forms of the galvanic process in mind.

What is important is not the particular products, but the role these products play in the larger circuit of processes. In the previous paragraph, Hegel had identified the first particular process as moving from undifferentiated bodies, by way of their animation, to neutrality. The galvanic process does not reach neutrality. It does introduce a differentiation that can then become the dynamic basis for a genuine chemical union. Oxides and hydrates become amenable to new kinds of chemical changes; pure potassium and pure chlorine are unstable in isolation; even the elements oxygen and hydrogen, what burns and what is burnable (§328), play an animating role. Galvanism is only the first step in the full dynamic of combination.

In this mixture of products, however, only one set can be identified as a distinctive class of chemical bodies. The elements, hydrogen, and oxygen, are abstract; the pure substances, sodium and chlorine, are unstable. Only the oxides and hydrates emerge as self-contained bodies in their own right. This is why they alone are included in the second species of corporeality.

Although in this paragraph Hegel is appealing to natural phenomena, he is organizing the data along logical lines. A metal is a simple, undifferentiated body: it is a kind of abstract universal. Water, as divisible, is a particular and particularizing substance. The resulting oxide, integrating oxygen and the metal, is a singular. Here nature provides a syllogism of Hegel's first figure, in which a particular mediates between universal and singular. The fact that galvanism offers an incarnation of this purely logical pattern makes it an appropriate starting point for investigating chemical experience.

23

§331

b / Feuerproceß	b / Combustion

b / Feuerproceß

Die im vorigen Processe nur *an sich* in der differenten Bestimmtheit der in Beziehung gebrachten Metalle *seyende* Thätigkeit, für sich als existirend gesetzt, ist das *Feuer*, wodurch das an sich *Verbrennliche* (wie *Schwefel*) – die *dritte Art* der Körperlichkeit – *befeuert*: überhaupt das in noch gleichgültiger abgestumpfter Differenz (wie in Neutralität) Befindliche zu *der chemischen Entgegensetzung*, der *Säure* und des (kaustischen) *Kalischen*, begeistet sind, – nicht sowohl einer eigenen Art von reeller Körperlichkeit, indem sie nicht für sich existiren können, als nur des *Gesetztseyns* der körperlichen Momente *dritter* Form.

b / Combustion

Once posited on its own account as existing, the activity in the previous process (*which is* only *implicit* in the differentiated determinacy of the metals brought in contact) is *fire*. Through it, what is inherently *combustible* (like *sulphur*) – the *third kind* of corporeality – is *ignited*: in general, what finds itself in a still indifferent and blunted differentiation (as in a neutrality) is stimulated to *the chemical opposition* of *acid* and (caustic) *calces*: an opposition, not of a distinctive kind of real corporeality (since they cannot exist on their own account), but only of the *being-posited* of the corporeal moments of the *third* form.

NOTES

Combustion Theoretical chemistry in the eighteenth century had primarily been concerned with questions of combustion, for 'fire brings out in bodies a great variety of alterations. It not only changes their form, but also often their mixture. So for a long time we have considered it to be an important means of achieving chemical operations.'[1] For much of the century, the dominant theory was that developed by Georg Ernst Stahl in 1697. 'Stahl explained combustion as the setting free of what is combustible; he made of this property a substance that is called phlogiston, which, on being separated, produces fire.'[2] Once it was recognized that the product (lacking phlogiston) was often heavier than the original combustible body (which contained it), it was claimed that phlogiston made the particles of the compound free-floating, so that the measurable weight is reduced.

The French chemist, Lavoisier, approached combustion with the conviction that mass or weight is a constant and can be neither increased nor destroyed. In 1777 he weighed phosphorus, and then weighed what remained after phosphorus was burned – the latter was heavier. At the same time, the air surrounding the phosphorus in a closed container was lighter by the same quantity of weight. It now lacked a component, called 'vital air,' which Joseph Priestley and C.W. Schelle had isolated shortly before.[3] Lavoisier theorized that vital air was necessary for all combustion, and that, far from being a separation, fire combined a part of vital air with the combustible substance. He further suspected that this part of vital air was an essential characteristic of all acids, so he gave it the name, oxygen (which means, the stuff of acid).

For Lavoisier, oxygen alone could not explain the phenomenon of combustion. Vital air was a compound of oxygen with caloric (or heat), an imponderable (weightless) element. Both components were essential for fire to burn:

We do not therefore affirm that vital air combines with metals to form metallic calces, because this manner of enunciating would not be sufficiently accurate; but we say, when a metal is heated to a certain temperature, and when its particles are separated from each other to a certain distance by heat, and their attraction to each other is sufficiently diminished, it becomes capable of decomposing vital air, from which it seizes the base, namely *oxigène*, and sets the other principle, namely the *caloric*, at liberty.[4]

Several aspects of this description are worth noting. It explains the distinction, maintained by chemists of the early nineteenth century, between oxygen and oxygen gas – the latter being a compound of oxygen and caloric. And it highlights the role that imponderable substances still played in Hegel's early days. Not only caloric, but also light, magnetism, and electricity were all considered at one time or another to be elements lacking weight.

By the time Hegel was writing, fire involved combining the oxygen from oxygen gas with a combustible body. (While he occasionally mentions caloric, it does not play a major role in his thought.) Bodies could burn without oxygen being present, though this was the exception rather than the rule. The products of the process were not only calces (or metallic oxides) but also alkalis and acids, depending on the combustible substance burned. Hegel here mentions only sulphur, which can combine, not only with oxygen and hydrogen to produce acids, but also with metals.[5]

Gesetzt/Gesetztseyn posited/being-posited Positing is an act of reflective thought. It makes explicit what was previously only implicit; but it does not generate anything new. What is posited is assumed to be immediate, even though one reaches it through an activity of thought. So it is the counterpart of the presupposing discussed in §329.[6]

In the philosophy of nature, positing is an intentional, external activity, brought to nature in such a way that something only implicit at one stage acquires a quasi-independent existence. This existence, now immediately present, was previously only implicit or presupposed. Thus, in this paragraph, fire is the explicit existence of the activity of oxidizing, basic to galvanism; and the division between acids and alkalis makes explicit aspects of the third kind of body.

The third kind of corporeality Hegel used this to gloss the participle: 'combustible.' Neither metals nor oxides (the two kinds of corporeality already mentioned) can be burnt, so neither can enter into the second chemical process. This latter starts from a distinctive kind of basic, or simple, stuff, to be distinguished from the metals of the first process.[7] This class appears to include not only what Berzelius called metalloids, such as carbon, sulphur, and phosphorus, but also the radicals of alkalis (or 'caustic calces'): potassium, sodium, lithium, ammonium, calcium, and so on.

More puzzling is the connection Hegel drew between this classification and the opposition between acids and alkalis. While combustion, he said, posits the 'indifferent, blunted differentiation' of combustible bodies in a sharpened, caustic form, this does not introduce a new basic classification, for the bodies that result are unstable.[8]

In other words, the class of bodies that can be burnt includes different sorts, but in their primary state these differences are only latent, since each thing is independent and has an aura of neutrality; they appear as simply a collection of diverse substances. Fire, however, sharpens the differences so that the resulting bodies stand in direct, antithetical relation. When the diverse come to be opposed, the products are unstable. They can be maintained in a pure state only with difficulty. The opposition of acids and alkalis, then, as a direct orientation of each towards its other, is a function of the original 'indifferent, blunted differentiation.' It does not represent a distinctive class, but only posits what was implicit in the class of combustible bodies.

COMMENTARY

According to Hegel, chemical bodies should be classified by their role as products of one kind of process and as conditions for another. So we might expect that oxides as the second kind of corporeality would provide the presuppositions for the next stage. But nature did not allow him to make this connection. The bodies transformed by combustion are not compounds, but another sort of basic substance, distinguished from metals in that they are burnable.[9] Because this gives their nature an implicit reference to chemical transformation, they are not as simple and immediate as metals.

Rather than establishing the systematic link by using the same substance as product of one process and presupposition of another, (as he could do when moving to the third and fourth stages of chemical union), Hegel had to rely on a more abstract connection. The activity of the first process has turned out to be oxidation. Fire, however, is oxidation pure and simple; it does not depend on electrical polarity or liquid medium. It is, then, the process on its own account, without reference to anything else.

Following Lavoisier, who had established that oxygen was added to the original substance in combustion, Hegel had described oxygen as the *burning* element (§328). But oxidation is also the result of the galvanic process. So the identification of the two processes was justified by analytic chemistry.

When we turn to Hegel's *Logic* we find that for him this move was not simply a contingent result in nature. As we noted in the chapter on chemism, the unsatisfactory results of the first chemical process (from differentiated objects to neutral product) led to isolating the negative activity as such. Separating the activity from its concrete conditions was an achievement of abstracting thought, an achievement instantiated in Lavoisier's analysis.

In the *Philosophy of Nature*, however, this theoretical move does not bridge combination and separation, as it had done in the *Logic*. Rather it has broken loose from its conceptual moorings, and now serves as a link between two kinds of combination. The contingencies of nature disrupt the systematic coherence of the logical argument, although still retaining enough of an analogy to suggest its own inherent rationality.

It is this combination of the theoretical with the contingent that is the achievement of the *Philosophy of Nature*. It takes phenomena seriously, but because of its self-conscious use of logical principles, it can recognize the logic inherent in phenomena even when circumstances are different.

Whereas combustible bodies are the presupposition for this process, fire is the mediating agent. For Hegel it is the physical element that is absolutely restless and devouring. While on its own it passes over into neutrality (§283), combined with this kind of body it destroys neutrality and posits an existing opposition or differentiation.

Yet fire was not mentioned as a potential mediator in the paragraph on the real process in general (§328). Only water and air appear there, the one for combination, the other for separation. Neither surfaces here.[10] But in 1817 Hegel had introduced air when talking about combustion. 'Fire,' he wrote, 'mediates the *inner differentiation* of the combustible body with its *being posited* (that is, its reality) through the physical element of abstract negativity, *air*, and animates [the body] into an *acid*. The air is thereby broken up into this, its negative principle, oxygen, and into the dead positive residue, *nitrogen*.'[11] The separation of air is, then, a function of combustion; indeed, Hegel admitted that fire is air *posited* (§283).

When he first talked about the middle terms of the chemical processes, he had said that air was the agent of separation, yet here he has listed combustion under the general category of combination or union. These two observations can be reconciled by noticing that combustion is a kind of chemical union that separates. It does not decompose compounds (other than air itself). But it introduces an explicit differentiation into the class of combustible bodies; it separates and opposes acids to alkalis.

It appears that, because of the limited space allowed him in the *Encyclopaedia*, Hegel did not take the time to remind us of all the physical elements involved at each stage. The paragraph on real process in general covered features that pertained to all such processes, and we are supposed to retain that information and apply it as we proceed. Because the separating role of air had already been mentioned, he could focus on fire, not as an additional kind of physical medium, but simply as the independent existence of pure activity.

Hegel defined combustion as the generation of acids and alkalis. In this he followed Lavoisier, who identified oxygen not only as the element necessary for combustion, but also as the common constituent of acids. More recent investigation had shown it to be a component of alkalis as well. Even before alkalis were decomposed, however, caustic lime and potash had been produced by fire, so that Hegel did not need to know of Humphrey Davy's experiments to write this paragraph in the terms he did.[12]

Nonetheless chemistry had come up with discoveries that did not fit with this basic analysis. As Hegel knew, hydrogen gas is inflammable in contact with oxygen, and the product is neither acidic nor alkaline, but neutral water. Some acids – for example, hydrochloric (muriatic), hydrogen sulphide, fluoric – do not contain oxygen. Combustion can take place without oxygen. And some acids and alkalis can be generated without recourse to fire. Once again, nature's abundance overwhelms the systematic schema.

All of this would probably not disturb Hegel. He knew that nature is bedevilled by contingency. Philosophy's task is to discover the basic principles, anticipating that their instantiation will be quite diverse. He was looking for a systematic pathway through the rich diversity of chemical phenomena. Once one had the pathway, one could acknowledge the exceptions, and in due course explain why they both fit the general classification and differ from the norm. That kind of detail, however, would introduce a more sophisticated analysis than the *Encyclopaedia* in outline, and the lectures based on it, could provide. It was sufficient that the process of combustion enabled him to organize into one complex classification combustible materials, acids, and caustic alkalis.

24

§332

c / Neutralisation, Wasserproceß

Das so Differente ist seinem Andern schlechthin entgegengesetzt, und dieß ist seine Qualität: so daß es wesentlich nur *ist* in seiner Beziehung auf dieß Andere, seine Körperlichkeit in selbstständiger getrennter Existenz daher nur ein gewaltsamer Zustand, und es in seiner Einseitigkeit an ihm selbst der Proceß (wenn auch nur mit der Luft, an der sich Säure und kaustisches Kali abstumpfen, d.i. zur formellen Neutralität reduciren) ist, sich mit dem Negativen seiner identisch zu setzen. Das Product ist das concrete *Neutrale*, ein *Salz*, – der *vierte*, und zwar als realer Körper.

c / Neutralization, Water process

What is differentiated in this way is completely opposed to its other, and this opposition is its quality. As a result it *exists* essentially only in its relation to this other; its corporeality in an independent, separated existence is thus only a state maintained by force; and in its one-sidedness, it is on its own the process of positing itself identical with its negative, (even if it is only with air that acid and caustic potash lose their force, or are reduced to a formal neutrality). The product is the concretely *neutral*, a salt – the *fourth* [kind of corporeality], indeed as a real body.

NOTES

Quality and other These terms are part of the logic of 'a being' (*Daseyn*). The argument develops along these lines: A quality is the way a being is – its immediate determination. A qualified being is something; the thought of 'something' inevitably leads to thinking 'something other,' and that shift in thinking can be called 'othering.' So something is qualified as much by its reference to another as by what it is in itself.[1]

The moves that the logic makes in going from one of these terms to the next are simple transitions; they do not involve the reflective stance that looks back on the pattern as a whole and recognizes a differentiation or opposition. But they provide the basis for that second-order consideration. Reflection takes the simple transitions of thought and holds them together in a totality. Thus it can see that something is not qualified with reference to another, but different from and indeed opposed to it. From this perspective, the two terms are complementary.

In this context, Hegel is pointing out that each of the bodies that emerged from the previous process – the acid or the alkali – is not simply one moment of a pair of opposition. It is also inherently qualified as one-sided, oriented towards something else. The fact that the other is not specifically defined means that body's basic determination is a simple quality, and explains why acids and alkalis neutralize even when brought in contact with air. Although they are unstable, they have some sort of basic immediacy.[2]

Neutralization Long before Lavoisier introduced his revolution into chemistry, chemists had talked about chemical combinations and chemical affinities. Not having isolated the four basic elements, they did not talk about the relation between oxygen or hydrogen and some radical. What they did explore was the way acids interacted with other substances to generate salts. Their sour taste, as well as the caustic quality of alkalis, was cancelled in this process, and new kinds of bodies were the result. Trommsdorff discussed this in §235 of his *Systematisches Handbuch*:

The acids are the most effective chemical instruments, which show themselves to be active particularly in decomposing and combining bodies; in part they combine with individual components of bodies, and thereby separate off others; in part they divest themselves of their oxygen, either completely or in part, to other substances, or dissolve them, and so on. There are primarily three classes of bodies with which acids prefer to combine; these are alkalis, earths and metals. With these bodies, acids produce extremely notable and useful combinations, which we call by the name 'salts.'

Metals do not enter into such combinations directly, but only to the extent that they are already oxidized.

Acids and alkalis have distinctive qualities: 'Acids evoke a peculiar taste on the tongue which we call sour; they also have as an essential mark the peculiarity that they colour several blue vegetable juices red, or indeed denude them of colour altogether' (§225). In contrast, alkalis 'evoke a particularly sharp, urine-like taste on the tongue; in their pure state they dissolve in water; they change several blue vegetable pigments to green, red vegetable colours into violet and yellow into brown; the blue vegetable juices that acids have turned to red, they turn back to blue; finally, in a condition of purity they exercise a strong dissolving force on all tissues and animal fibres' (§533).[3] All of the qualities mentioned in defining acids and alkalis on their own in fact describe their effects on something else. In other words, these substances were classified in terms of their reference to some other.

As Trommsdorff noted, neutralization occurs when acids combine, not only with alkalis, but also with metal oxides and 'earths' (by this he means silicates, magnesia, alum, glycerines, etc.) So when Hegel referred, at the beginning of this paragraph, to the objects differentiated 'in this way,' he was referring not only to the products of combustion, but also to the metallic oxides that resulted from the first kind of chemical combination, galvanism.

When an acid is united with an alkali or other oxide, a salt precipitates out of the solution, and the solution itself becomes more dilute. This means that water is produced as well.[4] This appears to have led Hegel to use 'water process' as well as 'neutralization' to name this third chemical operation. There is no mention of water in the substance of the paragraph. And the direct attack the more caustic substances make on their counterparts suggests that no explicit mediating body is required (as it was with galvanism).[5] In other words, water here functions as the abstract neutral product, whereas salt is the concrete one.[6]

In a sense, though, water does serve as mediator, because it explains the real difference in content between the bodies that go into the process and those that come out. Instead of being added, it is subtracted from the bodies to leave a salt.[7]

Real We have already met this adjective when distinguishing a real from a formal process. Here, however, it is used to modify a body or existing thing. The logical reference for this use is not found in the *Doctrine of Essence*, but in the *Doctrine of Being*. In the second edition of the *Logic* of 1831, reality is one moment within the discussion of quality. It is, in fact, quality, with the accent on being something *that is*, something positive that has set aside any suggestion of limitation or lack. (Negation, in contrast, is a quality determined as a non-being; that is, where a being is qualified by what it is not.)[8] The positive disregard of negativity explains why 'real' first emerges at this stage in the cycle of chemical processes. Acids and alkalis are qualities as negations – defined by their association with something other. The process of neutralization conceals this negative moment and leaves only something positive.

So the use of the term 'real' at the end of the paragraph completes the cycle begun by the use of 'quality' at the beginning. The process hides the one-sided negativity that initially qualified the acids and bases.

A further comment: Hegel's German allowed him two different forms – *reale* and *reelle*. The former, which is the cognate of *Realität* (the term discussed in the *Logic*), is used here. The latter appears twice in these paragraphs: in §330 as real activity and in §331 as real corporeality. In both of these cases it modifies abstract nouns. Whenever a concrete reference is involved – to bodies, to processes, to a differentiation that is realized – Hegel prefers the form *reale*.

The fourth kind of corporeality 'Salts,' writes Trommsdorff, 'are bodies that arise from the combination of acids with alkalis, earths and metallic oxides; the combination of acid with alkali is called an alkaline salt, with earth an earthy salt, and with metallic oxide, a metallic salt.'[9] Most such salts dissolve in water. When either an acid or a base is completely incorporated into such a combination, it is said to have reached a state of saturation. The proportions needed for saturation varied, depending on which acids or bases were used.

We have here, then, a good example of the kind of combinations Hegel had discussed in the logic of real measuring. One identifies, first, a particular affinity between an acid and a base to create a neutral salt and measures the specific weight of both the acid (for example) and the salt, setting these two figures into a ratio, using the specific weight of the acid as the denominator. One develops, in the second place, a series of such measurements, involving a particular acid and a number of other bases. Third, one goes through the same process for other acids. Fourth, one compares the acids by organizing the bases according to an 'order of alkalinity.'[10] And finally one compares the bases by developing a contrary set of second order ratios, involving their specific gravities and the specific gravities of the salts. This complexity develops, Hegel has suggested, when we want to specify by measurements the distinctive qualities of each acid and base. It is one way of making chemistry amenable to mathematical calculation.

COMMENTARY

The presuppositions for this third process of combination are the products of the two previous ones: oxides, acids, and alkalis;[11] the process is mediated by the one-sided, unstable quality of those initial bodies; its products are a salt and water. All of these aspects have been discussed under the notes. In the commentary I shall focus on the relationship between the three processes already discussed and the logical framework that sets them into a system.

As we have seen, the analysis of chemical process differs between the 1816 *Science of Logic* and the 1827 *Encyclopaedia*. In the former there are three processes: differentiated objects are combined into a neutral product by way of a neutral medium; a negative activity breaks apart a neutral product into its elements; elements are distributed among objects, thereby differentiating them. In the shorter form, only combination and separation are mentioned (with no reference to elements). But the one process of combination can be described as involving either particular mediation, singular mediation, or universal mediation.

In the chapter of the larger *Logic* on chemism, thought starts with the concept of a chemical object that is both independent and essentially oriented towards another such object. In the *Philosophy of Nature*, Hegel has started from immediate, simple, independent bodies, and shown how chemical processes, stimulated on the one hand by electricity and on the other by fire, produce chemical bodies whose distinctive quality is to be one-sided and unstable, directed towards some other body. Only at this point do we have bodies that capture the second moment in the definition of a chemical object: orientation towards another. The inherent affinity of the bodies is so strong, however, that it is hard to maintain the first moment: their independence. Because both acids and caustic alkalis are inclined to neutralize whenever they come in contact with something else, a real effort must be expended to keep them in a pure form.

This means that in none of the three processes examined so far do we have an exact replica of the chemical process discussed in the larger *Logic* (where two chemical objects, allowed to communicate through a neutral medium, combine to generate a neutral product). If the neutral medium had a role to play in galvanism, the metals that were its presupposition were not full chemical objects. If pure negative activity turned combustible substances into acids and alkalis, the products were neither neutral, nor abstract elements. If the third process moved from an unstable body, oriented towards another, to a neutral product, the initial bodies are not exact contraries under a single concept, nor is a formal neutrality necessary to bring the process about.

This may clarify why in the *Encyclopaedia* Hegel replaced the single syllogism of combination with a set of three alternative syllogisms, each of which describes the single logical process of chemical union. There is a fit between the three-fold pattern of particular, singular, and universal mediation and what we have just been considering. Water as a divisible (or particularized) medium mediates galvanism, fire as a (singular) pure activity mediates combustion, and the drive to overcome one-sided particularity is the universal that mediates neutralization.

Hegel, however, has not abandoned the earlier logical pattern; it is basic to the argument advanced in §328, in which a real process must be mediated (in contrast to a formal one, which is immediate). But nature, as he pointed out in §329, is not inherently logical. It is other than, and external to, pure thought, falling apart into particularity. Any rational pattern will be found implicit in a diverse range of contingent bodies and processes. So the logic is not instantiated directly; investigation must find what corresponds in nature to the logical pattern, though in a quite dispersed and incomplete way.

We have already seen that chemical processes have a range of products that do not fit neatly into any organized schema. While Hegel focused on general thematic patterns, he nonetheless recognized that each process generates substances that do not correspond to his basic classification of bodies. In a similar way, each particular process takes something from the logical pattern, but leaves much aside.

Water, for example, is not simply a formal medium, as suggested by the analysis in the larger *Logic*, but is itself divisible into elements. This compensates for the fact that in galvanism the bodies presupposed are not chemical objects opposed to each other, but are simple, solid, and undifferentiated metals. There, particularity finds natural existence not in the extremes of the 'syllogism,' but in a physical element that is *both* formal medium *and* divisible into opposites. So the galvanic process embodies in a rough way the structure of particular mediation, mentioned in the *Encyclopaedia*. Logic could not have expected that the formally neutral medium would also be a divisible particular. Nor could it have anticipated that water would re-emerge as a byproduct of the process of neutralization. Only certain features of chemical combination in the larger *Logic* are instantiated here and even that in an incomplete way.

Similarly, the larger *Logic* isolates a singular negative activity that then divides a neutral product into its indifferent elements. While in the theoretical introduction to the current discussion (§328) the medium of separation is identified with the physical element, air, the pure activity of the second process is fire, which exploits air in turning combustibles into acids and caustic alkalis. Although air is thereby divided, the product is a compound, not an element. To be sure, in the *Encyclopaedia* version, mediation by a singular activity is not a function of separation, but one way of understanding the process of combination. But from the logic there is no way of expecting that a pure independent activity will both generate compounds (acids and caustic alkalis) and produce bodies that are differentiated and antithetical to each other. Once again, the particular mode of chemical existence incorporates features of the various logical discussions in a way that is not directly logical. It could not be anticipated, but only discovered in experience.

To complicate the picture still further, there is a way in which galvanism and combustion represent not only forms of combination, but also illustrate the third syllogism in the larger *Logic*, in which elements are distributed among bodies to make them differentiated chemical objects, antagonistic to each other. Interestingly enough, this particular move in the larger *Logic* is not reproduced in the *Encyclopaedia*.

In the neutralization process, the fact that acids and alkalis can be maintained in a pure state only with difficulty is anticipated by a comment on chemical combination in the larger *Logic*: 'To the extent that each [object] is posited as self-contradictory with respect to itself and so self-cancelling, they are only maintained distinct from each other and from their mutual completion by an *external force*.'[12] As we have seen, while acids, alkalis, and oxides fit this description, they do not have the kind of independent and self-contained existence that was ascribed to chemical bodies in the *Logic*, and so they do not also require a shared means of communication. We have found those moments of the logical argument in galvanism.

Hegel, however, had gone on to say that the middle that brings the objects together could be thought of as the implicit nature of both, 'the whole concept, that each holds within itself.'[13] This latter remark is taken up in the *Encyclopaedia* under the third syllogism of chemical combination, which is mediated by the concrete universal. The only problem is that there is no single concept under which the oxides, acids, and alkalis all fit. The first are the second kind of corporeality; the others are posited forms of the third class. Nor does their instability inevitably direct them towards each other as contrary particulars under a general category. A simple quality drives each substance on its own towards neutralization.

In other words, for all the value of the logical analysis in providing ways of characterizing chemical phenomena, there is no one-to-one correlation. Experience alone can show what phenomena actually occur, and logic does its best to sort that confusion of data into a coherent framework.

d / Der Proceß in seiner Totalität	d / The Process in Its Totality

Diese neutralen Körper, wieder in Beziehung zu einander tretend, bilden den *vollständig realen* chemischen Proceß, da er zu seinen Seiten solche reale Körper hat. Zu ihrer Vermittlung bedürfen sie des Wassers, als des abstracten Mediums der Neutralität. Aber Beide, als neutral für sich, sind in keiner Differenz gegen einander. Es tritt hier die *Particularisation* der allgemeinen Neutralität, und damit ebenso die Besonderung der Differenzen der chemisch-begeisteten Körper gegen einander ein; die sogenannte *Wahlverwandschaft*, – Bildung anderer besonderer Neutralitäten durch Trennung vorhandener.

These neutral bodies, once again brought in contact with one another, generate the *real* chemical process *in its completeness*, since on each side it has such real bodies. For their mediation they require water, as the abstract medium of neutrality. However, the two of them, as each neutral on its own account, are not differentiated from each other. Here there enters the *particularization* of the universal neutrality, and thereby the dividing of the differentiations of the chemically animated bodies between them: what is called *elective affinity*, – generating other particular neutralities through the breaking up of those already present.

NOTES

Elective affinity This refers to the process that occurs when two neutral salts are combined in a solution of water and exchange their radicals, producing two quite different salts. The fact that the acid radical of one salt abandons its base radical to take up with another from another salt had earned it the name of 'elective affinity.' A definition of this process was given in Goethe's novel *Die Walhverwandschaften* of 1810: 'Think of an A that is closely united with a B and cannot be separated from it by many instruments or much force; think of a C that is related in the same way to a D; now bring the two pairs in contact; A is drawn to D, C to B without anyone being able to say who leaves the partner first, who is the first to have been united again with the other.'[1] The preferential order enabled the eighteenth-century Swedish chemist, Torbern Bergmann, to develop a table in which the power of affinity of various substances was organized in a series.[2]

In 1792 J.B. Richter viewed this as the basic type of all chemical procedures so that even combustion could be described as an elective affinity: a union of phosphorus and phlogiston was brought together with a union of oxygen and caloric (oxygen gas) and the products were phosphorus plus oxygen and phlogiston plus caloric (or fire).[3] Of more importance was another aspect of his investigations. Having studied at Königsberg, he took up Kant's challenge that chemistry was not a full-fledged natural science because it could not be reduced to mathematical laws. He discovered that 'when two neutral solutions are mixed, and decomposition follows, the new resulting products are almost without exception also neutral; the elements must, therefore, have among themselves a certain fixed ratio of mass.'[4] These fixed ratios made it possible to determine a number for each element in a salt. When these were inserted for three of the four elements in a process of double affinity, one could calculate the fourth.

The theory of fixed ratios had been advanced earlier by Proust and Kirwan. Proust, a Frenchman working in Spain, had shown that a metal forms only one or two oxides, each with a definite proportion. Where there was a continuous range of proportions, it was a sign that the combination was a mixture rather than a chemical union.[5] Kirwan then showed that 'the quantity of real acid, necessary to saturate a given weight of each base, is inversely as the affinity of each basis to such acid' and that 'the quantity of each basis, requisite to saturate a given quantity of each acid, is directly as the affinity of such acid to each basis.'[6] What Richter showed in addition was that, relying on the phenomenon of double affinity, the analysis of a few neutral salts could furnish by calculation the compositions of many others, a calculation that enabled the scientist to check the accuracy of his empirical analysis.

The French chemist Berthollet submitted the concept of chemical affinity to critical examination. He challenged the assumption of a single scale of preferences between elements, for he showed that the process of double affinity was affected by its governing conditions: temperature, solubility of the salt in water, cohesion, crystallization, and elasticity. 'I have made evident by direct experiments that the combinations that are considered to be produced by elective affinity, to which one attributes the greater superiority, give way to others which we had viewed as inferior, to the extent that one had weakened the circumstances that tend to maintain the former.'[7]

Berthollet argued as well that changed conditions could affect the proportions of elements that combine in a saturated salt. Nonetheless, he included a footnote, added by Fischer to the German edition of an earlier work of his, that ordered the figures developed by Richter on the proportions of the various acids that saturate a base.[8]

We have examined the logic of this concept in the chapter on real measuring. There it emerged as a way of measuring the distinctive quality of a particular thing – a simple quality that was in danger of being lost in an endless series of combinations. Yet in both 1812 and in 1831, as well as in the remark to this paragraph, Hegel cited Berthollet's evidence that the so-called elective affinity could be reversed by altering circumstances. This did not affect the logic, since one can still distinguish elective 'preferences' that some substances have for others by deliberately fixing the pressure and temperature. What is required, however, is a conscious initiative of thought; for in nature as given there is no single pattern of elective preferences. Though this term started out as a way of describing chemical phenomena and was transferred to the *Logic* by analogy, in Hegel's hands it became primarily a logical term that could be applied to nature only approximately.

Particularization Hegel stressed this word, because he here introduces the Latin form, whereas the German *Besonderheit* is more usual in his writings. (Indeed a cognate of this latter term appears later in the same sentence, translated here as 'dividing.') These two terms parallel the pair we noticed earlier: *Individualität* and *Einzelheit*. Like *Einzelheit Besonderheit* is one moment in the logic of conceiving – the act of determining a general concept by setting out the differences that specify it with reference to other particulars. The fact that Hegel underlined *Particularisation* indicates that he wanted to distinguish this natural process from the strictly logical move (even though it might also be read as an application of that concept). A neutral salt is something general; it is broken up into particulars, each one of which has a determinate function in the process of double affinity, for it exchanges its initial complement for another one. This movement in nature is conditioned by natural contingency. Just as individuals (*Individuen*) in nature are not strictly singulars (*Einzelne*) in the sense of being centred objects of reference, yet are sufficiently close that a virtual synonym can be used to describe them; so here the act of particularizing (*Particularisation*) is not so much a conceptual development of specific differences (*Besonderung*) but a natural breaking up of a thing into its constituents.

COMMENTARY

The three processes already discussed do not exhaust the kinds of chemical union one finds. Of considerable importance in the literature is what we can call double affinity: the process by which two salts, dissolved in water, exchange their radicals. As we have seen, Richter suggested that this was the pattern for all chemical operations and applied it to combustion. The chemical analysis of acids and bases had shown the process of neutralization to be a kind of double affinity as well, one product being the salt, the other, water. Hegel, however, was wary of overhasty generalization. He restricted his fourth process to the transformation from one pair of salts to another, because in this process salts are not only the bodies produced, but also the bodies presupposed. Water serves simply as a catalyst.

At the end of the previous paragraph, Hegel had identified salts as the 'genuinely real' chemical bodies. They have set aside any moment of negation, or reference to another. In this process, then, not only is the 'content grounded' *really* different from the 'content that grounds' (see above under §328),[9] but both the presuppositions and the products of this process are genuinely *real* bodies as well. Because 'reality' functions in both forms, Hegel called this the fully real chemical process.[10]

As well, no other process is presupposed either as condition or as consequent. Here both a uniting of differentiated components into compounds and a prior separation of compounds into their components are combined. Both moments identified in the early paragraphs of this section as aspects of the concept, differentiating and identifying, are present. Since the product is of the same class as the presupposition, and the process moves in both directions, this is a chemical transformation complete within itself. Therefore Hegel can call it the total process.

Earlier I discussed the significance of the term 'totality.' It serves as the stage of the singular on the one hand, but as the stage of the syllogism mediated by the universal on the other. The process of double affinity, then, is a single activity in which a whole breaks up its constituents into particular parts only to reconstitute itself again as a different kind of whole. Since both the presupposition and the product are not universals but par-

ticular combinations of salts, the process is not quite a logical particularizing, only a natural one.

In some ways this natural process fits best the logical description of combination. Bodies are brought together in the neutral medium of water,
which does nothing more than enable the product to emerge. In other
ways, however, the correspondence fails. For the presupposed bodies are
not differentiated from each other in any kind of polar opposition. They
are salts, complete in themselves, and *real*, in the sense of having a simple
positive quality that requires no reference to anything else. In addition,
there is no single neutral product, but two – the product is *particularized*.
We move from one set of neutral particulars to another.

Nor does it satisfy the criteria of a chemical separation, as specified earlier in the philosophy of nature. The parts into which the initial salts divide
never have an independent existence as bodies. They are simply moments
of the process and can be fixed only through conceptual abstraction. To
this extent they resemble the abstract elements of the logical analysis.

Hegel had said as much in 1817, when he had no separate paragraph on
separation, but included it under this concept of elective affinity: 'In terms
of what is specific to them, these processes are forceable separations of the
neutral into the abstractions out of whose processes they were produced –
reversions to the oxides and acids, and further as well, immediately and in
abstract form, to the undifferentiated bases, which in this way are presented as products' (§257). Thought discovers that the transformation takes
place because salts are compounds of basic chemical stuff that Richter
called 'stoicheia' and we now call elements. The ratios between these components are used to 'measure' the salts and to differentiate among them.
Whereas 'affinity' applies generally to the attraction of chemical bodies like
acids, oxides, and alkalis, only with reference to these abstract substances
can we discriminate among unions in terms of their strength and resistance
to tampering. This is why the concept of 'elective affinity' is appropriate
only here.

Hegel has thus introduced a new kind of 'chemical object' at this point:
simple substances that are inherently oriented towards something else.
These cannot be called bodies, since they do not exist independently in
nature. They are neither the presupposition nor the product of a process.
They are abstractions, analysed as moments within the dynamic of transformation: sodium and chlorine, phosphorus and sulphur, calcium and
potassium; these emerge from thought's careful analysis. The process of
double affinity shows that such abstract substances do function chemically,
are oriented towards each other, and stimulate combinations. In their being

isolated conceptually the way was opened for the law of definite proportions.

This fourth process is not, then, just an impure instantiation of the logic of chemical process. It offers reflective thought access to a full range of chemical elements (not in the limited sense in which Hegel uses that term, but in the current sense of basic simple substances). These are not themselves separated out in a pure state by the fourth kind of chemical union. They do, however, result from a conceptual (or analytic) understanding of what is going on therein.

26

2 / Scheidung

2 / Separation

§334

In der Auflösung des Neutralen beginnt der Rückgang zu den besondern chemischen bis zu den indifferenten Körpern, durch eine Reihe einerseits eigenthümlicher Processe; andererseits aber ist überhaupt jede solche Scheidung selbst untrennbar mit einer Vereinigung verknüpft, und ebenso enthalten die Processe, welche als dem Gange der Vereinigung angehörig angegeben worden, unmittelbar zugleich das andre Moment der Scheidung (§328). Für die *eigenthümliche Stelle*, welche jede besondere Form des Processes einnimmt, und damit für das Specifische unter den Producten, sind die Processe von *concreten* Agentien und ebenso in den *concreten* Producten zu betrachten. Abstracte Processe, wo die Agentien abstract sind (z.B. bloßes Wasser in Wirkung auf Metall, oder vollends Gase u.s.f.), enthalten *an sich* wohl die Totalität des Processes, aber stellen seine Momente nicht in expliciter Weise dar.

In the dissolution of the neutral begins the return to particular chemical bodies and on to undifferentiated ones: through a series of peculiar processes on the one hand; on the other hand, however, every such separation is in general itself indivisibly conjoined with a uniting. In the same way, the processes, which have been cited as belonging to the pathway of uniting, immediately contain at the same time the other moment of separation (§328). For the *peculiar place* that each particular form of the process occupies – and hence for what is specific about the products – we need to consider the processes from *concrete* agents and also into *concrete* products. Abstract processes, where the agents are abstract (for example, pure water working on metal, or purified gases etc.), *implicitly* contain the totality of the process to be sure, but do not set out its moments in an explicit way.

NOTES

Analytical chemistry When discussing the various basic substances, the chemical textbooks of the day would append a description of how they could be separated out in a pure form to a list of their sensory qualities and affinities. In many cases, a compound would be rendered unstable by altering heat, cohesion, or solubility (those conditions identified by Berthollet) and then passing it over some other substance that had an affinity for the secondary aspect of the compound, leaving the substance in question isolated.

Such a procedure has been used for some time to refine metals. Ores are melted into a solution with certain other chemicals that then unite with impurities into lighter compounds. When left to solidify, these compounds rise to the top, leaving the pure metal underneath. In a similar way, oxidized bodies are heated until they are gaseous, then passed over carbon or charcoal, which absorb the oxygen, leaving the other 'element' free.

Separation We need only recall the discussion of the second syllogism in Hegel's chapter on chemism.[1] A neutral object is the middle term, acted upon by a negative unity or independent chemical activity that transforms the neutral compound into something else. Hegel calls the product 'elements': isolated and abstract simple substances, basically indifferent to each other.

Abstract processes In §328 Hegel contrasted the abstract with the concrete modes of separation; here he points out that we distinguish between them by the kind of chemical agent involved. Whereas concrete separations enable us to classify both processes and products in terms of the natural bodies presupposed and produced, abstraction uses such things as distilled water and purified gases (not the physical elements of water and air) to isolate unstable, pure chemicals. These substances do not occur naturally as bodies, but are artificial products, the result of a controlled and conceptual manipulation of nature. They are used to break up compounds into abstracted substances that also do not appear normally in nature. Hegel used the term 'abstract' to refer to the chemical experiments that isolated substances not previously known, such as potassium, calcium, beryllium, etc.[2]

Yet among the chemical stuff listed in the remark appended to this paragraph, Hegel does not mention any of these newly discovered 'elements,' although he was acquainted with them. He refers, for example, to potassium and calcium in the remark to §330; and in his draft system of 1805–6 of the Jena years, he even mentioned osmium and iridium, whose discovery had been announced in the *Annals of Physics* only at the beginning of 1805.[3]

COMMENTARY

Within the process of double affinity, as we have noted, there is a moment of dissolution: compounds are broken up into chemically differentiated components on the way to being recombined with new partners. This process, then, is not only the final and most complete form of chemical union, but also the initial form of chemical separation. That second kind of process also functions independently, however, leaving as its final product an identifiable, simple chemical substance.

In the remark Hegel stressed that the separating processes are of different kinds – producing different classes of products. For all that the ultimate result may be a simple substance, metals are different from sulphur and phosphorus, and these are different again from the metalloids, both alkaline and earthy, not because of distinct surface qualities, but because they are derived from (and condition) different *kinds* of processes. They are organized into a series since the products of some separations can be used to separate other chemical materials. Thus, for example, pure sulphur will combine with impurities in metal ores, leaving the iron or tin in a 'reguline' form.[4]

In his lectures of 1819–20, Hegel pointed out that the process of separation uses affinity, fire, and even galvanism, the first three forms of uniting already discussed, to accomplish its ends.[5] There is no new kind of transformation involved. So in nature any separation is intimately connected with a contrary process of combination, because chemical analysis always exploits affinities and chemical union. To refine a substance out of a compound, we introduce some chemical body that, under altered circumstances, will unite with the other parts of the original compound and leave the substance in a pure form. Chemical union is inevitably conjoined with chemical separation.

Once we notice that the two basic kinds of process – union and separation – operate in tandem, we can recognize that the same thing was going on in the previous processes. Neutralization is a kind of double affinity, where hydrogen and oxygen are separated from the acids and bases to produce water, while the radicals of the initial two substances combine to make a salt. Combustion withdraws oxygen from the air, leaving in the main nitrogen. And galvanism, as we noted at the time, can be used to deoxidize certain materials and indeed to separate water itself into hydrogen gas and oxygen gas. In other words, not only does every separation require a union, but every union involves a separation.

The fact that the two sides of the conceptual pattern always occur together in nature is not something that we could have expected from our initial a priori analysis, with its talk of particular processes. Nor is it a function of the logic of chemical process. It is something we only discover when we consider chemical processes as they actually occur.

Nonetheless, we still do not have a *conceptual* circle. In any particular process, the elements separated are not the same as those that are combined. So we never end up where we started. Indeed, it is the differentiation between separating and uniting that defines the 'peculiar place' of each chemical operation: the specific form and distinctive character of a process is determined not only by the classes of bodies presupposed and produced, but also by what kind of concrete body combines with the 'impurities.'

Differences among combining agents provide a framework for organizing the processes of separation into a series. They also distinguish concrete processes from abstract ones. In standard separation, the agents used are forms of sulphur or charcoal found normally in our environment. Within the laboratory, however, agents are introduced that are themselves the result of abstract analysis. Only after they have been purified and refined are they used to generate other simple substances seldom, if ever, found in the natural order: chlorine or fluorine, calcium or sodium, potassium or beryllium. While these rigidly controlled experiments are also separations, their products are abstractions from natural bodies; they are not found 'concretely' in nature.

Like the fourth kind of union, these abstract processes form a totality. They presuppose an abstractly isolated substance as agent, and go through various forms of combination before producing an abstracted substance of another sort. Not only are both combination and separation involved, but the same kind of product is both presupposed and produced. So, just as the process of double affinity is a totality because it starts and ends up with neutral salts, here we have a totality that starts and ends with abstractly isolated substances. The abstract process represents such a totality only implicitly, however, for the various moments do not persist as independent bodies. This kind of separation is the work of analytic chemistry, not the natural functioning of nature.

27

§335

Der chemische Proceß ist zwar im Allgemeinen das *Leben*, der individuelle Körper wird ebenso in seiner Unmittelbarkeit *aufgehoben* als *hervorgebracht*: somit bleibt der Begriff nicht mehr innere Nothwendigkeit, sondern kommt zur *Erscheinung*. Aber durch die *Unmittelbarkeit* der Körperlichkeiten, die in den chemischen Proceß eingehen, ist er mit der Trennung überhaupt behaftet. Dadurch erscheinen seine Momente als äußerliche *Bedingungen*, das sich Scheidende zerfällt in gegen einander gleichgültige Producte, das Feuer und die Begeistung erlischt im Neutralen und facht sich in diesem nicht von selbst wieder an. Der *Anfang* und das *Ende* des Processes sind von einander verschieden; dieß macht seine Endlichkeit aus, welche ihn vom Leben abhält und unterscheidet.

In universal terms, to be sure, the chemical process is *life*; in its immediacy the individual body is both *cancelled* as well as *produced*. In this way the concept no longer remains simply an inner necessity, but emerges into *appearance*. Because of the *immediacy* of the corporealities that enter into the chemical process, though, it is in general encumbered with division. For this reason its moments appear to be external *conditions*; what is separated falls apart into mutually indifferent products; fire and the animating principle are exhausted in a neutral [product], and from there cannot rekindle themselves. The *beginning* and the *end* of the process are diverse from each other; this marks out its finitude, which keeps it apart, and different, from life.

NOTES

Life While vegetable and animal organisms have life, and spirit presupposes life as the basis on which it develops self-consciousness, life is also a logical concept that can be understood on strictly a priori terms.

This thought or idea develops from the opposition of concept and objectivity that plays a major part in mechanism, chemism and teleology.[1] Life represents the implicit union of the two sides: the concept permeates objectivity, and objectivity is organized, not just according to its own mechanical or chemical laws, but in such a way that the concept finds full expression.

In §326 we noticed that in abstract terms the concept is twofold: differences are identified and identities are differentiated. In the logic of chemism this finds expression in two processes: one where differentiated objects are combined into a neutral product; another where the neutral product is broken up into its abstract elements. There, however, the stages follow each other because of the external demands of the concept: first, the concept is the implicit identity of two independent objects; second, it is the moment of differentiation, not included in the neutral product.

In life, that division between concept and object has been overcome, and the two processes are part of a single dynamic. 'Life,' then, is not just a concept but an *idea*, a thought in which a concept is united with its actuality. In life, the diversity of the objective realm is integrated by the concept that permeates it. At the same time, the concept distinguishes within the object, not discrete parts, but members, each contributing a distinctive function to the basic unity. In teleological terms, the members are not just the means for realizing the concept, but also the end to be realized; they and their functioning constitute the realized concept. So the thought of life, like the thought of the concept, involves both identifying and differentiating in a single dynamic.

Life is what Hegel called a negative unity – a single dynamic that discriminates within itself and also separates itself from others. Its objective character involves self-determination.

Hegel took this logic further, analysing the concept of a living individual, the processes by which it relates to the objective realm excluded from it, and the way both are reincorporated into the genus. That detailed development, however, does not affect his discussion of chemistry.[2]

Aufhebung Hegel devoted a remark to this term in the larger *Logic*.[3] In German the word has two distinct meanings: 'retain' and 'bring to an end'; at times it also has a third sense: 'raise to a higher level.' Hegel delighted in this multi-layered sense because it suggested the complex dynamic of conceiving: identifying (or retaining), differentiating (or bringing to an end), and both united in a comprehensive, higher, perspective. The only English word that comes close to that plurality of meanings is the archaic 'sublate.'

Its first systematic appearance comes in the move from 'becoming' to 'a being' in the larger *Logic*. 'Becoming' turns out to be a circle of meanings: 'coming to be' moves from nothing to being; 'passing away' goes from being to nothing. When these two are combined as moments of a single concept, thought goes from nothing to being and back to nothing. That single, circular movement collapses into a single thought, which Hegel calls 'a being' (*Daseyn*). In that single thought, the various components of 'becoming' – being, nothing and the way thought moves from one to another – disappear into a unity. They are retained, yet cancelled; so the result is a new simple – and unmediated – concept. 'Aufhebung' names that moment of collapsing.

As used here, in the form of a past participle (*aufgehobene*),[4] Hegel counterposes it to *hervorgebracht*, or 'brought forward.' Thus what has been 'sublated' carries the negative sense of being cancelled and only implicitly retained.

Appearance While this term recalls the Kantian dualism between a thing in itself and the same thing as it appears, it also has its systematic place within the *Logic*, where Hegel articulates the reasoning that led Kant to his position. Appearance is an existence that is not taken just as it is, but as the reflection of something else that is its persisting essence. Indeed it is the transience of existence that points towards something more permanent, which defines and grounds what happens. So, when existing things and processes are considered as appearances, they are suggesting something more fundamental; they are symptoms of reality rather than reality itself.[5]

In this paragraph, Hegel is not talking about the logical move from transient existence by way of the concept of appearance to the world in itself, but rather the reverse move from the essential concept to appearance. Because chemical bodies dissolve into processes of transformation and thus lack permanence, they show themselves to be appearances of what is the inherent principle of their action: the concept.

Conditions This term comes from the logic of grounding and justification. Earlier we drew the distinction between a formal ground, with the same content in both ground and grounded, and a real ground, with a difference in content. The latter requires a middle term to introduce what is novel. When the logic explores this relationship in detail, the middle term becomes as much a ground of what ultimately emerges as the original real ground. On their own, neither of them can ground; only in combination do they do so. Then, they are no longer *grounds*, but *conditions*.

A condition is something that has an immediate existence on its own, but can, when brought together with other relevant conditions, become part of a ground or justification. We thus distinguish the conditions from the grounding relation, which produces the grounded result when sufficient conditions are present.

By talking about conditions we make both an advance on and a retreat from the language of real ground. On the one hand, we begin to do justice to all the content that ultimately emerges, and provide a justification or ground for it. On the other, a condition on its own is not a condition at all, but only one existing being among many. There is nothing inherent that points to any particular combination of conditions within a grounding relation. The synthesis that transforms it from a being to a condition has to be introduced from outside. Mere conditions are simply external to each other.[6]

COMMENTARY

Having considered all the relevant chemical material, Hegel now returns to philosophical matters. But he does not simply pick up were he left off at the end of §329; features have emerged that were not anticipated in those a priori reflections. In the first place, chemical processes have turned out to be both separations and combinations at the same time. In the second place, two types of processes – double affinity and using abstract agents to effect separation – manifest a kind of totality in that they not only couple combination with separation but also end up with the same class of substances they started with. (When described in general terms, using classes rather than individual chemicals, we have a pattern in which identifying and differentiating are two aspects of a single process: where aspects of the process are both the means used to achieve the result, as well as the results to be achieved.) In the third place, individual bodies do not persist as independent entities; they are both cancelled and produced. All of this fits the definition of the logical concept, 'life.'

This sounds as if Hegel was jumping into another genus: from simple or compound bodies to organisms. But the paragraph soon disabuses us of that preconception, for he went on to detail the ways by which chemical processes are far removed from actual living beings. The move suggested was not a natural but a conceptual one.

Once we think of chemistry as processes and not objects, once we classify chemical bodies in terms of their roles in the processes, and once we consider all of this together within a single perspective, we notice a conceptual pattern that resembles the logic of life. We have an analogy and nothing more, for the concept has not permeated objectivity in the way that life requires.[7] Rather, we philosophers have had to reflect on chemical process as a whole and talk in terms of sorts and kinds to discern the underlying pattern. Because the transience of the various bodies has shown them to be inessential, we have been led to look for what is essential. But the abstract circle described at the beginning of §329 is not yet embodied as such in nature, for no single chemical process returns to the point from which it started.

Nonetheless, the concept makes its appearance in chemical process, because no individual body is fixed in its independent existence: if it is a compound, it is broken up into its different constituents; if it is a simple substance, it unites with other substances to form compounds. It is dissolved into something else, and it is generated out of something else. The concept, with its identifying and differentiating, is no longer just an a priori principle governing our investigations; it has acquired a measure of public expression, however inadequate.

The discrepancy between chemical nature and the concept is evident from several perspectives. First, reflection has talked about classes of corporeality. But it is not corporeality in general that enters into a chemical process, only specific bodies do so. Bodies are simply there – immediately given to experience – and they are diverse from each other in a variety of ways. So even a class is an indescriminate range of particulars. There is nothing here that resembles the parts of a living individual.

Second, there are a number of conditions that have to coalesce to generate a chemical process. As Berthollet showed, it is not sufficient simply to allow the various bodies to establish contact; one needs to adjust the cohesiveness, the crystallization, the temperature, and the pressure to achieve the desired results. Each of these conditions is something that exists simply on its own, and a chemical process takes place only when an alien agent assembles them in an appropriate way.

Third, any process that separates out the constituents of a compound leaves them as indifferent products that have no relation to each other. So the status of independent existence applies not only to the various moments of the ground, but also to the various moments of what is grounded. In both chemical union and chemical analysis there remains a significant remnant of pure diversity.

Fourth, the processes themselves are finite. The dynamic activity, whether fire or oxygen, which transforms bodies into other bodies, is exhausted once the result is achieved and has no power to initiate anything further. So the processes, too, fall apart into a simple diversity.[8]

In all of these ways the integrity of the concept does not appear, and so life, although recognizable as a kind of implicit principle, is not in fact present. The end and the beginning of any single process are simply diverse; it cannot reconstitute its own beginning. So chemistry, despite the high hopes that Ritter had had in 1798[9] and the expectations of organic chemists even in Hegel's own day,[10] cannot explain life. The two phenomena are quite different from each other, for all their similarity. If chemistry cannot be reduced to the mechanical framework of matter in motion, as the chemical atomists seemed to want, neither does it have the integrity and self-determining momentum of the organic.[11]

28

§336

Es ist aber der chemische Proceß selbst dieß, jene unmittelbaren Voraussetzungen, die Grundlage seiner Äusserlichkeit und Endlichkeit, als negirte zu setzen, die Eigenschaften der Körper, die als Resultate einer besondern Stufe des Processes erscheinen, auf einer andern zu verändern, und jene Bedingungen zu Producten herabzusetzen. Was in ihm so im Allgemeinen *gesetzt* wird, ist die *Relativität* der unmittelbaren Substanzen und Eigenschaften. Das gleichgültig-bestehende Körperliche ist dadurch nur als *Moment* der Individualität gesetzt, und der Begriff in *der ihm entsprechende Realität*. Diese *in Einem* aus der Besonderung der unterschiedenen Körperlichkeiten sich hervorbringende *concrete Einheit* mit sich, welche die Thätigkeit ist, diese ihre einseitige Form der Beziehung auf sich zu negiren, sich in die Momente des Begriffs zu *dirimiren* und zu besondern, und diese ebenso in jene Einheit zurückzuführen, – so der unendliche sich selbst anfachende und unterhaltende Proceß, – ist *der Organismus.*

The chemical process, however, is just this: to posit as negated those immediate presuppositions that are the basis of its externality and finitude; to alter the properties of bodies, which appear as result in one particular stage of the process, at another stage; and to demote those conditions to products. In universal terms, what has thus been *posited* is the *relativity* of the immediate substances and properties. So the indifferently persisting corporeal is posited only as a *moment* of individuality, and the concept is posited within a *reality that corresponds to it.* This *concrete unity* with itself that 'in one go' produces itself out of the particularity of diverse corporealities, this unity, which is the activity of negating this its one-sided form of relating to itself, of *breaking itself up* and particularizing itself into the moments of the concept, and of bringing these back at the same time into that unity – in other words, the infinite, self-initiating, and self-maintaining process – is *the organism.*

NOTES

Relativity Hegel's use of 'absolute' as an adjective has led many people to assume that he rejects all relativism. But what is suggested here, and becomes explicit when one carefully analyses the chapters on absolute knowing, absolute idea, and absolute spirit, is that what is genuinely absolute is the way we show everything to be relative.[1] In understanding that something is not itself absolute, but conditioned by, and productive of, other things, we become aware of governing principles that are not themselves relative. But such absolute principles contain the means of correcting any partiality that they themselves produce; they show what is relative in their own particular formulations. Far from being a philosopher of the absolute, then, Hegel should be called the philosopher of the relative.

Infinite In a lengthy analysis from the larger *Logic*, Hegel worked through three different senses of the term 'infinite.' The first is a simple 'beyond' – that which lies on the other side of the finite's limit. Such a concept is, however, itself limited by the fact that it is simply other than the finite. So it is a finite infinite. As finite it pushes against its own limit, and a new 'beyond' emerges. And so the process continues *ad infinitum*. This concept of an infinite progress (or regress) is a second sense of the term 'infinite.' The third sense considers the governing principle of the infinite progress: the finite is defined by its limit, thought goes beyond to the infinite, the infinite becomes a finite again. Alternatively, the infinite is beyond the finite; as thus limited by the finite it is itself finite; and this in turn points beyond the limit to the infinite. We have two conceptual circles that are really one, since it is a matter of indifference whether one begins with the finite or the infinite. That circle is what Hegel calls the true infinite – a being on its own account that constitutes as its moments both determinate finites that press beyond to the infinite and infinites that are themselves limited and hence finite. In the concept 'being-on-its-own account' (*Fürsichseyn*) the diverse moments of the valid infinite are *aufgehoben* – cancelled yet preserved, and so they become *ideelle*.[2]

An organism, although in some sense finite and limited by its environment, nonetheless has a dynamic, self-constituting pattern as part of its internal constitution. Therefore 'infinite' is an appropriate term to characterize it.

Organism This is a key concept in the philosophy of nature, since a natural organism has a dynamic structure of self-determination that matches the self-contained processes of conceptual thought. Its importance was shown in Kant's *Critique of Teleological Judgment*, where he investigated our use of the concept of purpose in describing nature. 'A thing exists as a natural purpose if it is in a double sense both cause and effect of itself.'[3]

In the next paragraph Kant takes this provisional definition further:

In such a product of nature, every part is thought as existing only *by means of* the other parts and also as existing *for the sake of* the others and of the whole, that is, as an instrument or organ. This is not sufficient [as a definition] for it would also fit an artificial instrument and so would represent a possible purpose in general. Rather, [it needs to be] an organ that produces the other parts (and each of them reciprocally doing the same), which can be the case for no artificial instrument but only for a nature that supplies all the material for the instruments (even those of art). Only then can such a purpose be called a *natural purpose*, because it is an *organizing* and *self-organizing being*.[4]

For Schelling, these self-organizing beings (or organisms) provide evidence that the possibilities of transcendental thought are matched by the actualities of nature as directly intuited. Rather than reducing nature to the atomic particles of physics and their mechanical interaction (as was common among the natural scientists of his day) Schelling and his colleagues considered organisms to be the primary, comprehensive 'undifferentiated' reality within which are to be differentiated the mechanical moments of passivity and the magnetic, electrical, and chemical moments of activity.

In the drafts Hegel prepared at Jena, the organic continues to serve as the governing paradigm for nature, within which different subordinate moments are to be 'constructed.' By the time of the *Encyclopaedia*, however, chemical process is discussed on its own terms, taking account of the data from scientific investigation. Only at the end, when all the various aspects of those processes are considered together, does the *concept* of organism emerge. So, as in Kant, the move is to a new way of *thinking* about nature that will then govern subsequent investigations. The move is not, as in Schelling, to an intuition of undifferentiated reality that ultimately explains not only the chemical, but everything else that precedes.

COMMENTARY

The finitude of chemical process is not a new insight. In §335 Hegel showed that, for all that chemistry is an analogue of life, it nonetheless is not life. This reiterated the discussion in §329, where he argued that the pure conceptual pattern of a circular totality would appear in finite bodies and particular processes. Now, however, he has talked, not about particularity in general, but about the processes that actually occur in nature. Each has turned out to be both a separation and a combination; some have returned to the same kind of thing with which they began, forming a 'totality.' Within chemical particularity, then, nature has offered unexpected evidence that the concept governs the way concrete bodies function. As suggested by the logical idea of life, the concept permeates objectivity (albeit to a limited extent), and bodies organize themselves in a way that approximates the concept.

There is, says Hegel, a further aspect that emerges from the natural phenomena. When we consider all of them together, we realize that there is nothing that serves as an absolute or independent foundation for the whole process. Every single chemical body is both the product of a particular process and yet susceptible to chemical transformation. Its properties do not remain fixed and limited; for all that they are generated in one process, they alter and pass away in another. So what are stipulated to be conditions with some sort of immediate existence are, nonetheless, mediated products.[5]

In other words, the various bodies are not as independent and external as they seemed to be. For all that they are diverse, and for all that the chemical dynamic exhausts itself in a particular process and cannot start itself up again, there is nothing that is absolutely unmediated, no presupposition that is not also posited, no finitude that does not go beyond its limits into something else, no externality that is not cancelled and preserved in a chemical product.

The passing away of particular bodies, however, does not lead into an infinite regress, as happens in the mechanical realm, because the set of chemical processes make up a circle. Were we to start with iron, we can end up with iron again; were we to start with sulphuric acid, we can end up there as well. There is a sense in which the whole set of operations is self-contained.

Chemical process considered as a single whole establishes an important general principle: substances and properties that are taken to be immediate are nonetheless relative. They show their transience and conditioned nature. And they are all part of a single, circular pattern.

With this circle of relativity, we need no longer think of the different chemical bodies as thoroughly individuated. The only thing that has some kind of persistent existence is the total pattern of chemical interaction. It alone is a genuine individual; the bodies that claim indifferent persistence are only moments within its totality. This is why chemical process is analo-

gous to life. Despite all the residual diversity, the concept that unites identifying and differentiating in one self-determining process has found a sort
of corresponding reality.

What is missing is a basic integrity that unites all the various moments
within a single, self-perpetuating dynamic. This would be a process that
would be the source of its own activity. It would be a unity that generated
itself by differentiating within itself various bodily moments that are nonetheless constituents of its own concrete identity. It would be a dynamic
activity that would react against being simply a persisting entity, would
break itself up into particular moments that are complements, even opposites, of each other, and would at the same time reconstitute itself by rein-
corporating this particularity into its own unity.

Such a unified, active being would be what we could call an organism. Its
process would, in a genuinely infinite way, both generate finite particulars
and ensure that each such particular points beyond its limits to something
else; so that the process continually renews and maintains itself. By entertaining these possibilities reflection combines the various chemical processes into a single thought that is the concept of an organism.[6]

In other words, Hegel has effected a systematic transition to the philosophy of organic physics.

It is worth spending a bit of time to reflect on this transition. For the
critical question in any system is the move from one stage to the next – the
transformation of one way of understanding phenomena into another. If a
philosophy of nature fails to function at this point, it fails completely, falling apart into a set of diverse ways of viewing natural phenomena.

The transition here is not one that happens in nature. Hegel stresses that
chemical processes on their own do not convert into organic ones; they
continue to be finite and discrete. But the move is not strictly logical either;
we do not develop a concept to the point where its various distinct
moments presuppose and imply each other, so that they can then be cancelled and preserved in a more comprehensive concept. The mechanics of
the shift are more intricate than either mode of alteration on its own.

Chemical processes have been shown to have a number of distinct characteristics: (1) any separation is also a combination, and vice versa; (2) there
are processes of separation and combination that are totalities in that they
start and end with the same *kind* of chemical body. Further, when we look
at the total set of chemical processes, we discover (3) that we started from
pure metals and we ended up with the same metals;[7] and (4) that any particular body, although endowed with the appearance of self-contained independence, is not in fact unmediated but is produced by one kind of process

and absorbed and transformed in another. Therefore (5) the only thing that can really be firmly individuated is the set of processes as a whole.

These characteristics are not just given in nature. They are the way nature is *understood* to be. Not only have chemical bodies and chemical processes been *classified* according to certain general categories, but the full pattern becomes explicit only when we *think about* the total picture. Classification and reflection are functions of thought: not thought simply thinking its own concepts as in the *Logic*, but thought coming to terms with the givens of the natural order. Thought generalizes or classifies; it recognizes differences and takes care not to indulge in overhasty generalization; it considers how both the universal classes and the particular differences fit together into a totality. It is this kind of reflective comprehension of nature that recognizes in chemical process an individual totality whose dynamic activity involves both separation and combination; particular entities do not remain fixed, but are qualitatively transformed into something else and are generated by other such transformations; and a circular pattern, both in some individual processes and in the process as a whole, leads back to any particular starting point. Whereas, in the circle of double affinity, the identity is only formal and abstract according to kinds, in the whole process any individual body serves as both final product and initial condition. The only thing that holds chemical process back from moving on to life and organism is the fact that bodies remain diverse and processes particular. What has not found a natural expression is the unity of the process as a function of a single activity. The unity has been discerned only by external reflection. But that justifies a new philosophical move: looking to nature for unified processes that would perforce not be just chemical, but organic.

Notice that Hegel has not yet talked of that single activity as a body. What at first will emerge is the unity of the process only in general – the way the earth as a whole develops geologically.[8] Only later will he come to plants and animals – to living individual organisms. The systematic advance moves step by step; it does not leap.

This transition in the philosophy of nature is, then, the product of a reflective assessment of chemical phenomena that considers them as a totality. It presupposes a conceptual understanding that recognizes in nature's externality and contingency an inherently rational pattern. This is not nature observed; nor is it natural science. Only a philosophy of nature so integrates conceptual comprehension and natural fact that a single conceptual shift is necessary to move on to the next stage: the shift from a totality that retains an element of diversity to a totality that actively integrates its moments.

29

From 1817 to 1830

As part of the *Encyclopaedia of the Philosophical Sciences*, the *Philosophy of Nature* went through three editions at Hegel's hands.[1] The section on chemical process started out in 1817 two paragraphs shorter than 1827 and with a different title: 'The Process of Singularizing.'[2] By 1827, however, the basic structure of the final version was in place, and Hegel's changes in 1830 were more editorial than substantive. I shall review the differences in general terms, and then draw some conclusions about Hegel's motivations for making the changes.

In 1817 Hegel grouped chemical processes into a set of three, rather than the four-plus-one of the later editions. The numbering, however, was deceptive; under (1) he talked about both metals being oxidized by means of the abstract neutrality of water and combustible bodies being burned in air.[3] Separation did not have a separate paragraph, but was introduced as a moment within the discussion of double affinity.

The description of actual processes started in the first sentence of the first paragraph after a comment that 'the chemical process has its products as its presuppositions.' There was no discussion of the conceptual pattern of identifying and differentiating, of real as distinct from formal process, of the finitude of particular processes, and of abstract as opposed to concrete processes. Amalgamation was not mentioned at all, and the role of mediation was covered by a separate paragraph within the discussion of metallic oxidation.

Also of interest is the fact that the oxidation of metals, while taking up three full paragraphs rather than one, made no mention of galvanism, since that had already been discussed under electricity. As well, the elements oxygen, hydrogen, and nitrogen emerged from the division of water and air, functioning as middle terms in oxidation and combustion, and carbon was added in a summary paragraph about all four elements at the end of (1).[4]

The lectures we have from 1819–20 show that Hegel soon moved to the later pattern.[5] Galvanism now provided the bridge into chemical process and was numbered separately from combustion.[6] Amalgamation was mentioned with reference to Winterl; and separation was said to involve nothing more than the three already cited processes: galvanism, combustion, and neutralization. While the student taking the notes did not always grasp the significance of Hegel's more theoretical comments, it is clear that Hegel spent some time at the beginning talking about chemical process as an analogue of life, detailing both similarities and differences.

The changes from 1827 to 1830 are not as major. Three basic themes emerge: the first distinguishes an abstract from a concrete process; the second articulates the grounds for, and application of, a genuinely chemical classification; the third stresses how a chemical is different from an electrical process. While all of these concerns had been implicit in the remarks of the earlier editions, they are now included in the main text.

What can these revisions tell us about Hegel's philosophical method? Why did he make these changes? We can identify two different explanations: in 1827 reflection had led Hegel to make discriminations previously overlooked; in 1830 he was motivated by polemical concerns.

Consider that in 1827 Hegel added to the beginning of the section four paragraphs that discussed theoretical questions. As his philosophy of nature developed over the years, he had learned the importance of distinguishing the a priori and systematic discussion from the appeal to more empirical data. While the latter was still expressed in the abstract language of philosophy, the justification for the statements made there came, not from reflective discriminations, but from the actual discoveries of chemistry. It was important to keep these two kinds of contribution to a philosophy of nature separate. As a result he wanted to set the stage with a more explicit and detailed analysis.

This move had several implications. First, as he became more self-conscious about the organizing role of theoretical thought, Hegel noticed that it licensed the distinction between the 'formal' process of amalgamation and the 'real' process of chemistry. Second, the abstract discussion of middle terms in a real process no longer needed to be embedded within the analysis of oxidation. Third, the logic of chemism required a separate handling of separation, even if it involved no new kind of chemical process. Fourth, by distinguishing between the a priori and the a posteriori the latter could fall away from a rigid three-part schema: union included really four kinds of processes; union and separation were two contrary moves. Nature's 'impotence' left things scattered in a diversity that did not fit neatly into the conceptual structure.[7]

Only one change reflected empirical considerations: the decision to integrate the discussion of galvanism with that of metallic oxidation. It appears that Hegel had been convinced, perhaps by his colleague Pohl, that the galvanic process was primarily chemical, for all of its electrical features. As such it provided the paradigm for the oxidation of metals.

The need to defend this last decision led to a further change, added in 1830: a sentence identified how the activity of water transformed a merely electrical process into a chemical one. The polemic was elaborated in Hegel's written remarks. At the same time, his disagreement with the chemists who classified all chemical substances as elements of the same order led him to include both the explicit language of classification and a more precise discrimination between abstract and concrete processes in the final version.

For Hegel, chemistry was distinguished from mechanics and physics in that it talked about the transformation of bodies. It was not just a question of 'investigating the qualitative and quantitative relations in which the various components of bodies stand with respect to each other' as Trommsdorff said;[8] nor was it just the 'science of the composition of bodies and of their relation to each other,' as Berzelius suggested.[9] Simple talk of relations suggested that the terms had an independent and continuing existence outside of the relation. But the chemical surfaced as a separate area of investigation precisely because bodies were changed; they lost their original properties and became something else.

Since it is as process, not as simple relation, that the chemical has a role to play, any philosophy that wants to set it within an overall view of nature must work from that dynamic. It should not assume static entities that are simply interrelated. Chemical bodies are rather implicitly and explicitly active: they need to be classified according to the kind of activity they generate and the kind of activity by which they are produced.

This not only justified Hegel's stress on a proper classification; it was a reason for distinguishing abstract from concrete. The abstract substances of distilled water and purified gas, the abstract products of hydrogen and nitrogen, potassium and chlorine, never occur in nature as dynamic bodies. They are the results of theoretical abstraction, using the techniques of analytic chemistry. It was legitimate to isolate them, but the philosophy of nature was not concerned with what they are like in isolation, but with the bodies that change when they are added or subtracted from compounds.

The distinction between concrete separations and abstract ones becomes important once separation is identified as a process distinct from uniting. The *logic* of chemism had shown that when an independent activity was applied to a neutral product it produced abstracted and fixed elements. In just this way, analytical chemists used oxidation, combustion, and neutralization, not primarily to create new compounds, but to draw off some substances from compounds already present and leave others in their pure state. Abstraction was the form separation took when it was governed by these analytical demands of logical thought.

While abstract analysis was the primary interest of chemists in the early decades of the nineteenth century, Hegel's philosophy of chemical process focused on actual transformations of natural bodies. He was not concerned with the laboratory, but with nature as the sphere of human experience. The abstract and theoretical results of science may throw light on the 'mechanics' of the process, but they do not do justice to its 'chemics' – to the dynamic of bodily transformation.

In the 1830 text, then, Hegel sharpens the references to classification and abstraction to make clear how his philosophy of chemical process diverged from the directions being taken by empirical chemistry. We have yet to see whether he intended thereby to pass judgment on the explanations proposed by the chemists, or whether he was simply distinguishing his discipline from theirs.

30

The Remarks

Hegel's conception of a philosophy of nature emerges from the remarks he added to the paragraphs on chemical process. Since these are more accessible than the main paragraphs, a summary of their contents will serve to introduce a discussion of how chemistry is related to philosophy.

In 1817 there were three remarks, one appended to the discussion of oxidation (§253), a second to the paragraph on double affinity (§257), and a third to the penultimate paragraph on the distinction between chemical process and life (§258). In 1827 the first of these disappeared and was replaced by a discussion of galvanism (§330). The second was divided in two and connected to the paragraphs on separation (§334) and double affinity (§333). The third remained relatively unchanged (§335). The only major alteration in 1830 was that the remark on galvanism (§330) increased eightfold in length.

Since the first remark of 1817 is not readily available, it is worth outlining its content.[1] Hegel points out that, though some metals become oxides and thus chemical bodies oriented towards acids, nature's 'impotence' means that there is no hard and fast rule. While alkalis (such as lime and soda) and earths (like strontion and baryte) have also been shown to be oxides, some oxides of metals turn out to be acids, on the other side of the chemical divide.

The second half of the remark explains why oxygen and hydrogen are to be considered abstractions. Isolated as gases, they permeate each other much as light does, without any genuine combination. They are thus 'raised to immateriality.' In addition, any chemical character is not intrinsic, but emerges only when these gases become components of compound, individuated bodies. So, for example, oxygen is just as much a constituent of metallic oxides and alkalis as of acids, and some acids have been identified that have only hydrogen; Lavoisier's assumption that oxygen is the necessary chemical in acidity had been proven wrong on two counts.

The new remark to §330 in 1827 makes two points: The first, almost an aside, points out that there is no uniformity in the functioning of nature, since acids and alkalis can be substituted for the water of the galvanic process, and the same effects can be achieved with two liquids and one metal as with two metals and a liquid. The second stresses that the language of (passive) electrical conductors cannot do justice to the dynamic transformations that take place in galvanism.[2]

By 1830, the active role of water has become the theme of a lengthy polemic, supported by Pohl's evidence, against the electrochemical theory of Berzelius. Hegel lists the phenomena not explained by that theory, accuses its proponents of overhasty generalization, and uses galvanism to illustrate the 'impotence' of nature, in that it has both electrical and chemical characteristics.

The remark to §333 (which started out as the second half of the 1817 remark to §257) not only cites Richter's contributions to the laws of definite proportion, but also cites Berthollet's evidence on elective affinity to reinforce the point that, in its 'impotence,' nature allows a wide variation from any norm.[3]

The remark to §334, extended somewhat from its 1817 version, challenges the predisposition of chemists to lump all chemical substances together in a single classification, thereby ignoring their physical diversity and the difference between abstract and real process. The attempt to explain organic processes in chemical terms is also set aside, although it does refute the prevailing metaphysical assumption that basic stuff is unalterable. Hegel's polemic derives from the fact that chemistry is the science of the *transformation* of bodies. Metals might be able to exist independently, but all other chemical bodies are defined by the way they function in the processes of chemical change. From this perspective the difference between Hegel's four chemical elements and the noble metals is so great that it is surprising that anyone could even consider placing them on the same level. Hegel ends by stressing that we should consider chemical process in its totality, rather than focus on specific products and specific reactions.[4]

The final remark, appended to §335, refers to the process, already cited in the *Science of Logic* of 1816, where an oxide adjusts its degree of oxidation so that one part can combine with an acid, leaving the other free.[5] This, says Hegel, is an anticipation of purposiveness, and is the one point where the logic of teleology surfaces in the philosophy of nature.[6]

There are several themes that emerge from these remarks. The first concerns the 'impotence' of nature. The second highlights the dangers of over-hasty generalization. The third points out that the philosophy of nature considers all the relevant material together as a whole, and in this way establishes its systematic significance. I shall discuss each in turn.

1 / Oxidation produces not only metallic oxides and alkalis, but also acids. Galvanism can occur with two liquids and one metal as well as with two metals and a liquid. Whereas water is needed as a catalyst for some oxidation, there are metalloids that oxidize in air. Processes do not divide neatly into electrical and chemical. Elective affinity can be reversed by altering temperature and pressure.

In his remarks Hegel cites all this as evidence that nature is 'impotent' – that its rich diversity overwhelms the regularity of philosophical thought. Unlike natural science, philosophy cannot lose itself in the details of concrete phenomena; it is concerned instead with the essential core of what goes on, not the range of variations.[7]

This means, however, that it has to reflect on the wide-ranging 'show' of appearance to discern what is essential. Of all the different forms of galvanism, which is closest to the 'real thing'? Which is the normative model for oxidation? Why is 'elective affinity' the appropriate concept for salts exchanging their radicals? Neither nature nor natural science can answer these questions. Nature is simply diverse, while chemistry examines 'the particular behaviour of bodies and their peculiarlyqualified processes.'[8]

When we look more closely we find that Hegel is using logical norms to 'measure' nature's variety. In the discussion of real measure we saw how measuring uses quantities to specify qualities; in the same way the philosophy of nature uses the abstract categories of thought to identify what is distinctive about natural phenomena. Galvanism and oxidation involve the particularization of a mediating term; they correspond to the first type of syllogism; elective affinity measures the distinctive quality of a particular entity. In this way concepts, derived from the logical patterns of pure thought, become the principles that discriminate what is significant from contingent variations.

This does not mean that nature is forced into a Procrustean bed. Many conceptual possibilities are developed throughout the logic, and nature's diversity instantiates different ones in different contexts. Therefore a philosophy of nature cannot simply deduce what ought to be. Rational patterns have to be discerned in the wide-ranging variety of nature. The chemical distinction between amalgamation and union fits the logical distinction between formal and real ground, a distinction made in the logic of essence. Water in galvanism, fire in combustion, and mutual affinity in neutralization correspond to different sorts of syllogistic mediation; together they make up a full set of the three discussed under conceiving. The ratios discovered by Richter follow the logic of real measuring in the *Doctrine of Being*. The concepts used come from quite diverse spots in the *Science of Logic*, and cannot simply be derived from one other.

Once a match between concept and reality has been found, however, anything that diverges from this basic pattern can be recognized as a variation on the theme. So, even though thought is external to nature, it nonetheless uses reflective criteria to discriminate the chemically essential from the inessential.[9]

The diversity of the non-essential reflects the alien givenness of nature. It is external, contingent and particular; we cannot expect it to be otherwise. Nonetheless, within that externality we trace the implicit hand of reason and discover the principles that allow nature to be considered within a systematic philosophy.

2 / In a sarcastic comment in the remark on galvanism, Hegel challenged the electrochemical theory of Berzelius:

A previous practice of natural philosophy, which has attributed (or rather damned and trivialized) the system and process of animal reproduction to magnetism, or the system of vessels to electricity, did not schematize more superficially than the way this reduction of concrete corporeal opposition is constructed. With justice in those cases such a practice of being short with the concrete, of overlooking what is distinctive and of fleeing into abstractions is repudiated. Why not also in the present one?[10]

The charge is of overhasty generalization.

For all that the logic enables us to discern what is essential in the rich diversity of nature's impotence, the philosopher has also to take the concrete seriously, to pay attention to distinctions, and to be wary of abstract universals.

This holds not only for keeping the permanent results of chemical activity distinct from the transient products of electricity. It also applies to the distinction between independent metals and chemicals like sulphur and phosphorus, and even more between solid inert substances like gold and silver and abstracted elements like oxygen and hydrogen. To comprehend nature we must recognize the importance of differences.

Here Hegel is appealing not to the a priori principles of the *Logic*, but to differences and distinctions in the natural order. An oxide is quite different as product from a spark, a substance that burns should not be confused with an impervious solid, and elements that can be abstracted from many different compounds need to be kept distinct from natural bodies (such as silver and gold) that resist qualitative transformation.

Taking differences seriously provides a necessary corrective to the logical identification of what is essential discussed in our first point. The diversity of nature includes not only impotent variations but also significant differences that reflect distinctive categories The way solid metals are transformed in galvanism is different from the way combustibles burn, even though both involve oxidation; the substances presupposed have contrary characteristics, and the substances produced stand on opposite sides of the tension between acids and bases.

Just as, however, classification not only applies a priori logical categories but also takes account of the distinctive traits of nature, so differentiation reflects not only natural differences but also conceptual ones. Galvanism and combustion are distinct sorts of mediation: one by way of particularization, the other by means of a synthesizing singular. Similarly, chemically fixing a persisting product conforms to the conceptual activity of understanding concepts, whereas the electrical resolution of opposites matches the speculative achievements of reflection. The natural differences to be taken seriously are those that correspond to conceptual distinctions.[11]

Because logic enables the philosopher to identify significant differences, Hegel not only defends his stance against the scientists of his day, but also attacks. With regard to the elements, to atomic theory, to electrochemistry, and to organic chemistry, scientists had not considered empirical differences carefully enough; they were too concerned to find a single, abstract unity, to reduce chemistry to mechanics or physics.

So in the match between nature and thought, not only can some of the diversity of nature be set aside, but other differences need to be taken more seriously than was current in the scientific laboratories.[12]

3 / For Hegel, what distinguishes a philosophy of nature from empirical chemistry is not found primarily in the way category and experience interact when the investigator classifies or discriminates. Scientists also develop conceptual hypotheses to explain phenomena, and these preconceptions determine what experiments they construct and what they count as significant disconfirmation. What philosophy brings in addition is a consideration of the total picture:

Here as elsewhere it is necessary to take chemical process in its complete totality. To isolate particular parts or formal and abstract processes leads to the abstract representation of chemical process in general as merely the *influence* of one substance on another; which means that much else that occurs – such as abstract neutralization (production of water) and abstract generation (development of gases) – appears as an almost secondary and contingent result, or at least as only externally connected, not considered as an essential moment in the relation of the whole. A complete working through of chemical process in its totality demands, however, more precisely that it be explicated as a real syllogism, indeed as a triad of syllogisms intimately involved with each other – syllogisms that are not only a combination in general of their terms, but as activities are the negation of the terms' determinations, and in their interconnection would have to display uniting and separating integrated within one process.[13]

Being open to the situation as a whole means that, in any single process, one does not focus on a particular result, but on everything that happens. Water as well as salt emerges from neutralization; hydrogen as well as oxides are produced by galvanism; division as well as union occurs in double affinity. A conceptual grasp of which classifications and differences are significant can only be derived from that overall perspective. For only then can one see how the various moments embody the logical pattern of syllogistic mediation by way of singulars, particulars, and universals.

More important, it means considering the whole sphere of chemical activity: the separating as well as the uniting, acidification as well as oxidation, particularizing into opposed extremes as well as neutralization.

This overall perspective determines what logical concepts are to be used for classifying and discriminating. By considering all the processes together, one notices how a particular substance functions at one time as presupposition, at another as result. One distinguishes between the mediating agency of water in galvanism, of fire and air in combustion, of the bond between acids and bases in neutralization. Furthermore, one notices how separating and uniting are sides of a single, complex dynamic.

It is considering the picture as a whole that enables one to identify the essential moments and to distinguish contrary and distinctive operations. The *single* process that incorporates all the others is not a simple generalization, then, but rather an intricate network of relations binding quite distinctive and different processes and entities together. In this way a complete comprehension articulates not only classes and differentiations, but also how they are interconnected by way of intermediate, dynamic terms.

This sense of a differentiated whole gives Hegel his response to the electrochemical theory. As part of the impotence of nature, galvanism confuses electrical with chemical phenomena. But considering the whole, one distinguishes a transient electrical charge from a dynamic chemical transformation. For Hegel, a full explanation never reduces one to the other but, while keeping the distinctions clear, discerns how the essential moment is chemical.

A philosophy of nature, then, is distinguished from empirical chemistry by the way it considers the total picture, not in a single intuition, nor in a collection of discrete analyses, but as a network of interconnected moments.[14]

The three themes we have drawn from Hegel's remarks together serve to distinguish the approach of a philosophy of nature from that of empirical chemistry. They are summarized in a comment Hegel made in his lectures:

The particular behaviour of the body and its peculiarly qualified process is the subject-matter of chemistry. In contrast, we have to consider the process in its totality, and how it separates off the classes of bodies and identifies them as stages of its passage, which have become fixed.[15]

31

How Chemical Process Is Systematic

In the logic of chemism, as in the logic of real measure, the key systematic move is the transition to a new concept: to teleology or to the undifferentiated background of the 'real' thing. In both cases we discover a network of relations in which terms mutually condition each other, so that the total complex comes to be considered as a single, self-contained unit. In one, the concept organizes objectivity for its own purposes; in the other, the reciprocal shift from a qualitative beyond to a quantitative infinite and back again points to an underlying, undifferentiated reality.

Similarly, in the philosophy of chemical process the critical move lies at the end, when reflection effects the transition to organism and organic physics. Even in the edition of 1817, where Hegel jumped into the oxidation of metals halfway through the first sentence of the section, he needed two paragraphs at the end for the systematic transition to the next stage.

As we have seen, this shift is not something observed in nature. It comes from considering chemical process as a whole. One notices that the same processes both unite and separate, that any single body is both product and presupposition, that no body can resist dissolution, and that the process as a whole has a self-contained and self-generating pattern. Considering that picture as a whole sets the scene for the next stage of natural philosophy.

A similar act of reflective synthesis generates the move to chemical process. Since that occurs in the paragraph preceding the section we have been discussing, it has not yet merited our attention. To make the systematic character of the philosophy of nature clear, however, we need to look at it:

§325

Die *Besonderung* des individuellen Körpers bleibt aber nicht bei der trägen Verschiedenheit und Selbstätigkeit der Verschiedenen stehen, aus welcher die abstrakte reine Selbstischkeit, das Lichtprinzip, zum Prozess, zu Spannung Entgegengesetzter und Aufheben derselben in ihrer Indifferenz heraustritt. Da die besondern Eigenschaften nur die Realität dieses einfachen Begriffes, der Leib ihrer Seele, des *Lichtes*, sind und der Komplex derEigenschaften, der besondere Körper, nicht wahrhaft selbständig ist, so geht die *ganze* Körperlichkeit in die Spannung und in den Prozess ein, welcher zugleich das Werden des individuellen Körpers ist. Die Gestalt, welche zunächst nur aus dem Begriffe hervorging, somit nur *an sich* gesetzt war, geht nun auch aus dem existierenden Prozesse hervor und stellt sich als das aus der Existenz Gesetzte dar, – der *chemische Prozess*.	The *particularizing* of the individual bodies, however, does not remain with the indolent diversity and self-activity of the diverse, out of which the abstract pure self-ishness, the light principle, emerges into process, generating tension between opposites and sublating them into indifferentiation. Since the particular properties are only the reality of this simple concept, the flesh of their soul, of *light*, and since the complex of properties,the particular body, is not genuinely independent, so the *whole* corporeality enters into the tension and into the process, which at the same time is the becoming of the individual bodies. The form, which at first only emerged from the concept, and so was only posited *implicitly*, now proceeds as well from the existing process and presents itself as what is posited in existence – *chemical process*.

Immediately preceding this paragraph the discussion had talked of how individual bodies are distinguished from each other, or particularized: through density, colour, smell, and taste. When bodies differentiated in this way are brought together and then allowed to rub against each other, a different kind of differentiation occurs: they acquire contrary electrical charges whose opposition is resolved by a spark of light.[1]

In §325 thought considers all these factors together: the 'indolent diversity' of colour, the 'self-activity' of smell and taste, and the electrical process by which tension is both generated and released. Two features emerge, which Hegel presents in the crucial 'since' clauses. First, the sensed properties are the public expression of the inherent nature that develops electrical charges. They are, so to speak, the outside of its inside; they are the body for its soul.[2] Second, the various secondary properties form a complex; they distinguish a particular physical body. Electricity has shown that this body is not radically independent but, when brought into contact with others, develops a tensed opposition and release. In this dynamic, different sensed qualities, and different colours, tastes, and smells are generated. (One thinks, for example, not only of the spark but also of the acid or caustic taste that results from completing a galvanic circuit by means of an eye or tongue.) So the process not only presupposes particular bodies, but also generates new qualities, which should then serve to particularize different bodies.

Considering all this as a totality, reflection integrates the various moments into a single, encompassing perspective. One thereby conceives of a process that would involve *whole bodies* being distinguished or particularized from each other, and in which oppositions are both produced and overcome. A dynamic of that sort would fit the concept of chemical process already developed in the logic of chemism.

The abstract vocabulary of §325 is ambiguous: is this move the work of simple reflection or is Hegel claiming that nature in fact, by means of electricity, transforms indolent diversity into chemical opposition? Certainly the galvanic process appears to do so. But, as we have seen, Hegel attributes the combination of the chemical and the electrical to the 'impotence' of nature, and strenuously argues against conflating their role in galvanism. Since they are to be kept distinct, the move here can only be from one conceptual stage to another. The various features identified in the use of density, colour, smell, taste, and electricity to distinguish bodies are all integrated together into a single thought.

This analysis confirms Hegel's claim in the introduction to the *Philosophy of Nature* that its transitions are systematic rather than natural: 'Nature is to be considered as a *system of stages*, in which one necessarily proceeds from another and is its proximate truth. It results, not in the sense that it is generated *naturally* from the other, but rather within the inner idea that amounts to the ground of nature.' He went on to distance himself explicitly from Goethe's theory of metamorphosis by pointing out that any change occurs only conceptually, not within natural bodies.[3]

The synthesis of the various moments described in §325 is, then, not a proposal for a scientific experiment, but rather the product of reflective thought, considering the ways bodies are differentiated 'in their complete totality.'[4] Since theoretical considerations provide the premises for the argument from 'since' to 'so,' the shift from one stage to the next is an inference of thought, not a movement of nature.[5]

Once reflection sets the new stage, thought (in §§326–9) explores its theoretical structure: identifying differences and differentiating identities, formal combinations and real mediations, concrete transformations and abstract separations. In addition thought expects that this theoretical model will be instantiated in a variety of particular natural processes that in their 'impotence' will not strictly conform to pure theory.

In my commentary I called a priori those reflections that initiated the section on chemical process. Now we can see that they themselves are generated a posteriori from reflection on earlier experience, from both seeing how bodies are in fact differentiated from each other and considering the total picture. At any one stage in the philosophy of nature, what serves as its a priori setting has been derived from thinking about what experience has offered in the previous stage.

These reflections enable the philosopher to focus on what is significant about the phenomena now in question. So, for example, the new process is concerned with transformation of bodies from one particular form to another. Since chemistry has been distinguished from physics and mechanics in that it talks of how non-living substances change, it is the appropriate science to provide empirical data.

In developing their theories, chemists had tried to explain this dynamic using static models: the theory of atoms, elements distinguished only in terms of their specific gravity or inherent electrical charge. Even when they considered what was dynamic, they wanted to reduce the chemical to the electrical. They were not prepared to consider chemical processes on their own terms, as required by the philosophy of nature.

Once one does take nature on its own terms, one has a basis for organizing the phenomena that chemistry describes. One can distinguish various processes depending on the kind of mediation involved; one can classify bodies in terms of the processes they condition and are produced by; one can investigate whether separating requires a different process from uniting. In sum, having worked out the implications of any stage where processes of differentiation and identification involve whole bodies as both conditions and products, one looks to nature to see what particular processes do in fact fit this perspective.

Despite using prior principles of organization, then, the philosophy of nature does not reach its conclusions about chemical process by imposing rational categories on recalcitrant experience. When making its systematic shifts, the philosophy of nature does not just follow the logic, but goes its own way.

As we have seen, in the *Logic* the demise of chemism gave rise to teleology, where an external subjective concept uses objective means to attain its end. Apart from an aside, added as a remark to §335, purposiveness and teleology do not surface at all in the move to organic physics; and Hegel points out at the very beginning of the *Philosophy of Nature*, that teleology reflects the way humans use nature in practice, not the way nature itself functions.[6]

Instead, in the *Philosophy of Nature* the concept that begins to emerge out of chemical process is life, a term investigated in the *Logic* only after teleology has had its day. Indeed, the first organism that is investigated is not in fact living at all, but rather the planet earth as a whole.

We can see the reason for this difference in systematic development by comparing what happens to chemical process in the two disciplines. In the *Logic*, the three key processes are: combination into a neutral product (which can be read in three ways), separation of elements, and distribution of elements among differentiated bodies. The move from one to the other is determined by a conceptual dissatisfaction when we discover that any particular sort of chemical objectivity is theoretically incomplete. Teleology makes explicit this governing role of conceptual thought in organizing the objective realm.

In the *Philosophy of Nature*, however, no one process exactly fits the logical description of combination; in addition, the same process may be used both to unite and separate. Certainly, when driven by theoretical considerations,[7] nature can be made to conform to the logical model: elements can be isolated that, in being distributed among bodies, generate chemical differences. But this involves abstracting from nature, forcing it to fit the requirements of conceptual thought; it does not represent its concrete existence.

When we consider chemical reality 'in its complete totality,' we discover that any chemical substance may serve as the condition as well as the product of a process. As a result, though all the processes together make a kind of circle, the circle is not the one articulated in the *Logic*, from differentiated objects to differentiated objects, but one that goes from iron, for example, back to iron. Though chemical bodies are able to persist independently, they nonetheless pass away into something else only to re-emerge later on.

Reflective thought recognizes in the synthesis of all these experienced characteristics the self-generating and self-maintaining pattern that the *Logic* defined as life. Were that dynamic to be constituted as a single body, it goes on to say, we would have an organism. But as yet in the systematic development that is only a proposal of thought; it has not been instantiated by empirical data.

In other words, it is the evidence that nature itself provides of circles returning to their starting point that determines the next stage of the *Philosophy of Nature*. Conceptual thought, coming from sensory differences and electricity, had told the philosopher to look to chemistry; but what was then found empirically determined where thought should look next.[8]

So, considered as a whole, the section on chemical process follows the moments of the concept. Initial reflection explores the general or universal characteristics of this stage (§§326–9). Then the various particular processes are identified in experience and described in philosophical language (§§330–4). Finally, all are brought together into a totality and integrated into a single perspective (§§335–6). This triggers a conceptual shift to a new general concept and a new exploration of experience.

Unlike the *Science of Logic*, the *Philosophy of Nature* is a system, not because thought thinks through the implications of its own concepts, but because thought learns that it should look to nature in a certain way, then considers every experience relevant to that perspective, and finally discerns in the synthesis of all the resulting descriptions patterns that point forward to the next plateau.

32

Conclusion

I have come to the end of my project. Three chapters from Hegel's philosophy have provided an insight into his use of chemical concepts and his understanding of chemical phenomena. I have offered an interpretation of the texts, and proposed explanations for the changes he introduced and the positions he took. It is now time to tie the various strands together and consider what all this tells us about Hegel's systematic project.

Let us start with the difference between his argument in the *Science of Logic* and that of the *Philosophy of Nature*. The first works entirely in the sphere of pure concepts; the latter appeals to experience.[1]

In the *Science of Logic*, philosophy analyses concepts. When any concept shows itself to be incomplete, thought explores what has been left out; if two aspects of its meaning conflict with each other, thought resolves the contradiction by investigating its ground or sufficient reason. Each of these moves leads on to more adequate definitions of the original concept, which in turn are subjected to critical analysis.

At its limits, however, a concept begins to break down. When its various moments are precisely defined and their mutual relationship identified, the original meaning has all but disappeared. The nodal line expresses a relation that is measureless; the fully developed set of three syllogisms marks the demise of chemism. For the various constituents of its meaning have turned out to imply or require each other; and this reciprocal interconnection constitutes a single network of meanings that integrates the various aspects of the previous concept into a qualitatively distinct, new, and simple concept. The former moments are 'sublated' (to use Hegelian jargon) into something more comprehensive. In this way real measure prepares the way for essence, and chemism's demise opens the door for teleology.

In all of this, thought simply uses its own resources. It considers a partic-

ular concept, defines it exhaustively in terms of other concepts, explores
the conceptual relations between various moments. It is, as Hegel himself
said, thought thinking itself, but doing so in a way that not only takes
account of every nuance but also reviews the action as a whole, seeing how
it all fits together.

In working out a concept thought becomes aware of what is missing, and
goes looking to fill the gap. When it comes to the end of the logical project
as a whole the same thing happens.

At that point the logic reaches a concept that captures the full nature of
its own activity, that incorporates and sums up all the various moments
that have gone before into a single, highly potent, pattern. Thought now
understands its own dynamic, in which various moments are distinguished,
then related, then 'sublated.' This 'idea' of logic is no longer relative to
other concepts or ideas, but absolute.

All this, however, has taken place within the realm of thought. Whatever
emerged as an opposite was nonetheless a function of conceptual reflection.
So there was a kind of necessity to its path. Everything could be incorporated into a single, comprehensive, and universal perspective.

As soon as thought has in this way self-reflectively identified the nature
of its own systematic development, it notices what is missing. What about a
realm that is radically other than thought, that has all the characteristics
that thought lacks? Such a realm would be external, not only to thought,
but also in the way its various constituents are related to each other; there
would be no internal relations. It would be multiple and diverse, rather
than integrated and united. Instead of a necessary development, it would be
bedevilled by contingency.

Thought's desire to be fully comprehensive makes it want to incorporate
this realm of otherness. But it is prevented from doing so. Because this
other could never appear as another moment in thought's internal history,
it is simply a possibility entertained. For it has been defined as that which is
completely other than thought. Whatever is other in this way will remain
other and will never become a moment within thought's own internal
dynamic. It cannot be domesticated into a network of necessary, integrated
relations. In other words, thought has come to its limits. If it wants to comprehend this other it must abandon its own self-determining operations
and open itself completely to the alien. It must decide to let itself go.

While doing so, however, it retains instruments it can continue to use.
For in the course of its own development concepts have emerged with
which it can describe what this possible other would be like: 'possibility'
and 'other,' to be sure, but also 'external,' 'diverse,' 'finite,' 'contingent,'

'particular.' In the *Logic* all of these have acquired definition; and all have required, as counterparts to their meaning, related concepts: 'actuality,' 'relation,' 'internal,' 'ground,' 'infinite,' 'necessity,' 'universal.' So pure thought can hope and expect that this realm of otherness will instantiate terms it already knows, and that there will be clues of implicit patterns and necessary relations. As a result, reflection will eventually be able to understand and explain, using integrated and universal terms, what is going on.[2]

Nature is the realm that is radically other than thought: multiple and diverse, contingent and finite, its variety related only externally. While thought may anticipate that it can discover an inherent necessity there, that is not at all evident a priori. How can thought hope to comprehend it? Will it simply introduce its own expectations, forcing this alien material into its own Procrustean form?

To do justice to nature, thought must abandon its own pretensions. It must let nature be itself. It must decide to be thoroughly empirical.

Some comments on Aristotle, in Hegel's *Lectures on the History of Philosophy*, offer an idea of what he means by this:

Aristotle is a thorough-going empiricist, that is, at the same time one who thinks. Empiricist in that he takes up the determinations of the object of observation as we know it in our ordinary consciousness; he disproves empirical conceptions, earlier theories, and holds firmly to what must be retained from the empirical. By connecting all these determinations and holding them together, he constructs the concept. He is speculative to the highest degree, to the extent that he shows himself to be empirical. That is quite peculiar to Aristotle. His empiricism is total; that is, he does not leave out determinations; he does not hold first to one determination, and later on to another in the way understanding reflection does, which has identity as its rule and can break out of it only because, in the one determination, it always forgets and sets aside the other. Rather, Aristotle holds the determinations together in one.[3]

Reflective thought is tempted to anticipate, reading its own presuppositions into nature. It likes to simplify: having discovered one pattern that makes logical sense it assumes that everything else can be understood on its terms. So it reduces the variety of nature to a simple formula and thereby focuses on some bits of experience, ignoring the rest. It assumes that whatever is of immediate interest can be taken on its own, without reference to anything else.

This is how natural science frequently functions. When it formulates hypotheses it appeals to models and analogies that are familiar. It tries to reduce complex phenomena to simple terms, so that, for example, chemical processes, even life itself, are explained in strictly mechanical terms. It focuses on one particular kind of thing, one particular sort of relation, and assumes that nothing else need be considered to reach the truth.

Aristotle, says Hegel, did none of this. He was genuinely empirical in that he observed objects in ordinary experience. He did not leave out determinations. He did not hold first to one and then to another; he looked at all the determinations together, noticing the relations they have to each other. In this way he 'constructed the concept.'

Thought can systematically comprehend nature, suggested Hegel in this observation, only when it takes a thoroughgoing empirical approach, without anticipations and pre-judgments.

This, however, appears to land him on the other horn of a dilemma. If thought cannot take the initiative, then it is confronted with a booming, buzzing confusion, a plethora of diversity. No patterns leap to view – only a chaos of rich variety.

Thought grasps the horns of this dilemma by looking at nature as a whole, apart from any determinations at all. It takes account of all the givens in nature, but it also reflects on them, considering first their most abstract features and only gradually focusing in on more complex structures.[4]

Thus, for example, thought starts from the most general characteristics of nature. As other than thought, nature is a realm of external relations. Experience shows that this involves points and the three dimensions of space. Lines and planes are *other* than points, yet *develop out of* them.[5]

When it synthesizes these two considerations, thought comes up with the concept of 'developing otherness,' which it then experiences instantiated in time, where an 'is not' becomes an 'is,' and an 'is' becomes an 'is not.'[6]

Now thought thinks of space and time together: it conceives of a *point* that *comes to be.* Experience in turn offers place and movement to fit this schema. Similarly the synthesis of place and movement enables thought to notice matter. And so it goes.

At each stage thought considers all that experience tells us about nature together with all the determinations identified previously. This provides the schema for its next appeal to experience. Since thought is not to anticipate, it scrupulously avoids looking for anything that has not been justified by previous reflection. It takes account of particular determinations only when it has a reason to look for a certain kind of thing. So, for example, only after thought has recognized both development and otherness in space, can thought, considering both of these characteristics together, look for and discover the instantiation of this new concept in time. And only once it thinks both 'point' and 'coming to be' together, does it have a basis for noticing the significance of place and movement.

In this way the philosophy of nature develops ever more complex concepts, each one of which incorporates everything that has gone before. By the time we come to 'chemical body,' this term includes all the characteristics of space and time, matter and motion, physical elements, specific weight, colour and density, but in a new, and integrated way.

The only things that thought brings to this investigation are the expectation that nature will be a realm of external relations and the conviction that it should be considered, not selectively, but as a whole. Approached in this radically empirical way, nature turns out to have an implicit systematic structure. 'Grasping the empirical in its synthesis,' says Hegel, 'is the speculative concept.'[7]

Logic, as the process of thought thinking through the implications of its own concepts, turns out to be directed towards nature as an alien other. Nature, when considered in its totality turns out to have an inherent logic. Here we have two 'objects' that are oriented towards each other. Although independent realities, they are not complete in themselves. So together they satisfy the definition of 'chemical object' we encountered in the *Logic*. That concept is instantiated, not only within the realms of nature and spirit, but also at this macroscopic level.

To follow through the logic of chemism, the process of bringing logic and nature together is the work of philosophy, using the abstract neutral medium of language. Its product is the philosophy of nature.

The two 'objects,' however, are not strictly equivalent. For thought is active, even at the point of deciding to abandon itself to nature. In order to be genuinely empirical, it must constantly restrain its impulses to anticipate, to take possibilities as actualities, to select. Nature on the other hand is passive. It is simply there as an alien other. We may discover movement and process, but any change simply happens; nature does not convert itself into something else. Using the language of chemism again, we can say that logic is an animating principle, nature is animated. Both contribute to the ultimate neutral product, but only thought maintains the separations, isolates the elements, and shows how they contribute to both opposition and resolution.

Using the language of the other concept we analysed, logic measures, but nature is measured. For nature is simple, qualified reality. Logic, with its arsenal of concepts, each precisely defined, and with its distinction between discrete terms and continuous relations, is the realm of quantity. So we can say that, in the philosophy of nature, logic is measuring something real.

It starts out by looking for a simple relation or ratio (between points or chemical substances, for example), only to find that much more is needed – that nature is a series of measured ratios. So it focuses on a particular ratio that is preferred, an 'elective affinity,' that might be matter in motion, chemical process, or organism. But these turn out to form a nodal line, a series of stages where each is qualitatively distinct from the preceding even though thought, by reflecting on the totality of each stage, has shown the quantitative continuity that leads from one to another.

So logic and nature can be understood as related to each other, not only as chemical objects entering into a process, but also as the quantitative measuring the real as qualitative. The concepts we have analysed from the two chapters of the *Science of Logic* describe the overall framework of our study.

Both concepts, however, were shown to be incomplete. Chemism presupposed a distinction between a governing concept and objectivity. In our present context this means that the relation between logic and nature presupposes a distinction between their objective interrelationship and a reality that governs and controls it. Similarly, real measuring ends up with the measureless leap that points towards an underlying 'real' thing.

What is the 'real' thing that underlies logic's measurement of nature? What is the governing concept whose subjective intention uses the chemical process by which logic and nature interact to accomplish its ends? While the material we have analysed in this study enables us to ask those questions, it does not provide any answers. We must look further afield and include more for a complete perspective.

To do so we must ask two questions: First, how can the logic be true of the world? – why is it able to animate nature and expose its inherent rationality? Second, what is the final stage to which our understanding of alien otherness leads us? – what is the complete context of nature?

At this stage in our investigations, we can only suggest Hegel's answers to these questions, for they lead us far beyond the three chapters of our study into the framework of his philosophy as a whole. Nonetheless the answer is not unfamiliar: there is a reality that is more inclusive than either logic or nature, which can overreach the otherness of nature and from which thought abstracts its logic. Hegel called it spirit.

Consider the first question about logic's truth. As I have expounded the text, I have considered simply the implications of each concept and followed the logic inherent in them. It could be, however, that the pure possibilities of thought have nothing at all to do with the actualities of the real world. Kant raised this suspicion when he claimed that there is a radical breakbetween concepts and existence, and that thought can fit the real things 'out there' only schematically.

Hegel's response was to analyse the various claims to knowledge (including Kant's) as confident convictions of truth. In the *Phenomenology of Spirit* he showed how each such claim learned through experience of its internal inconsistency, and was thereby pointed towards a more appropriate kind of knowledge. Through this experiential development, self-conscious beings learn from their failures and become subtler and more sophisticated in their epistemological assertions, taking greater account of the way the environment interacts with their subjectivity. In the end it turns out that all one can claim to know is the process of learning itself: making a claim, discovering its strengths and its weaknesses, accepting the failure, and starting again with a more adequate approach. This, however, is a discovery, not an abstract hypothesis. It is the product of human experience over time; it distils all of that past into a potent and effective liqueur.

That done, humans can reflect on the moments of the process of learning and abstract them from the variety of contexts in which they appear. These abstractions, and the way they lead from one to another, become the *Science of Logic*. Considered in isolation, they are nothing more than the insubstantial conceptions of pure thought, but if the *Phenomenology of Spirit* has proved its case, they are more. They encapsulate the inherent principles of all our experience of reality. Any conception that might be partial or inappropriate has had its inadequacies exposed. Because its concepts concentrate the learned results of all human experience, the Logic can lay claim to truth.

Now for the second question: what is the complete understanding of nature?

As we have seen, at the end of chemical process in the philosophy of nature we were pointed towards organisms. That theoretical possibility turns out to be incarnate in the earth as a whole, in plants and in animals. The latter are self-active beings that reproduce their own generic kind and die. The synthesis of those characteristics gives us the idea of a being that, through death, generates a universal. Since such a being does not simply submit to death but constitutes itself thereby, we have a new kind of possibility: a centred being who is able to determine itself, a spirit.

From now on the totality of nature includes more than passive otherness; it involves a self-determining activity that can constitute *itself* as other even to that which it is like – to thought itself – and can nonetheless overreach the otherness of nature and alien spirits to incorporate them into its more comprehensive life.

Spirit, too, manifests stages, but these stages are not simply external to each other, to be connected by reflection. They are the product of its own self-determined development. Its most comprehensive achievement is not the integrated individual, but society – the nation state, the international community, and finally all human history. Here we have a fully comprehensive perspective of the realm that is other than pure thought. But it is now not totally alien. For the capacity to think has emerged as one way (along with willing) by which spirit comes to terms with itself and with its environment. Thought now thinks of the whole realm of thinking and willing beings. Indeed, these 'finite spirits' can use thought to tell them how to act in a way that would destroy any previous reflective synthesis. Otherness now does not just happen; it is willed.

So even the overall perspective of human history has its limits. Humans, for all of their overreaching power, are nonetheless finite, one species on a single planet. Aware of this they have a sense of something beyond, something more comprehensive; and this finds expression in great works of art, in the cultic practices of religion, and finally in disciplined and self-reflective thought.

Philosophy, as this last achievement, articulates not only the achievements of the human species, but also its limitations; its dependence as well as its independence. Reflecting on this overall picture, it can distinguish the pure principles of its own thinking from the radical otherness of nature. And it can both work out thought's internal implications and allow an alien nature to be itself through a genuine empiricism.

By means of philosophy, then, spirit combines and separates the 'chemical objects' of logic and nature, uses logic to measure nature, and thereby comes to know itself as the governing concept and 'real' thing that integrates all reality.

In the last analysis it is the capacity of finite subjective spirits to become part of a world community and to reflect on their own achievements and limitations that ultimately grounds the systematic structure of Hegel's philosophy. As members of the universal intellectual community, they are the agents who are able to unite logical thought and empirical chemistry using the real process that is Hegel's philosophy of nature.

Notes

1: Hegel's System

1 *Phän. HGW*, 9, 21; (Miller) 13
2 Such as Findlay, who in the appendix to *Hegel: A Re-examination* reconstructs such sections as 'Chemical Process' to fit a threefold pattern. A similar approach to the same section is taken by Mark Peterson in his dissertation, 'Volcanos in the Sky.'
3 For a critique of this terminology see G.E. Müller, 'The Hegel Legend of "Thesis-Antithesis-Synthesis,"' *Journal of the History of Ideas* 19 (1958), 411–14.
4 See, for example, E.E. Harris, *An Interpretation of the Logic of Hegel*, xii: 'The general principle of the dialectic, so often and so variously misrepresented, is the fundamental holism which grounds it and of which it is the expression, and when this is clearly and firmly grasped, many difficulties and obscurities melt away, and what (at first sight) seem arbitrary connexions and transitions are seen to be in place.' See as well Harris's *The Spirit of Hegel*, 142: 'The essential feature of Hegelian dialectic is not the triadic arrangement of opposites so much as the holism from which the triadic structure results.'
5 For example, Stace, *The Philosophy of Hegel* (see in particular 297–311), and Wandschneider, 'Nature and the Dialectic of Nature in Hegel's Objective Idealism,' 30–51.
6 Braun, in *Realität und Reflexion* 50, shows how this relationship between the *Logic* and the *Philosophy of Nature* is captured in the logic of 'inner' and 'outer' as developed in *The Science of Logic, HGW*, 11, 364–8; (Miller) 523–6. André Lécrivain discusses some of the relationships between the logic and the philosophy of nature in 'Pensée spéculative et philosophie de la nature.'
7 While E.E. Harris recognizes that Hegel took contemporary science seriously, he nonetheless sees nature as part of the whole, or absolute, mind, out of which

all division and triplicity emerges. 'Philosophy, therefore, returns to Nature as revealed in empirical science and gives a new reflective account of it as the implicit Idea – the Idea in the form of externality or other-being – the manifestation of spirit as the world in space and time' (*The Spirit of Hegel*, 133).

8 Basing his judgment solely on Hegel's dissertation of 1801, Karl Popper dismissed the whole of Hegel's philosophy of nature on these grounds: 'He even accomplished the deduction of the actual position of the planets, thereby proving that no planet could be situated between Mars and Jupiter (unfortunately it had escaped his notice that such a planet had been discovered a few months earlier)' (*The Open Society and Its Enemies* [Princeton: Princeton University Press, 1966] II, 27).

In the first edition of the *Encyclopaedia* of 1817 (remark to §224) Hegel explicitly disavowed the approach taken in 1801, although he dropped this clause in the later editions (§280). For a discussion of Hegel's likely reasons for making these changes, see Ferrini, 'Framing Hypotheses: Numbers in Nature and the Logic of Measure in the Development of Hegel's System.'

9 Von Engelhardt has shown how Hegel endeavoured to provide a systematic framework for the mixture of elements, affinities, and processes that made up early nineteenth-century chemistry. In this he undertook a task that also concerned the chemists, but he placed it in a larger perspective. See von Engelhardt's 'The Chemical System of Substances, Forces and Processes in Hegel's Philosophy of Nature and the Science of His Time,' 41–54. See also his 'Müller und Hegel: Zum Verhältnis von Naturwissenschaft und Naturphilosophie im deutschen Idealismus,' 85–103.

10 In *Hegel und die Chemie*, von Engelhardt has provided a good account not only of the chemistry of Hegel's day and how it found expression in Hegel's philosophy of nature, but also of contemporary developments in the philosophy of nature. The following study presupposes von Engelhardt's groundbreaking work, and takes up the task he mentions but sets aside: 'Eine besondere Analyse verlangt Hegels Verwendung chemischer Kategorien in der Logik, nur aber in einer Bedeutung, die auch für die Welt des Geistes Gültigkeit besitzt. Diese Analyse könnte aber nur im Rahmen einer allgemeinen Erörterung des Verhältnisses vom Naturphilosophe und Logik durchgeführt werden; das ist hier nicht möglich' (85).

11 We can get some idea of how much of the systematic movement from stage to stage is missing in the brief, numbered paragraphs by comparing the *Encyclopaedia Logic* with the fully expanded text of the *Science of Logic*, using the number of pages in the Lasson edition of the *Logic* and the Nicolin and Pöggeler edition of the *Encyclopaedia*, published in the same series by Meiner. The *Encyclopaedia Logic*, without its introductory material, is 161 paragraphs and 93 pages. (Were

the spacing between paragraphs removed, this would be much less.) In contrast the full *Science of Logic* is two volumes of just over 850 pages in total.

12 Hegel lectured on the *Philosophy of Nature* in 1819–20, 1821–2, 1823–4, 1825–6, 1828, and 1830.

13 He thus adopted the governing principle of the early collected edition: that Hegel was someone whose thought was of eternal significance. Notice the last word in the title of this edition: 'G.W.F. Hegel, *Werke. Vollständigen Ausgabe durch einen Verein von Freunden des Verewigten.*' At one point in the discussion of animal organism, Michelet ignored the changes Hegel introduced into his text in 1830 because the lecture notes he wanted to use followed the earlier text of 1827.

14 Hegel, *Naturphilosophie. Band I Die Vorlesung von 1819/20.* See also W. Bonsiepen's review of the extant manuscripts on the *Philosophy of Nature*, 'Hegels Vorlesungen über Naturphilosophie,' 40–54; and his outline of parts of some of these manuscripts: 'Hegels Raum-Zeit-Lehre,' 9–78, and 'Veränderungen in der Einleitung zur Naturphilosophie 1823/4–1828,' 213–18.

15 With respect to the *Logic*, see his preface to the second edition, where he suggests that the *Logic* handles the determinations of thought that 'run through our spirit in an instinctive and unconscious way' (*WL HGW*, 21, 17:34–5; (Miller) 39). On this, see Braun, *Realität und Reflexion*, 53.

16 In making this hermeneutical claim, I am distancing myself from the relativism of recent hermeneutical and deconstructionist theories. I am not thereby affirming that I already *have* the unequivocal focus of adequate interpretation. Rather, reason has tools for establishing the inadequacy of its interpretations by appealing to the words actually written in the text and to the natural and logical implications of careful thought. As soon as an interpretation has been shown to be relative and inadequate it has lost authority. This process of showing how previous positions are relative uses ways of connecting and distinguishing ideas that are inherent and common to rational thought itself. Were this not the case, it would be pointless for postmodernist theorists to advance their claims in published works and lectures that, at least ostensibly, are designed to persuade or convince an audience.

17 *Enz.*, §79–§82; *HGW*, 20, 118–20. See also the preface to the first edition of the *Science of Logic*: *HGW*, 11, 7:29–8:7, and 21, 8:2–19; (Miller) 28. Compare chapters 3 and 4 in Burbidge, *Hegel on Logic and Religion*.

18 Another option is to make of Hegel's language a set of technical terms that have their own bizarre life. They thereby lose any sense of expressing something rational and universal.

19 See, for example, M. Inwood, *Hegel* (London: Routledge, 1983), 310: 'Concepts and their interrelationships are static in a way that our thinking is not.'

20 This could be the basis for Hegel's comment about the speculative sentence in the preface to the *Phenomenology of Spirit*, *HGW*, 9, 43–4; (Miller) 61–2. Since Frege, logicians have used the charge of 'psychologism' as a reason for rejecting any logical theory that is inherently dynamic. I have found no argument to justify this charge. Because 'psychologism' is such a vague term, it can be used not only against the contingencies of personal, subjective consciousness (legitimately) but also against the developmental process that is covered by such logical terms as 'implying,' 'concluding,' 'defining,' and even 'referring,' all of which are operations (as are 'disjoining,' 'conjoining,' 'identifying,' and 'distinguishing.') The result is a failure to explicate and justify how an argument *moves* from its premises to its conclusion. Since that has been assigned to the realm of caprice and contingency, a valid argument becomes a brute fact that cannot be explained.

21 Since the translators have used varied conventions and, when unsure, had to propose their own interpretations, which often hide as much as they reveal of Hegel's original text.

22 When a group of scholars met to translate Hegel's *Jena System, 1804–5: Logic and Metaphysics*, we frequently ran across a difficult passage and initially assumed that Hegel had written carelessly. Inevitably, often after half a day's discussion, we discovered a reading that did justice to the actual words Hegel had used – a reading that was more subtle and more interesting than the one we started with. We came away with the conviction that we should beware of resorting to the crutch that Hegel did not quite know what he was doing.

23 In the Nicolin and Pöggeler edition, it is all over in thirteen pages.

24 Hegel's decision not to publish a complete philosophy of nature may have been deliberate. The sciences were constantly coming up with new discoveries, and any detailed text that tried to do justice to the most recent conclusions would be out of date almost as soon as it was in print. Much better to rely on the spoken word that shares transience with time and must be reconstituted afresh each time the lectures are given. As I have noted, such diffidence was not shared by Michelet.

25 'The text is intended to be intelligible by itself. But for it to become intelligible one must have followed two divergent routes: the one the study of Hegelian Logic, the other a careful attention to the natural sciences simply as they are for the scientists. What is then sought is to show that in all the sciences there are difficulties of a logical order – an inadequacy of method to experience – such as have their solution only in the recognition that the Hegelian logic is the logic of nature' (Doull, 'Hegel's Philosophy of Nature,' 381–2).

     Charles Taylor makes the same point: Hegel's hermeneutical dialectic 'presupposes what has been proven in the *Logic*, and also what has been shown by natural science and shows how one reflects the other. Rather than a proof, it provides an exposition of the agreement of nature with the Idea' (*Hegel*, 352). Unfortunately, Taylor goes on to talk about Hegel deducing both 'the triplicity of dimensions' of space (356) and 'gravity' (357).

26 Of interest here is Max Wundt's *Hegels Logik und die moderne Physik*, which shows how Hegel's logic of contradiction and his epistemology of subject-object interdependence can explain the way modern physics is faced with contradictions between the corpuscular and the wave theory of light, and the interaction of the measuring and the measured in Heisenberg's indeterminacy principle.

Von Engelhardt has explored the impact Hegel had on some scientists in the nineteenth century in 'Chemie zwischen Metaphysik und Empirie zu Beginn des 19. Jahrhundert,' 217–26; 'Philosophie und Theorie der Chemie um 1800,' 223–37; and 'Müller und Hegel,' 82–103.

For an attempt to reconstruct Hegel's philosophy of nature in terms of twentieth-century science, see E.E. Harris, 'The *Naturphilosophie* Updated,' in *The Spirit of Hegel*, 141–54.

2: The Background

1 For a philosophical discussion of the development from Kant by way of Fichte and Schelling to Hegel see Kröner's classic work, *Von Kant bis Hegel*.

2 *Metaphysiches Anfangsgrund der Naturwissenschaften* (1794), x; *Werke*, viii, 15. See *Metaphysical Foundations of Natural Science*, trans. J.W. Ellington (Indianapolis: Hackett 1985), 7–8.

3 Schelling cites Buffon, who follows Newton's suggestion in identifying chemical affinities with the universal law of gravitation. See *Ideen zu einer Philosophie der Natur*, 2nd. ed.(1803), book 2, chapter 7; *Ideas for a Philosophy of Nature*, 208ff.

4 See J.W.G. Fichte, *Grundlage der gesammten Wissenschaftslehre (1794)*, in *Fichtes Werke*, ed. I.H. Fichte (Berlin: de Gruyter, 1971), I, 91–123; *Science of Knowledge*, trans. P. Heath and J. Lachs (New York: Appleton, 1970), 93–119.

5 This becomes explicit in Fichte's more popular work, *Die Bestimmung des Menschen (1800)*, in *Werke*, II, 165–320; *The Vocation of Man*, trans. P. Preuss (Indianapolis: Hackett, 1987).

6 For a useful discussion of the way Schelling's philosophy of nature developed, see Schmied-Kowarzik, 'Thesen zur Entstehung und Begründung der Naturphilosophie Schellings,' 67–100.

7 See *Ideas*, book II, chapters 4 and 5. For a fuller discussion of Schelling's handling of chemistry in his philosophy of nature, see Moiso, 'Die Hegelsche Theorie der Physik und der Chemie,' 54–87. For a general discussion of his

philosophy of nature, its background, and its influence, see Esposito, *Schelling's Idealism and Philosophy of Nature*.

8 Di Giovanni shows that Kant, in the *Nachlaß*, was also working along these lines, and that Schelling in the *Ideen* was continuing the Kantian critical philosophy, not reverting to a pre-critical metaphysics. See 'Kant's Metaphysics of Nature and Schelling's *Ideas for a Philosophy of Nature*,' 197–215.

9 On the relation between Fichte and Schelling, see Maesschalck, 'Construction et réduction.' On the importance of Fichte's *Science of Knowledge* for Schelling's philosophy of nature, see Küppers, *Natur als Organismus*.

10 *Ideen*, book 2, chapter 9

11 That Schelling relied on Richter is indicated by his oblique reference to 'the acuity of a German author' who discovered the 'constant arithmetical progression of the alkalis, in relation to every acid, and of the geometrical progression of the acids to every alkali,' at the end of the supplement to book II, chapter 7. Richter's theory of heat is explicitly cited in book II, chapter 8.

12 Compare here a passage from Michelet's additions to Hegel's *Encyclopaedia*, §326: 'If the structure is the unity of the concept and reality, then magnetism, as merely the first abstract activity, is the concept of the structure; the second – the particularizing of the structure within itself and vis-à-vis others – is electricity; the unrest that realizes itself is, third, chemical process as the genuine reality of the concept in this sphere.'

13 It has perhaps not gone unnoticed that the three implications we have drawn from the intellectual intuition of matter also represent the three potencies of activity, passivity, and undifferentiated union.

14 That the two positions were contrary aspects of a single philosophy was the basic theme of one of Hegel's early essays, title of which should properly be translated as: 'Differentiation in the Fichtian and Schellingian System of Philosophy.'

In 'Einfluß der Schellingschen Naturphilosophie auf die Systembildung bei Hegel: Selbstorganisation versus rekursive Logik' (in Gloy and Burger, eds., *Die Naturphilosophie*, 238–66), Wolfgang Neuser argues that even in his first lectures of 1801 Hegel appropriated Schelling's philosophy of nature of 1797–8, while seeking to give it a logical structure. Bernard Mabille provides a useful comparison of the two philosophies of nature in 'Sens de la contingence naturelle et liberté de l'absolu chez Hegel et Schelling.'

15 In *HGW*, 6

16 This text is found in *HGW*, 7. The English translation of this volume, *G.W.F. Hegel: The Jena System, 1804–5: Logic and Metaphysics*, by Burbidge, Giovanni, et al., stopped after the metaphysics, as did the translation with commentary prepared under the direction of F. Chieregin, *Logica e metafisica di Jena*

(1804–1805). For a detailed commentary on Hegel's discussion of chemistry in this material, see H.S. Harris, *Hegel's Development: Night Thoughts*, 265–79.

17 *HGW*, 8. This volume also contains a summary of some sections ascribed to the fall of 1805. For a discussion of the ways in which this differs from the earlier text, see H.S. Harris, *Hegel's Development: Night Thoughts*, 429–41.

18 I shall not discuss at any great length the earlier material from 1803–4 since our purpose is not to trace each step in Hegel's development. The 1804–5 discussion, because it includes the logic and metaphysics, provides the best picture of Hegel's systematic perspective during the Jena years. On the background of Hegel's early system in Schelling's thought, see Moiso, 'Die Hegelsche Theorie der Physik und der Chemie, 54–87.

19 By discussing the 1804–5 *Philosophy of Nature* material before turning to the *Logic and Metaphysics*, H.S. Harris fails to notice how the discussion of construction and proof in the latter provides the organizing principles for the former.

20 A number of chemists at the time, including Lavoisier, thought the gases were not simple elements but chemical unions of the elements with heat (or caloric).

21 Hegel's language is ambiguous. It reads as if he were describing a natural cycle of transformations. A charitable reading, however, would suggest that he was showing how the *ideal* construction was infinite and so self-maintaining. See in the 1803–4 text: 'This their absolute relation, which is posited absolutely through the idea itself, *is not tied to the empirical presentation of these elements* ...; so if the empirical presentation should alter, so would what is now found to be simple have to express the indicated relation' (*HGW*, 6, 50–1).

   In the text, Hegel did not explicitly name the element that is the base of carbon dioxide gas (which he calls carbonic acid gas). For a time during the latter part of the eighteenth century some chemists were unsure whether it could be distinguished from nitrogen, since both were inert and extinguished candles and life.

   For a full discussion of Hegel's use of 'element' and its context, see chapter 20.

22 In 1803–4, Hegel saw all chemical processes as expressions of the physical element of fire, and listed the phenomenal forms of fire's activity as: flame, acidity, differentiated bodies (as in galvanism), and static electricity (*HGW*, 6, 143–6).

23 *HGW*, 8, 107

24 The only reference to chemical matters in the *Phenomenology of Spirit* occurs in the chapter on 'Observing Reason,' where the attempt to know things in terms of their defining qualities came to grief with the chemical experience that a thing comes to be something other than it was originally. So the processes of chemical transformation led consciousness to abandon the claim that truth lies

in defining characteristics, and to adopt the view that truth is found in the laws that processes exemplify (*HGW*, 9, 141:8–12; (Miller) 149–50).

Nadler, in 'Die Enwicklung des Naturbegriffs in Hegels Philosophie,' 138–9, attributes the break with the Jena version of the philosophy of nature to the discussion of observing reason in the *Phenomenology*: 'Hegel beschreibt hier die Beobachtung der Naturdinge, des Organischen und der Natur als eines organischen Ganzen. Das Leben tritt dabei auf als die zufällige Vernunft. Und damit ist wiederum ein wichtiges Schritt in der Entwicklung des Naturbegriffs bezeichnet. Das Reich der Natur ist für Hegel das Reich des Zufälligen und Willkürlichen ... So ergibt es sich schliesslich für Hegel, in der Philosophie die Notwendigkeit der Natur zu erweisen, während er es den Naturwissenschaften überlässt, die Zufälligkeiten zu erforschen.'

25 Note that cognition (*Erkennen*), as opposed to knowing (*Wissen*), reappears as one side of the penultimate section of the *Logic*.

26 Von Engelhardt (*Hegel und die Chemie*) shows how Hegel's is to be distinguished from both the romantic (Schelling's) and the transcendental (Kant's) philosophy of nature: 'Die Philosophie der Chemie entwickelt als begrifflich-reale Konstruktion der Natur ein chemisches System, das die Fülle der chemischen Erscheinungen ebensosehr zu orden erlaubt als es sich aus diesen bildet' (114). Briedbach stresses how the final *Philosophy of Nature* leaves the romantic features of the early Jena system behind. See *Das Organische in Hegels Denken*, 206.

Hegel may have become convinced of the need to respect the results of scientific investigation as a result of his own reading in this area. See the letter to Paulus of July 30, 1814: 'You know that I have occupied myself too much not only with ancient literature but also with mathematics and recently with higher analysis, differential calculus, physics, natural history, [and] chemistry to be affected by that humbug in natural philosophy which consists in philosophizing without knowledge by the power of imagination, and in regarding empty brainstorms born of conceit as thought' (Letter #235. This can be found in *Hegel: The Letters*, trans. Butler and Seiler, 309).

27 See in particular, *HGW*, 12, 269.

28 That this is not as curious as it might at first appear is evident from Hegel's *Differenzschrift*.

3: Specific Quantity

1 When Hegel died, only the first of the three books of the *Science of Logic* had been revised. Since this revision has been used in most subsequent editions, the reader should be aware that there is a considerable regression in the stage of Hegel's own development when we move from the first to the second book of

the larger *Logic*. Ferrini's 'Logica e filosofia della natura' provides a detailed discussion of the various versions of the logic of measure and its implications for the logical development from 'being' to 'essence.' Some of this material is also contained in her 'On the Relation between "Mode" and "Measure."'

2 Hegel himself admitted the second time round that this chapter was one of the most difficult in the whole *Logic* (*WL, HGW*, 21, 327:18–19; (Miller) 331), and that the development of the pure concept benefits from using illustrations from science and the philosophy of nature. While I follow his recommendation to a certain extent, I shall keep the purely logical movement of thought distinct from the illustrations used to help the mind unpractised in pure thinking.

In the final paragraph of the remark to §259 (concerning time) of 1827 (and 1830) Hegel notes that 'the valid philosophical science of mathematics as a study of magnitude would be the science of *measure*, but this presupposes the real particularity of things, which only takes place in concrete nature. Because of the external nature of magnitude, however, it would be the most difficult science' (*HGW*, 19, 195; 20, 251; (Miller) 39, (Petry) I, 235).

The difficulty of this section led E.E. Harris to abandon the *Science of Logic* at this point and focus only on the *Encyclopaedia*: 'The precise relationship of the subdivisions in this complicated list to one another, and even what some of them mean, is difficult to divine. Some of them recur at different levels without obvious regularity, and the scientific phenomena to which they are supposed to apply are obscure. I shall make no serious attempt to sort all this out and shall simply do what I can to follow the sequence of the *Encyclopaedia*' (*An Interpretation of the Logic of Hegel*, 145).

3 At this point Hegel is starting to use concepts that have been discussed in the first chapters of the *Logic*: 'something,' 'quality,' 'determination,' 'limit,' and so on. It is worth remarking that in the *Logic* Hegel uses three different German terms, all of which could be translated by our English word 'thing': *Etwas* (something or somewhat), *Ding* (a thing that has properties) and *Sache* (the *real* thing or, as I have suggested in *On Hegel's Logic*, the heart of the matter). While in the early stages of this chapter the first one is primarily used, the second does, on occasion, appear. The third emerges as a crucial term at the end (where I call it the 'real' thing, using quotation marks). Both *Ding* and *Sache* are explicitly discussed in the second book of the *Logic*, on Essence. Here, whenever I use 'thing' I am using it in the first, vague, sense, where it can be used for anything we are thinking about.

4: When Two Measures Are Combined

1 For this chapter see *WL, HGW*, 21, 347–8; (Miller) 349–51. Useful commen-

taries for the section on real measure inthe larger *Logic* can be found in Biard et al., *Introduction à la Lecture de la Science de la Logique de Hegel*, vol 1; and Doz's translation, *La Théorie de la Mesure*. Since the *Encyclopaedia* omits this discussion, the commentaries that are based on the shorter *Logic* are of little value.

2 Hegel's example here is specific gravity, in which space or volume is used to establish the units, or denominator, and weight or mass is counted relative to those units. Space is an abstract and obvious feature that can easily be delimited. Moiso, in 'Die Hegelsche Theorie der Physik und der Chemie, 60–1, points out that in 1797 Eschenmayer had understood differences in quality as a function of variations in the specific density of matter.

3 Hegel frequently makes a general observation from the standpoint of someone outside the process, before moving into the detailed analysis of how the conceptual analysis itself leads in that same direction.

4 It is important to remember that all we have are the meanings so far defined. We are not representing particular things that have a whole set of diverse qualities that are not included in the measurement. So the move does not reflect a changing body in nature, but rather the fact that the thought of something allows for an alteration in that concept, so it moves on to something else, other than the first. At this point this otherness is nothing but another measured ratio.

5 Hegel's comment that we do not need to consider what conditions make such a combination possible reinforces my point that he is not talking about an actual natural process, but the logic that is inherent in such a process of measuring. Some of the a priori conditions are spelled out in the chapter on chemism. A posteriori conditions are investigated by natural science with respect to particular phenomena.

6 Doz, in his commentary *La Théorie de la Mesure*, 145–8, takes the measurement of the combination to be the ratio between the figures for each of the two things being combined. Figures differ only with respect to which one is taken as the denominator of the fraction. This will not quite fit what Hegel is about, since he spends some time on the specific internal ratio for the combination, and says it cannot be derived by a simple addition from the figures of the two independently. For the comparison to genuinely specify the original thing, it must use the product of the combination, and not the figure for the other object, as the numerator of the ratio. Were it simply a question of the latter, any object whatsover would do for the comparison, and there would be no basis for introducing the subsequent discussion of affinity. In due course (when we come to elective affinity) a particular combination can also be measured by the quantity of each of the things that unite to make a fully saturated combination. But that ratio is not a relation between internal ratios, such as we have been discussing in this section.

7 This need for a recalculation of what is the specifying ratio confirms Hegel's original observation that the numbers used in measuring, even though they specify what a thing is, are nonetheless abstractions and, therefore, in some sense indifferentto what it is inherently. When they are used to measure a feature that is not peculiar to the thing, but serve as an abstract way of measuring anything at all (such as space or time), they are less inherent and more subject to change when alterations are introduced than when they measure what a thing is within itself (such as mass or weight). Even Archimedes' original experiment on the specific density of gold and silver did not pretend to establish what the specific ratio of gold to silver was in the crown, only that it was neither pure gold nor pure silver.

It is worth noting at this point that in Hegel's a priori analysis thought cannot anticipate measurements (by adding, for example), but is dependent on empirical evidence. Reason itself shows the need for experience to provide specific content.

8 This is certainly the case in social statistics. The operationalization of a concept into countable units at the first stage of developing a statistical study is in some sense arbitrary. Those numbers become less arbitrary when they are converted, at first into percentages (a first-order ratio), and then into correlations between percentages (between a control group and an experimental group, for example). Quantitative social science had not developed its sophistication when Hegel was writing, but his analysis of the way in which measuring becomes more precisely defined by measuring ratios of ratios applies to its procedure as well.

5: Measuring Involves Series of Measured Ratios

1 This chapter discusses *WL HGW*, 21, 348–52; (Miller) 351–4.
2 Notice that Hegel's first sentence in this sub-section is in the conditional mood, whereas the second is in the indicative.
3 Or, as Hegel now says, neutralizations. The product of the combination is neutral, intermediate between the two extremes with their distinctive ratios. Thus he takes up the language of neutralization that he had used in the first edition to describe the whole process of combination.
4 One can notice in the chemical textbooks of the early nineteenth century how the definitions of chemical entities move from being descriptions of their secondary qualities (such as taste, feel, colour, shape, and so on) to being accounts of the way they interact with other entities when combined with them. Then, through the influence of Richter and others, the texts used the measured proportions when in combination.
5 Hegel is not limited to a psychological or subjective context for the verb

'compare.' The process of putting two things together to see how they are both similar and dissimilar can be achieved through the entities themselves. The comparison is effected by measurements that generate distinct ratios both for the things being compared and for their combination.

6 Hegel does not use the word *Ordnung* here, but only when reviewing this move at the end of the chapter.

7 A possible diagram:

	A	B	C	D
a	x	x	x	x
b	x	x	*	x
c	x	x	x	x
d	x	x	x	x

The intersection marked * would generate a second-order ratio */b in one series and */C in the other.

8 Notice that each series is indeterminate in the sense that it could be extended to other objects not yet identified. That indeterminacy is relativized into the fixed, or constant, order. Any new item that emerges should be fitted into that regular pattern. So Hegel has not done away with contingency, but instead incorporated it into a broader perspective.

When describing this threefold function, Hegel uses the word *Zahl*, usually translated as 'number.' But it cannot be a particular numerical exponent, since that exponent changes, depending on what is the numerator and what the denominator, and no exponent as such names the ordered location in any series. In any event, the second-order ratios are not between the exponents of the two things in combination, but between each and the ratio for the neutral product; so that the second-order ratios could not be the inverse of each other. Because of this difficulty, I have interpreted Zahl as referring to a member of a series.

9 We have already made such a shift within the discussion of real measure. We used specific gravity to illustrate the first-order ratio. But when we refined this kind of measuring to overcome its weaknesses, we found ourselves thinking of something that applied more to chemical affinities and neutralization.

Because nature is diverse and incomplete, an intellectually unsatisfactory method of measurement may still be appropriate for a certain purpose. At the same time, the fact that one kind of measuring fits one set of data does not mean that the conceptual possibilities of measuring specific qualities as such are fixed and cannot be developed further. Indeed, investigators are continually looking for new ways of measuring when they discover that traditional modes have their limitations. Such quests are not primarily the result of observed data, but stem from reflection on the inherent weaknesses of the methods already used to organize experiments conceptually.

10 At that point Hegel was not interested in using quanta to *measure* something, but simply working out the logic of magnitudes considered on their own.

11 In Hegel's abstract language this is an act of negating an original negation. 'Negation' is a very general term that covers all uses of the particle 'not.'

6: Elective Affinity

1 Goethe, for example, used it (ironically) for the relationship between the sexes in the novel entitled *Elective Affinity*. This chapter examines *WL HGW*, 21, 352–4; (Miller) 354–6.

2 There are a lot of phenomena that could be described in these terms as well. 'Chemical object' need not be restricted to the elements and compounds of chemistry.

3 In 'Chemische Einsichten wider Willen,' Ulrich Ruschig takes this discussion as 'eine Deduktion der Voraussetzung der Relationen aus diesen selbst' (177) and faults Hegel for claiming that a specific quality can be precisely measured. He misses the fact that Hegel is not primarily concerned here with chemical operations, but with the process of measuring, whose self-appointed task it is to define a quality quantitatively. His systematic concern is to show how the failure to measure precisely at each stage drives the logic forward to its next stage.

4 Hegel has not explicitly said that a specific quantity of each element is needed to attain a neutralized compound, but it is implicit in his earlier discussion. The specific weight of any single combination has a ratio distinct from that of either original element as well as from the simple addition of those two original fractions. Since it is to specify by measurement, it is not generated out of indifferent quantities of the two components. A unit of the first will always be matched by a specific quantity of the second to generate both the neutralized compound and its measurement. So when the various members of the opposing series generate products with different specific ratios, one can expect that different quantities of those things will be involved in the combination.

   In his lectures of 1819–20 Hegel cites five different forms of saturated compounds where measurements of the components show that they combine in multiples of whole numbers: oxidation, oxygen to the radical of an acid, acid to oxide, unions without oxygen, and acids to alkalis. These measurements show that combinations are exclusive; they do not follow any proportion whatever. 'The laws discovered are only empirical since they concern quantities,' he says; 'so they do not yet display the concept but are a preparation for doing so' (G.W.F. Hegel, *Naturphilosophie 1819–20*, 98–9).

5 Earlier I mentioned that an intensive magnitude or degree could be converted into an extensive one once it was compared with other similar degrees. At this stage an extensive magnitude converts into an intensive one to the extent that it generates something qualitatively distinct.

6 Hegel here introduces a remark on the way recent chemical theory had developed its analysis of elective affinity. Because we are here concerned only with the systematic nature of the logic, it is not appropriate to spend time on this remark now. I return to it in chapter 11.

7: The Nodal Line

1 This chapter explores *WL HGW*, 21, 364–6; (Miller) 366–8.

2 I have been helped in understanding this section by the analysis of Dr Cinzia Ferrini in 'La teoria della misura nella *Scienza della Logica* di Hegel.' If I have altered her approach at all, it is in tracing the a priori logical pattern, rather than relying on chemical examples, to make it work.

3 I am using 'element' here as a synonym for the components of a compound, not in the sense of its being elementary, itself unresolvable into further elements. Compare here the explicit use that Hegel himself has for the term 'element' in his discussion of chemism (chapter 14) and in the *Philosophy of Nature* (chapter 20).

4 To illustrate: the earlier discussion of elective affinity talked about what happens when oxygen combines with carbon (CO_2), nitrogen (NO_3) and hydrogen (H_2O). We have now moved to a kind of measuring that examines different proportions of the same elements (NO_2, NO_3, N_2O_5, etc.). When Hegel was writing, the relationship of definite proportions was being systematized by empirical chemistry, although the symbols I have used in this note had not yet been generally accepted. Compare the comments in his lectures of 1819–20: 'A basic law concerns the various stages of oxidation of a base; when two bodies combine in several ratios, these amounts are in a very simple progression of 1, 1½, 2, 4, 8, etc.' (*Naturphilosophie, 1819/20*, 99).

   It should be noted that this kind of measuring is not restricted to chemistry. In his remark Hegel refers as well to the number system (in which, for example, some numbers are products or compounds and some are prime) and to harmonies. Cinzia Ferrini has drawn my attention to Hegel's reference to nodes in his doctoral dissertation, *De orbitis planetarum*, where it refers to 'the point at which the orbit of a planet or a comet intersects the plane of the sun's apparent annual path.' (See G.W.F. Hegel, *Philosophical Dissertation on the Orbits of the Planets (1801) Preceded by the 12 Theses Defended on August 27, 1901*, translated, with foreword and notes, by Pierre Adler, *Graduate Faculty Philosophy*

Journal 12 (1987) 295, and note 24 on 307. The original Latin with a German translation can be found in *Dissertatio Philosophica de Orbitis Planetarum / Philosophische Erörterung über die Planetenbahnen*, translation, introduction, and commentary by Wolfgang Neuser, *Acta Humaniora* VCH, 1986.] Although this example is not cited in the text from the *Science of Logic*, Ferrini suggests that a connecting link can be found in Hegel's reference to the harmonies of the musical scale, for Kepler's *Harmonice Mundi* interpreted the orbits of the planets under the analogy of harmonies.

5 In his lecture notes of 1803–4, Hegel offers some examples of this: 'The transition of the oxidation of mercury, for example, does not move from the first stage, where it is green (black), into becoming progressively brighter, but it passes over into quite another colour, red, and becomes a semi-glazed oxide; grey lead oxide equally does not pass into merely something brighter, but into something yellow, then into bright red (where it is glazed) and then into a completely glazed, honey-yellow oxide.' *HGW*, 6, 166. Hegel refers to this as well in his lectures on the *Logic* in 1817 (*Vorlesungen über Logik und Metaphysik*, 107).

6 It is just this indefinite extension of possibilities that encourages chemists to experiment with creating ever new, qualitatively distinct, compounds of the same basic elements.

7 Hegel here introduces another remark that takes up the conventional wisdom that there are no leaps in nature. This analysis, together with a related one that occurs earlier in the discussion of specific quantity, provided Engels with one of his laws of dialectic: that quantitative change converts into a qualitative one and vice versa. See Engels, *Dialectics of Nature*, 83.

8: What Cannot Be Measured

1 This chapter is an analysis of *WL HGW*, 21, 369–72; (Miller) 371–4. Important background for Hegel's discussion of the measureless can be found in §26 of Kant's *Critique of Judgment*.

2 This recapitulates the move from bad to valid infinite in the discussion of qualitative infinity. See *WL HGW*, 21, 124–37; (Miller) 137–50; and my effort to expound that text in *On Hegel's Logic*, 53–8. Of equal significance, the repeated pattern captures the ability of imagination to apprehend the infinite regress in Kant's analysis of the sublime. When imagination cannot comprehend it, reason must introduce its idea of totality to comprehend it. It is this Kantian move of reason that Hegel captures here in the shift to a valid infinite.

3 See *WL HGW*, 21, 218–36; (Miller) 225–40.

4 This kind of shift is strictly conceptual. It cannot be illustrated either by referring to something in the world, or through imagination. A concept, when fully

analysed, turns out to involve several distinct components, each one of which is defined by its relation to the others. It is either implied by the other, or it cancels the other. Since all of that is a pattern of thought, it can be considered as a whole – as a network of mutual relations – to get at its fundamental principles. The complex, on close examination, collapses into a single concept, whose distinctive character requires a new name. So the whole logical process of definition and implication can then start all over again. This collapsing of a complex interconnection into a simple unit is the logical process to which Hegel gives the name, 'sublation,' the German *Aufhebung* (see *WL HGW*, 21, 94–5; (Miller) 106–8).

5 Here is Hegel's logical derivation of the concept of the supersensible that plays such a role in Kant's theory of the sublime.

6 This substratum must *be* something, it must be *manifest* in the process, and it must *establish* or determine the process. These three italicized words, which encapsulate the three aspects of the substratum's basic meaning, together define how it can be specified by the principle of the measureless. Compare once again Kant's 'Analytic of the Sublime' in the *Critique of Judgment*.

9: A Systematic Review

1 *WL HGW*, 21, 371:24–372:13; (Miller) 373–4

2 It is interesting to note how this kind of analysis provides a logical anticipation of the way chemistry and physics, in the years after Hegel, explained chemical phenomena by grounding them in a single, 'supersensible' base, called 'energy.' Hegel is showing how the quest for such an explanation is inherent in the attempt to be consistently logical, even though he does not anticipate what its theoretical solution would actually look like. That can only be determined by integrating this logical demand with the specific characteristics of the substances being investigated.

3 This self-referential character of the *Logic* was brought to my attention by E. Halper's article, 'Self-Relation in Hegel's *Science of Logic*,' *Philosophy Research Archives* 7 (1981), 1443.

4 See in particular Hegel's introduction to the whole section on measure: *WL HGW*, 11, 189–91; 21, 323–8; (Miller) 327–32. Ferrini's article, 'Logica e filosofia della natura,' already referred to, explores the connections between Hegel's discussion of measure and Spinoza's and Kant's reliance on modes.

10: From 1812 to 1831

1 *WL HGW*, 21, 327:18–19; (Miller) 331

2 Although some features did emerge in his Heidelberg lectures of 1817, *Vorlesungen über Logik und Metaphysik*, ed. K. Gloy, 107–8

3 In her article, 'Logica e filosofia della natura,' Ferrini discusses the significance of the various versions of the whole section on measure for the transitions both from the logic to nature and from being to essence.

4 This contrasts with what he did in the chapter on *Daseyn*, where he kept on rearranging the order of the concepts throughout the three editions of the *Encyclopaedia* and into the 1831 edition of the larger *Logic*. On this, see my 'Transition or Reflection,' in *Hegel on Logic and Religion*, 19–27.

5 In the next chapter I shall discuss some of the reasons for Hegel's abandoning the use of 'neutralization' as a general term here.

6 See the observation that J.M.E. McTaggart made: 'Hegel does not merely introduce into this category the pure idea which is implied in, and specially characteristic of, the facts of chemistry. He also introduces empirical chemical details, which could not form part of the dialectical process of pure thought at any stage, and he introduces them as part of the argument' (*A Commentary on Hegel's Logic* [New York: Russell and Russell, 1964], 81).

7 *Bestimmung* and *Beschaffenheit*

8 *WL HGW*, 21, 110–6; (Miller) 122–9

9 In drawing an analogy to an earlier logical discussion to explicate the systematic development, Hegel was adapting the strategy he had used extensively in the *Encyclopaedia Logic*. There, forced to reduce the logical argument to a skeleton, he found analogies made the conceptual transitions plausible in a short compass.

10 In changes introduced to the remark on elective affinity, Hegel acknowledged the contribution of Berzelius in this area.

11 So much so that it took me several agonizing runs at this text before I caught the nuances.

12 At the same time, the changes in the logical argument made it more difficult to fit in the examples he cited in his unaltered remark. It may be possible to talk of various harmonies as combinations of basically the same moments using diverse ratios on a continuum, but can that be said for the number system? When a multiple is factored, its components do not remain the same when their ratio is changed, since numbers cease to be when one adds to, or subtracts from, them. Similarly, the analysis in terms of moments does not apply as easily to the transformations from ice to water to vapour, where the continuum is one of temperature, not of the ratio between components of a compound. Hegel's moral examples, in which an action pushed to an extreme becomes a crime, or a state enlarged too much converts from a republic to an empire, are too complicated to allow an easy analysis into moments in proportion. In these cases it is not at all clear what is to be measured.

13 As we shall see, it was also scientific considerations that led to a changed emphasis on neutralization.

14 See *WL HGW*, 11, 316–22; (Miller) 472–8; and *On Hegel's Logic*, 100–5. In the latter text *die Sache selbst* is translated as 'the heart of the matter,' a locution I have also found in Merold Westphal's *Hegel, Freedom and Modernity* (Albany: SUNY Press, 1992), 110.

15 §§147–8 of the second and third editions. Interestingly enough, the manuscript from the Heidelberg lectures on the Logic report that Hegel used *Sache* in the same context, even though the term had not appeared in the 1817 *Encyclopaedia* on which the lectures were based. See *Vorlesungen über Logik und Metaphysik*, 132.

16 In 1817 Hegel appears to have decided that there was no reason for two discussions of conditioning (one in 'ground' and one in 'real possibility') and combined them in the section on 'actuality,' adding *Sache* to this context in 1827. Then in 1831 he saw that *Sache*, as underlying the structure of conditioning, intersected with the supersensible in Kant's discussion of the measureless. The term could then be relocated to the *Doctrine of Being*, independent of the context of conditioning altogether.

17 This shift from a fully determinate concluding concept to an indeterminate anticipation needs to be explored further. For *die Sache* is not an insignificant weapon in Hegel's arsenal. It plays a major role in the *Phenomenology of Spirit* and is called upon frequently in Hegel's lectures.

18 In this paragraph I have suggested that this recursive activity is a function of the logic itself even though the evidence points only to Hegel correcting his own analysis. So it could be that he simply got it wrong the first time, and was endeavouring to correct his idiosyncratic mistakes. To the extent that the logic follows an inherent rational pattern, however, there is nothing that would prevent others, who notice possibilities for simplification or elaboration, from using the same procedures to perfect it further. After all, as I noted in the introduction, Hegel claimed to be advancing the one philosophy, not propounding a system peculiar to himself.

19 This play between 'representative names' and 'names as such' is a main plot in John McCumber's *The Company of Words* (Evanston: Northwestern University Press, 1993).

20 This is made explicit at the beginning of the *Science of Logic* (*WL HGW*, 21, 32; (Miller) 48), where Hegel points out that the *Phenomenology of Spirit* justifies the concept of science. The experience of consciousness, which incorporates the historical moments of Greek and Roman social life, of the Renaissance, the Enlightenment and the French Revolution, is in the end distilled into its essence as absolute knowing; and the *Logic* articulates the structure of that pure know-

ing. Although the logical moves are justified intrinsically, they nonetheless emerge out of the cultural past.

21 For a useful discussion of the ways in which the natural sciences interact with the philosophy of nature see Gloy, 'Goethes und Hegels Kritik an Newtons Farbentheorie,' in *Die Naturphilosophie im Deutschen Idealismus*, 323–59.

22 *WL HGW*, 21, 38:17–20; (Miller) 54

11: The Remarks

1 The reader is directed to the notes in part II on the *Philosophy of Nature* for background on the stage chemistry had reached while Hegel was working.

2 §327 and §328 of the second and third editions

3 Winterl's term is used in this remark in both editions. Hegel introduced it into the *Encyclopaedia* of 1827 but dropped it in 1830. The term had not caught on with the scientific community.

4 On Hegel's use of Berthollet, see Snelders, 'Hegel und die Bertholletsche Affinitätslehre,' 88–102.

5 *WL HGW*, 21, 359:16–20; (Miller) 362

6 *La Théorie de la mesure*, 150–1

7 Though, as Hegel himself points out (*WL HGW*, 21, 355:25–9), Fischer had added a remark to his translation of Berthollet's *Treatise on the Laws of Chemical Affinity* that not only detailed the work of Richter, but also presented a single table of the proportions of acids and bases that combine to form a salt, using sulphuric acid as a base. This note was included without amendment in Berthollet's *Essai de Statique Chimique*.

8 Berzelius, *Essai sur la théorie des proportions chimiques*, 20–1. While Hegel cites this short text in his remark to §330 of the *Encyclopaedia*, in the present remark he refers to the full German edition, *Lehrbuch der Chemie*, trans. Wohler (Dresden: Arnold 1825), where the shorter text is part 1 of book III.

9 *WL HGW*, 21, 358–9; (Miller) 36

10 In his *Metaphysical Principles for Natural Science*, Kant argued that all physics was based on the dynamic interplay of attractive and repulsive forces. So he could be as much the target of Berzelius' attack as Schelling's *Naturphilosophie*. In his introduction to the German edition of Berthollet's *Essai de Statique Chimique*, the chemist E.G. Fischer contrasts the atomic to the dynamic theory, and expresses his preference for the latter. See Berthollet, *Versuch einer chemischen Statik*, 27–30. Richter also belonged to the Kantian 'dynamic' school.

William Whewell, in his *History of the Inductive Sciences* of 1837 (only six years after Hegel's text), reports that Berzelius first began to think about these things after reading Richter: 'In 1807 Berzelius, intending to publish a system of

chemistry, went through several works little read, and among others the trea-
tises of Richter. He was astonished, he tells us, at the light which was there
thrown upon composition and decomposition, and which had never been
turned to profit. He was led to a long train of experimental research, and, when
he received information of Dalton's ideas concerning multiple proportions he
found, in his own collection of analyses, a full confirmation of this theory' (cited
from the 3rd edition of 1857, iii, 131).

11 Fischer's remarks to Berthollet's *Essay* organized these figures systematically.

12 *WL HGW*, 21, 355–6; (Miller) 358

13 *Essai*, 12. Since Berzelius's definition of 'atom' was that which would not be further divided by *mechanical* means, he could refer here to atoms of *chemical* compounds. Berzelius went on to propose the chemical symbolism still in use today.

14 *Naturphilosophie 1819–20*, 99

15 To show that Hegel was not alone, however, in acknowledging definite proportions while rejecting atomism, one need only cite William Whewell in 1837:
'The general laws of chemical combination announced by Mr. Dalton are truths
of the highest importance in the science, and are nowhere contested; but the
view of matter as constituted of *atoms*, which he has employed in conveying
those laws, and in expressing his opinion of their cause, is neither as important
or as certain. In the place which I here assign to his discovery, as one of the great
events of the history of chemistry, I speak only of the *law of phenomena*, the
rules which govern the quantities in which elements combine' (*History of the
Inductive Sciences*, 1967, iii, 127).
    On Hegel's critique of Berzelius' atomism see Buchdahl, 'Conceptual Analy-
sis and Scientific Theory, 19–21.

16 *WL HGW*, 21, 362–3; (Miller) 365. The same challenge applied to the series of
chemical affinities that Bergman and Berzelius had tried to systematize.

17 See K.R. Popper, *The Open Society and Its Enemies* (Princeton: Princeton University Press 1966), II, 27.

18 Kepler provided Hegel with a prime example of a scientist who struggled
through many conceptual drafts until he arrived at the principles that governed
the locations of the planets over time. This was why his achievement was
greater, in Hegel's eyes, than that of Newton.

19 To be discussed in chapter 30

20 Both points also made in the remark to §330.

21 Of interest again is Whewell's comment in 1837: 'I must, however, state, as a
further appeal to the reader's indulgence, that, even if the great principles of
electrochemistry have now been brought out in their due form and extent, the
discovery is but a very few years, I might rather say a few months, old; and that

their novelty adds materially to the difficulty of estimating previous attempts from the point of view to which we are led. It is only slowly and by degrees that the mind becomes sufficiently imbued with these new truths, of which the office is, to change the face of science' (*History of the Inductive Sciences*, 1967, iii, 136). The recent discoveries he is referring to are those of Faraday.

12: Mechanism

1 Although Hegel used the term 'chemism' in his lecture notes from 1803–4 to refer to the chemical aspects of nature (*HGW*, 6, 42), by the time of his developed system, it referred to a way of conceiving objectivity. It thus became a logical rather than a natural concept.

A reliable commentary on this chapter can be found in the third volume of Biard et al., *Introduction à la lecture de la Science de la Logique de Hegel*, 288–302. It does not, however, undertake to trace the inherent logical moves from one stage to the next – the task we have undertaken here.

2 See *WL HGW*, 12, 32:3–5, 41:13–43:6; (Miller) 600, 610–12; and my article, 'Where is the Place of Understanding?' in *Hegel on Logic and Religion*, 29–38.

3 There are two German terms that are translated by the English word 'object': *Objekt* and *Gegenstand*. Hegel uses the former to express the way we *conceive* the relation to be, the latter to represent the object we actually encounter. In this chapter he uses *Objekt* almost exclusively, although he introduces *Gegenstand* in an aside at *WL HGW*, 12, 151:11–12 ('allgemeines Natur des Gegenstandes'; (Miller) 730: 'universal nature of the object').

Several commentators have questioned Hegel's including a discussion of mechanical, chemical, and teleological objectivity within the confines of the *Science of Logic*. Thus Hösle writes: 'Man kann also zusammenfassend sagen, daß Mechanismus, Chemismus und Leben nicht in eine als Ontologie und Logik gefasste Fundamentalphilosophie gehören' (*Hegels System*, 1, 247). Similarly K. Düsing writes: 'Die Objektivität ist nicht der Gegenstand als Begriff, in dem die Subjektivität sich selbst erkennt, wie dies aus Hegels Schlußlehre zu erwarten wäre, sondern das Anderssein des Begriffs insgesamt' (*Das Problem der Subjektivität in Hegels Logik* [Bonn: Bouvier, 1976] 289).

These approaches misunderstand the distinctive character of Hegel's *Logic*. Thought is exploring the implications of certain concepts; so, once the subjective understanding articulates its own functioning in terms of judging and inferring, it realizes that this is only one-sided – that there is an objectivity to be understood (or conceived). Mechanism, chemism, and teleology are the ways we conceive an objective realm. The logic of that kind of conceiving itself needs to be explored, together with its implications.

Objectivity, as the way subjective conceiving understands objectivity, is thus to be distinguished from more basic concepts, such as reality or actuality where the thought abstracts from the role of subjective conceiving or understanding.

4 These ways of understanding objects are not limited to natural phenomena. Hobbes, for example, understands not only human society in a mechanical way, but also mental processes. Similarly, John Stuart Mill identifies a law of association in which, 'when an association has acquired this character of inseparability – when the bond between the two ideas has been thus firmly riveted, not only does the idea called up by the association become, in our consciousness, inseparable from the idea which suggested it, but the facts or phaenomena answering to those ideas come at last to seem inseparable in existence' ('Of Belief in an External World,' in *An Examination of Sir William Hamilton's Philosophy*, 2nd ed. [London, 1865], 191). In other words, ideas are thought of as subject to a combination that is more chemical than mechanical. This then enables a collection of possible sensations to be joined together; 'And as this happens in turn to all of them, the group as a whole presents itself to the mind as permanent, in contrast not solely with the temporariness of my bodily presence, but also with the temporary character of each of the sensations composing the group' (194). For all, then, that he dismisses a 'chemical' understanding of society (*A System of Logic*, book VI, chapter 7), Mill is led to affirm a 'chemical' mode of conceiving that understands thoughts as combining into integrated unities that have their own distinctive character.

13: The Chemical Object

1 This chapter discusses *WL HGW*, 12, 148–9; (Miller) 727–8.
2 This implicit bond between two separate objects makes this general notion the counterpart, at this stage, of the subjective act of judging. Notice that frequently I shall use the term 'differentiation' (in German, *Differenz*) to express this relationship of contrasting objects that are yet oriented towards each other.
3 Hegel here introduces a paragraph discussing how this concept can be used not only in chemistry but also for meteorological phenomena, the relation between the sexes in biology, and (from certain formal perspectives) love and friendship.
4 Here Hegel adds another note that shows how this description fits the legal concept of a person.
5 Hegel's term is 'absolute.' When he uses that adjective, he is not becoming a Bradleyian metaphysician. He means that a concept is considered on its own,

apart from all relations. Absolute is a term that can be defined negatively: what is absolute is not relative. Frequently, then, it has the same sense as 'abstract.'

14: Process

1 This chapter discusses *WL HGW*, 12, 149–52; (Miller) 728–31. This section is very difficult and compressed. One suspects that Hegel would have reworked it considerably had he had the chance to revise it. Our *exposition de texte* follows all the meanderings of his discussion.

2 See the discussion of neutralization in chapter 11.

3 Although Hegel does not explicitly refer to the passage here, this reproduces the argument he develops when discussing the concept of 'real ground.' See below in the discussion of §327 from the *Philosophy of Nature*, chapter 19; and *On Hegel's Logic*, 93–4.

4 Hegel here refers to water and signs as two illustrations of such a mediating element. The latter, including language, perform this function only when one views social phenomena as *analogous to* chemical ones.

5 For an analysis of Hegel's discussion of syllogism, see *On Hegel's Logic*, 158–92.

6 Using the language of *singular, particular*, and *universal*: S-P, S-U, so P-U. Hegel calls this the second figure.

7 For Hegel, induction shares with Aristotle's third figure the pattern P-S-U, since the act of bringing the particulars together is singular. As we shall see, in 1830 Hegel explicitly identifies this whole discussion of chemism with reflection.

8 In the first syllogism, understanding started out with the particular objects as one extreme, and the combined product as the other, and had to discover what could serve as a middle term. Here, in contrast, we have the middle term and one extreme, and we need to figure out the second extreme.

9 For some reason Hegel here uses *Gegenstand* rather than *Objekt*. The discussion of syllogisms here is sufficiently obscure that it is hard to identify clearly what Hegel intends.

10 Since it serves both as subject and predicate in the premises.

15: Chemism's Demise

1 Often in the *Science of Logic*, as here, Hegel does not separate his remarks from the main text. One can distinguish them only by his use of representations, rather than concepts.

This chapter is an analysis of *WL HGW*, 12, 152–3; (Miller) 731–3.

2 A colleague in chemistry has suggested that this describes the phenomenon

called 'disproportionation.' Examples are: $2HClO_2 \rightarrow HClO + ClO_3 + H$; or $3OCl \rightarrow 2Cl + ClO_3$. Hegel uses the same illustration in a remark to §335 of the *Philosophy of Nature* to suggest that one can find instances of teleological purposiveness in nature.

3 This is misleading. Considered as a syllogism, the extremes are the universal determination and the two particular objects.

4 What is interesting here is the way Hegel describes this move in his lectures of 1817: 'Finite mechanism and chemism as well have their result and product in their beginning. Only in them the concept is only as inherent or implicit; what is there is a circle of conditions and circumstances external to each other. The concrete result is not present on its own account as the unity of a whole. Purpose, however, is the being of the concept as something subjective which has objectivity within itself, so that the result is the ground of the activity and the return of the concept into the product is posited within itself' (Hegel, *Vorlesungen über Logik und Metaphysik*, 171).

The move Hegel makes here is a very small one. In the next chapter he will not be saying that the object is intrinsically purposive; that concept will only be found when we come to 'life.' All that has been established at this point, and all that 'teleology' discusses, is the notion that objects are intrinsically amenable to being manipulated for purposive ends, introduced externally by a subject.

16: From 1807 to 1830

1 Taking five paragraphs in 1817: §§148–52; four in 1827 and 1830, §§200–3.

2 Though, as we have seen in the discussion of the second syllogism, both universality and particularity are considered as mediating.

3 The lecture notes from 1817 appear to be working in the earlier framework: 'The chemical moments – the undifferentiated, differentiated and neutral – are 1) presupposed or immediate in the process. But 2) they are equally product or mediated; the expiration of the activity in products is thus the positing of a determination, or of something differentiated in itself, which thus is opposed to the process. [In German *widersetzt*. This might have been misunderstood by the auditor, for it makes sense to read *wieder setzt*: 'which thus posits the process again.'] The undifferentiated and neutral conditions are themselves of this nature; they are only singular moments of the whole, which is therefore a cycle of processes – absolute chemism, which in nature is the meteorological process' (Hegel, *Vorlesungen über Logik und Metaphysik*, 170. Michelet's addition to §326 also refers to the meterological process as the 'chemism' of the earth.

4 On the constraints Hegel faced in writing the first edition, see *Hegel: The Letters*, 261; Hoffmeister, *Briefe von und an Hegel*, §198, 393; and O. Pöggeler,

'Nachwort zu Entwicklungsgeschichte von Hegels Logik,' *Hegelstudien*, 2, (1963) 47–70.

5 There also appears to have been a conscious introduction of the three syllogisms into this part of the *Logic*. See in the 1817 edition §148, §151, and §158; in 1830 §198, §201, §207, and §217.

6 He did not have an independent discussion of separation.

7 This explanation would support Karen Gloy's third alternative for the interplay between science and the philosophy of nature: 'Die dritte Variante nimmt nicht nur die partiale Angewiesenheit auf die Naturwissenschaft und die empirische Forschung an, sondern die totale; sie sieht die schlechthinnige Abhängigkeit von dieser vor. Das Hegelsche Begriffssystem ist dann als theoretischer Überbau zu deuten, der mit den empirischen Ergebnissen und Methoden steht und fällt und sich ihnen gemäß ständig ändert' ('Goethes und Hegels Kritik an Newtons Farbentheorie,' 358).

8 In the *Philosophy of Nature*, the animating of indifferent bodies turns out to be a function of combination, not an independent kind of process.

9 As we have seen, in 1816 this is what results when the subjective concept is removed from the circle of syllogisms towards the end of 'Chemism's Demise.'

10 See *WL HGW*, 11, 249–57; (Miller) 399–408; and *On Hegel's Logic*, 67–72. This discussion is removed from the main logical development in the *Encyclopaedia* of both 1817 and 1830 to become simply a part of the introduction to the *Doctrine of Essence* (§§64–5 and §§113–4); but the fact that Hegel refines his argument here by referring to reflection suggests that it was not to be abandoned altogether.

11 'The process is the going to and fro from one form to another, which yet at the same time remain external to each other' (§202). Passages cited here and in the next three notes are additions in 1827 or 1830.

12 'As the relation of reflection with respect to objectivity, chemism has, along with the differentiated nature of the objects, their *immediate* independence as a presupposition.' Again, the animating principle of differentiation does not exist in the product 'as sunk back into immediacy' (both from §202).

13 'As posited totality of the concept' the object is the contradiction between its totality and its existence (§200). This phrase is, in fact, introduced in 1830. The 1827 text read: 'As the concept in itself.'

14 'Inversely, the product shows the presupposed immediacy of the differentiated objects to be null and void. Through this negation of the externality and immediacy in which it was immersed as object, the concept is posited free and on its own account over against that externality and immediacy – as purpose' (§203).

15 The same thing happened when he revised the chapter on *Daseyn* from the *Science of Logic*, where, in 1831, he drew a distinction between the simple

transitions of thought and reflection in rewriting the moves from a being to infinity. See my article 'Transition or Reflection,' in *Hegel on Logic and Religion*, chapter 3.

16 On the parallels between reflection and speculation and between understanding and conceiving, see 'Where is the Place of Understanding?' in *Hegel on Logic and Religion*, chapter 4. The third parallel is between dialectic and transition.

17 See *HGW*, 12, 265–71; and the editorial discussion on 329–31.

18 See *WL HGW*, 11, 327–9; (Miller) 484–7. The only possible exception to this claim about vocabulary is the use of 'pure metallity' at 12, 267:21, which refers to the realm of metals, though in abstract terms.

19 This term is not more precisely defined, although 'metallity' is glossed by 'elementarity.'

20 Compare this with his later use of 'a being' and 'reflection' to name the first two types of syllogisms.

17: How Chemism Is Systematic

1 In *The Company of Words: Hegel, Language and Systematic Philosophy* (Evanston: Northwestern University Press, 1993), John McCumber has two independent discussions of the logical development in the chapter on chemism. The first, in chapter 4 (140) sees it as a formal operation that identifies a set of previous markers with a new single term, and then argues for the mutual implication of the set with the new term. This makes it possible to include the latter in a new, more inclusive set, triggering a move to the next logical concept. On this analysis, however, there is no consideration of how the mutual implication that chemism introduces is any different from that of mechanism. And the teleology that results is organic (more appropriate to Hegel's logic of life) rather than subjective intention using objective means to realize its concept, which is in fact Hegel's next step.

In chapter 10 (312) McCumber does bring in the distinctively chemical features, but he does so not in conceptual terms, but by using actual empirical chemicals: acids, bases, and salts (examples that Hegel studiously avoids here, introducing them only in the philosophy of nature). In addition, he identifies only two processes: from acids and bases to salts and back again; rather than Hegel's three-fold pattern: from differentiated objects to compounds, to elements of the compounds, and only then back to differentiated objects. As a result McCumber does not allow for the differentiation between the concept of chemism and the chemical object, which not only is the motive principle of this section, but also leads into finite teleology.

18: §326

1 The table of contents says simply 'Organics.'
2 *Naturphilosophie: Band I: Die Vorlesungen von 1819/20*, 108: 'Der höchste Punkt der Besonderung ist die Individualität.'
3 This fits not only the term's sense in the *Philosophy of Nature*, but also its use in the logic of life.
4 Outside of the *Logic, Einzelne* does not emerge in the *Encyclopaedia* until the chapter on phenomenology in the section on subjective spirit.
5 This also can be said for the appearance of singulars and singularity in the *Phenomenology*, which lies between the *Anthropology* and the *Psychology*.
6 Compare the passage from Michelet's addition to this paragraph: 'In magnetism the difference emerges in *one* body. In electricity each differentiation belongs to its own body; each differentiation is independent and the whole body does not enter into this process. Chemical process is the totality of the life of inorganic individuality; for here we have complete, physically determinate structures.'
7 'Ground is essence as totality' (*Enz.*, §121–2). In the first edition of the *Science of Logic* this analysis describes the absolutely unconditioned, or the 'real' thing (*die Sache selbst*). As we have seen, in the second edition the latter concept has been moved earlier in the development.
8 See §263 in the *Philosophy of Nature*.
9 The exceptions are §332, §334, and §336.
10 Even 'animate' can say too much. It suggests that the process 'comes to life.' Chemical processes are not yet living ones.
11 See in the *Encyclopaedia Logic*, §161: 'The advance of the concept is no longer a transition or a showing-in-another, but a development, since the different is immediately posited as the identical with its other and with the whole, and determinacy is to be a free being of the whole concept.'
12 The phrase 'quite particular bodies' is introduced in 1830. Note that Hegel also moved *different* to modify *Momente*, a shift that was not retained in Nicolin and Pöggeler's edition of 1959.
13 *Philosophy of Nature*, §314
14 I have argued elsewhere ('Where is the Place of Understanding?' in *Hegel on Logic and Religion*, chapter 4) for the identification of conceiving and understanding. That argument was based simply on the *Logic*. In the *Phenomenology* the process of understanding becomes fully articulate in explanation, which has the pattern I have sketched out here. This mutual structure of identifying and differentiating is also the culminating stage of the logic of subjective conceiving, since a disjunction involves not only an either/or (difference) but also a both/

and (identity). Because of understanding's ability to articulate comprehensive disjunctions it can take the reflective syntheses of speculative reason and integrate them into a simple concept.

15 One of the greatest temptations for intepreters of Hegel's systematic argument is to make intuitive leaps that are not strictly justified by the stage reached. It takes discipline to identify the plodding, step by step advance that Hegel sees is necessary.

19: §327

1 This distinction is developed only in the larger *Logic*, not in the *Encyclopaedia* (*WL HGW*, 11, 302–12; (Miller) 456–66). Compare *On Hegel's Logic* 91–4. See also the logical discussion of chemical process chapter in 14.

2 *WL HGW*, 267–90; (Miller) 418–43; *Enz* §§117–20. Compare *On Hegel's Logic*, 74–83

3 In an opposition there is frequently the sense that the conflict or tension has been brought in from outside. Somebody or something introduces the concept within which one body is opposed to another. Once we move to contradiction that external third is removed, and two things that are identical are nonetheless opposed to each other without reference to anything else.

4 This is the point Hegel made in his reference to chemistry in the *Phenomenology*. See chapter 2, note 24, above.

5 *Prolusiones ad chemiam saeculi*, 111–12

6 German translation, I, 693

7 *Essai sur la théorie des proportions chimiques*, 7. This essay was the first part of volume III of his *Lehrbuch*, published separately.

8 In his lectures of 1819–20 (*Naturphilosophie*, 85:30), Hegel described this process using the language of chemical classifications, developed below. An amalgamation has, as both presupposition and product, bodies of the same class; yet, unlike the exchange of salts in the process of double affinity, there is no transformation in the process.

9 Notice that a 'synsomatic' combination is not absolutely unmediated. A mixture frequently comes about because some outside agent brings the two bodies together. Nothing, however, needs to be added to the bodies themselves to effect the combination. The agent cause is external to the natural bodies and to the characteristics that enter into play in the process.

20: §328

1 It is this act of particularizing that is characteristic of the process of understanding. See *WL HGW*, 12, 41–3; (Miller) 610–12.

2 Hegel's third thesis associated with his dissertation, *De orbitis planetarum*, of 1801 was: 'The square is the law of nature, the triangle is the law of mind.' Hegel, *Philosophical Dissertation on the Orbits of the Planets (1801) Preceded by the 12 Theses Defended on August 27, 1901*, translated, with foreword and notes, by Pierre Adler, *Graduate Faculty Philosophy Journal* 12 (1987), 1 and 2, 276. The original Latin with a German translation can be found in *Dissertatio Philosophica de Orbitis Planetarum / Philosophische Erörterung über die Planetenbahnen*, translation, introduction, and commentary by Wolfgang Neuser, *Acta Humaniora* VCH, 1986.

3 In his *Anfangsgründe der Stöchyometrie* (Breslau and Hirschberg, 1792), 3–7

4 In his last work in 1830, Humphrey Davy noted that 'the test of a body being indecomposable is, that in all chemical changes it increases in weight, or its changes result from its combining with new matter,' while 'the test of a body being compound is, that in assuming new forms it loses weight' (cited from Partington, *A History of Chemistry*, IV, 51).

5 See his Remark to *Enz. PN*, §281.

6 Compare the Lectures of 1819: 'We can now clarify the opposition between a physical and a chemical element. The latter is something concrete in itself because it persists on its own account, though not yet individuated; the physical is the final abstraction' (*Naturphilosophie*, I, 93.5ff.). In the lectures of 1803–4 the physical elements are derived from the chemical ones; whereas in the 1817 *Encyclopaedia* the chemical elements are identified as the components of water and air, discussed earlier.

7 In the lectures of 1803–4, Hegel identifies these physical elements in terms of their functions: 'Fire is the sublating of the chemical elements; water is the fluid that has been sublated; air is the sublating in the form of having been sublated; if it emerges as sublating it is fire, if as having been sublated, it is water' (*HGW*, 6, 74). Earth is the three taken together as a unity (75).

8 Until our modern technological world started producing artificial chemicals far more abundantly than the environment could easily absorb.

9 But compare the comment of Färber in 'Hegels Philosophie der Chemie,' 107: The four physical elements 'sind philosophisch, aber sie sind nicht Elemente. Luft, Feuer, Wasser, Erde sind zu Allegorien geworden, in denen die allgemeinsten Veränderungen der Stoffe zusammengefaßt werden sollen; das aus ihnen gesponnen Netz ist noch zu weit, so daß die Wirklichkeiten damit nicht einzufangen sind.'

10 By the early nineteenth century it had been established that the proportions of nitrogen, oxygen, and carbon dioxide in the air of the atmosphere did not vary significantly between high and low, or between different regions of the earth, even though air was not strictly a compound, but a mixture.

11 This last sentence is an effort to do justice to a sentence in §282: 'As *negative universality*, this identity is the unsuspected, yet surreptitious and devouring power over whatever is individual and organic.' I have highlighted this destructive capacity of air, because it becomes important in the text of the paragraph we are currently discussing.

12 The counterpart to evaporation is the water produced when hydrogen is burned in oxygen.

13 Metals were compounds of these 'metallic earths' and phlogiston.

14 *Anfangsgründe der Stöchyometrie*, 3–7

15 *Systematisches Handbuch der gesammten Chemie*, I, §22. Other volumes were published in later years. In this caution he followed Lavoisier, who defined an 'element or principle' as 'the last point which analysis is capable of reaching.' Any conclusion is tentative: 'since we have not hitherto discovered the means of separating them, they are with respect to us as simple substances; and we ought never to suppose them compounded until experiment and observation has proved them to be so' (cited in Partington, *A History of Chemistry*, III, 485).

16 First Swedish edition in 1811; the German translation used for reference here was that made by F. Wöhler and published by Arnold in Dresden in 1825.

17 Berzelius, agreeing with Humphrey Davy, was not prepared to affirm unequivocally that nitrogen was an element. Its inert status suggested that it might be a compound of a radical, nitre, with oxygen.

18 It should be noted that this classification of metalloids did not agree with that of Hegel. In his remarks in the 1830 *Encyclopaedia* Hegel used the term for calcium (§330) and simply replaces 'earths' with 'metalloids' in a list of chemical material (§334), suggesting that the term covered radicals like potassium and sodium, aluminium and beryllium, all of which Berzelius listed as metals. See as well Michelet's addition to §330 where metalloid is used for metals that are scarcely found in a reguline state.

19 In due course it was shown that organisms appropriated these metals in such minute quantities that earlier instruments had not been able to detect them.
    Berthollet in 1803 defined metals this way: 'Their distinctive properties are principally derived: from the reciprocal affinity (or cohesion) by which they can combine among themselves, while they do establish a union with only a small number of other substances; from their specific weight, which is much larger ...; but in particular from the affinity they have with oxygen, and from the results of this oxidation, which acquires properties equally distinct from those of other combinations' (*Essai de Statique Chimique*, I, 339).

20 He had by 1831, because he cited the full German edition in his remark on elective affinity in the larger *Logic*. In the remark to §330 of 1830, he quoted from Berzelius' shorter *Essai sur la théorie des proportions chimiques* in its French

version of 1819 (even though it had been translated into German in 1820), which was a separate issue of the first part of the third volume of the *Lehrbuch*. If he had had the full edition in 1830, one would have expected him to cite Berzelius (in the remark to §330) in German rather than French. The shorter essay did not outline the detailed results of electrochemical analysis, but instead defended Berzelius' theory concerning the nature of the galvanic process. Therefore it does not discuss the elements.

21 See remark to §330. *HGW*, 20, 336:6–10; (Miller) 250; (Petry) II, 197:20–4.

22 See first edition, §253–5

23 In 1803–4, Hegel justified this distinction by pointing out that nitrogen, oxygen, and hydrogen do not have any cohesion on their own. 'Cohesion as a particularizing of specific weight is found only in them all together, but they lack just this totality as well as its unit status. So they are not to be put in the same list as those things that are equally simple for analytic chemistry, but in another potency. For with the undecomposed earths, sulphur, phosphorous, acids, metals, it is to posit something earthy and real. [The chemical elements] are in quite a different sense simple and undecomposable – simple as moments of the earthly or of carbon; these others are again determinations of the earthly, and coherent when separated within themselves' (*HGW*, 6, 49–50). Compare a passage from Michelet's addition to this paragraph: 'While carbon alone has subsistence on its own account, the others [nitrogen, oxygen and hydrogen] come to existence only through force and thus have only a momentary existence.' In their gaseous form, N, O, and H were considered by many in 1803 to be compounds of the element and caloric.

24 In the lectures of 1803–4, Hegel points out that the four elements do not remain identical in chemical transformation but are fundamentally altered. See *HGW*, 6, 68–9.

Had he been talking about organic chemistry, the emphasis on just these four elements would have made a good deal of sense. Compare J.W. Ritter, *Physisch-Chemische Abhandlungen in chronologischer Folge* (Leipzig, 1806), I, xix: 'Chemistry has succeeded out of the most noble and diverse organic forms to extract little more than hydrogen, carbon, nitrogen and oxygen, in scarcely different ratios ...' But Hegel dismissed organic chemistry in his remark to §334: 'Animal and vegetable substances belong to a completely different order; their nature can so little be understood out of chemical processes, that they are rather destroyed thereby, and only the way of *their death* is grasped.' (This point is made as well in the logical discussion of life: *WL HGW*, 12, 183:34–184:4; (Miller) 766.) The rest of Ritter's sentence thus came into its own: '... without, in contrast, being in the condition of being able to put back together from them, in any happy state, even the simplest destroyed member.'

Once again we see the significance of process for Hegel: animal and vegetable substances 'should at the most serve to work against the metaphysics, which is dominant in both chemistry and physics, namely the thoughts, or rather confused conceptions, of the unalterability of matter under all circumstances, as well as the categories of the assembling and the maintenance of bodies out of such stuff' (remark to §334).

25 It is interesting to note that mass, cohesion, and heat are three variable conditions that are particularly stressed by Berthollet in arguing against elective affinity. See below in the discussion of §333.

26 Of course the references both to real process and to concrete totality have been justified on the basis of a posteriori considerations. They are the conceptual counterparts of what turned out to be partial and inadequate phenomena. So I am using 'a priori' here not in any absolute sense, but rather looking at what is known prior to the particular paragraph we are currently discussing.

27 An example might help. We say, for example, that a certain virus is the real ground of a cold. There is an identity of content between the two. But we still have to explain why some people, exposed to the virus, develop a cold and others do not. A real ground is always an incomplete explanation.

28 It is interesting that Nicolin and Pöggeler leave this adjective out of their edition. There seems no particular reason, other than the fact that Hegel did not use it in 1827.

29 'Bezeichnungen wie 'das reine Allgemeine' für den Stickstoff, das 'reine Besondere' für den Kohlenstoff wurden von Steffens geschaffen. Mit etwas Einfühlungsvermögen stellt man leicht ihren Ursprung fest: Stickstoff ist in der Luft überall verbreitet, ohne sich wie Sauerstoff an chemischen Geschehen überall zu beteiligen; Kohlenstoff ist die Grundlage in den mannigfaltigen besonderten Stoffen aus Pflanzen und Tierreich. Man sieht dabei zugleich, wie wenig zwingend und vor allem wie gering an Inhalt diese metaphysischen Ansichten sind. Dieselbe Methode wird auch auf Wasserstoff und Sauerstoff angewandt. Sie sind ganz offenbar, der Heftigkeit der Knallexplosion wegen, die allgemeinen Repräsenten der potenzierten Attraktiv- und Repulsionskraft' (Färber, 'Hegels Philosophie der Chemie,' 95–6).

In 1830, Hegel made a slight amendment at this point that suggests (a) this organization of the elements is the subjective application of the concept, and (b) it was in some sense peculiar to his immediate culture. By inserting two words he changed 'In this way the chemical elements have ...' to 'In this way we have as the chemical elements ...' For some reason Nicolin and Pöggeler reverted to the 1827 version, which is more awkward grammatically.

(It is worth mentioning one other change they made in this paragraph. They reintroduce aber, 'however,' into the first sentence. Hegel had removed it, because the new introduction to the previous paragraph had identified it as an aside, so that this one moved directly on from §326.)

21: §329

1 On the logic of judgment see *WL HGW*, 12, 53–89; (Miller) 623–63; and *On Hegel's Logic*, 125–57.
2 See *WL HGW*, 21, 116–24; (Miller) 129–37. The complex logic of infinity follows. See as well *On Hegel's Logic*, 52–8.
3 On the logic of reflection, see *WL HGW*, 11, 249–57; (Miller) 399–408; *On Hegel's Logic*, 67–72.
4 Michelet's addition to §329
5 To §257; to §334 in the second and third
6 See Michelet's addition to §329: 'The nature of a body depends on its position in relation to the various processes in which it plays the part of generator, determinant, or product. True it is also capable of entering into still other processes, but it is not the determining factor in them. Thus in the galvanic process, pure metal is the determining factor; it does indeed also pass over into the process of fire as alkali and acid, but these do not give it its place in the total process. Sulphur also has a relationship to acid and is effective as so related; but it is in its relationship to fire that it is a determining factor' ((Miller) 243).
7 *Essai*, I, 60 and II, 4
8 Trommsdorff, *Systematisches Handbuch*, §596 and §853
9 *HGW*, vi, 114 and 369. The editors of the critical edition cite as a basis for this reference the work of Paracelsus. Compare what William Whewell wrote in 1837: 'But in order to point out the chemical bearing of the next subjects of our narrative, we may further observe, that *metals, earths, salts*, are spoken of as known *classes* of substances; and in like manner the newly-discovered elements, which form the last trophies of chemistry, have been distributed into such classes according to their analogies; thus *potassium, sodium, barium*, have been asserted to be metals; *iodine, bromine, fluorine*, have been arranged as analogical to *chlorine*. Yet there is something vague and indefinite in the boundaries of such classification and analogies, and it is precisely where this vagueness falls, that the science is still obscure and doubtful' (*History of the Inductive Sciences*, iii, 125–6). Not until Mendeleev developed the periodic table in t he 1860s would there be a sound basis for classifying chemicals.

22: 1 / Union §330   a / galvanism

1 In 1817, he placed galvanism within the section on electricity, and talked only

about oxidation under chemistry. By the time of his lectures in 1819, galvanism provided the bridge to his discussion of chemistry.

2 The German is *selbstisch*.

3 Remark to §330, *HGW*, 20, 333:28–31; (Miller) 248. Hegel reaffirms this distinction between electricity as fleeting and chemical change as more permanent in the remark on elective affinity in the 1831 *Logic*: *WL HGW*, 21, 360:15–20; (Miller) 363.

4 Partington, *A History of Chemistry*, IV, 5–6

5 Ritter, *Beweis daß ein beständiger Galvanismus den Lebensproceß in dem Thierreich begleite*. Further evidence for his thesis was the natural form of electricity in certain fish.

6 See Partington, *History*, IV, 12–13.

7 The term came from the column formed by the discs, laid on top of each other. Another name for the contraption was 'artificial electrical organ,' because it imitated the torpedo fish.

8 Berzelius, *Lehrbuch*, 129. Compare Partington, *History*, IV, 24.

9 Hegel cites this claim several times in his lectures of 1819. See *Naturphilosophie I*, 89.9f and 90.16–8.

10 See Berzelius, *Lehrbuch*, 127f.

11 Berzelius, *Lehrbuch*, 128

12 He developed this theory in the first part of the third volume of his *Lehrbuch*, which was published separately in both French and German before the complete work. It was the French version of this shorter treatise (*Essai sur la théorie des proportions chimiques*) that Hegel cited in his remark to this paragraph.

13 It was not necessary to be an atomist to accept the theory of definite proportions. Gay-Lussac in 1809 had shown similar ratios for volumes of gases. See Berzelius, *Essai*, 13–14.

14 This appears to have been Davy's concern. See Partington, *History*, IV, 17.

15 See Ritter, *Physisch-Chemische Abhandlungen in chronologischer Folge* (Leipzig, 1806) I, 219ff

16 In *Der Proceß der galvanischen Kette*

17 *Process*, 471–9; see Partington, *History*, IV 135.

18 Pohl, *Process*, 27

19 Pohl, *Process*, 70. The use of terms that evoke Hegel's discussion of chemical process is not accidental. Pohl held that the speculative penchant of the Germans would lead to a more reliable scientific theory than atomism's throw of dice and the superficiality of bare appearances. See *Process*, 32–34 and 363ff. While teaching in a Berlin gymnasium, he had attended Hegel's lectures.

In his *History of the Inductive Sciences*, iii, 139f., William Whewell points out that the experiments Pohl cited posed problems with Davy's hypothesis 'that chemical and electrical attractions were produced by the same cause, acting in the one case on particles, in the other on masses; ... and that the same property, under different modifications, was the cause of all the phenomena exhibited by different voltaic combinations ... That there remained something to be done, in order to give full evidence and consistency to the theory, appears from this; – that some of the most important parts of Davy's results struck his followers as extraordinary paradoxes; – for instance, the fact that the decomposed elements are transferred from one part of the circuit to another, in a form which escapes the cognizance of our senses, through intervening substances for which they have astrong affinity. It was found afterwards [by Faraday] that the circumstance which appeared to make the process so wonderful was, in fact, the condition for its going on at all.' Only in 1833 when Faraday proved that the electric current could be described as an axis of power was Davy's thesis established. That was two years after Hegel's death.

20 Several lengthy quotations from these polemics can be found in my 'Hegel and Galvanism,' in *Hegel on the Modern World*.

21 This appears to be the reason why, in 1827, the phrase about fluidity stood *outside* the parenthesis, which then became a gloss on 'fluidity' and not on 'solid unity.'

22 *Essai de Statique Chimique*, II, 361, 393

23 Since there is no reference to galvanism in the first edition of 1817 (though the products of the first process are oxides §253), the use of earths in this context is peculiar to 1827. See, however, Michelet's addition to this paragraph: 'To the metal calces which are the result of the galvanic process belong the earths as well: silica, chalk, baryte, soda, potash; for what appears as earth has in general a metallic base.'

24 In the sentence just analysed Hegel suggests that the various qualities and capacities of metal fit into a comprehensible, interconnected framework. Reflective thought, he implies, can explain why the contact of metals produces electrical polarity. This does not mean, however, that empirical properties are being deduced a priori. An explanation emerges only a posteriori, as a way of integrating an apparent diversity or resolving an experienced contradiction. But from a good explanation, once proposed, one should be able to derive what essentially defines the empirical phenomena.

25 In his lectures of 1819–20, Hegel associated this process with air as individualized and differentiated, in the same way that the next two processes were then called the 'circle of fire' and the 'circle of water' (in the 1827 edition they were called 'fire-process' and 'water-process'). Oxidation takes place, he suggested, because water is reduced to its two elements, both of which become gases. (He also added the strange statement that hydrogen is the basis of air.) (*Naturphilosophie*, I, 104.17ff.).

The qualification 'yet divisible' with respect to water was added in 1830. Hegel thus explicitly distanced himself from the Ritter-Pohl thesis that water is simple, uniting with positive or negative electricity to compose oxygen or hydrogen. In the fifth volume of his *Handbuch* (1803), Trommsdorff reported that 'Humphrey Davy's experiments confirmed the separation of the types of gases that make up water (which had already been done by other means) so that no doubt remains' (V, 40).

26 Michelet's addition to this paragraph spends some time distinguishing the electrical from the chemical factors.

27 In the literature of the time, chemists distinguished hydrogen, oxygen, and nitrogen as such, which can be components of liquids and solids as well as gases, from those substances in their gaseous form, which are called hydrogen gas or oxygen gas. Some thought that the gases were combinations of the elements with caloric. Indeed, in his *Naturphilosophie* of 1804, a younger Hegel pointed out that nitrogen only becomes material when it is united with caloric and becomes nitrogen gas. So when referring to the material product here, Hegel talks of gases, but uses the abstract names for the elements in §328.

23: §331 b / Combustion

1 Trommsdorff, *Systematisches Handbuch*, I, §56
2 Berzelius, *Essai*, 57
3 Hegel cited this experiment in his lectures of 1819, *Naturphilosophie*, 92.1ff.
4 Cited from Kirwan's *Essay on Phlogiston* (1789) 13f., in Partington, *A History of Chemistry*, III, 423. Other bits of the citation are also interesting: 'This ... is not an hypothesis, but the result of facts ... No supposition enters into these explanations; the whole is proved by weight and measure ... The property of burning is nothing else but the property which certain substances possess of decomposing vital air by the great affinity they have for the oxigenous principle ... An inflammable body is nothing else but a body which has the property of decomposing vital air, and taking the base from the caloric and light, that is to say, the *oxigène* which was united to them ...; it is principally and almost entirely from such substances [vital air] that the caloric and light are disengaged.'

Phlogiston continued to be used in explanations of fire even after the role of oxygen was recognized. Thus Richter thought the phlogiston from the original body united with the caloric tied to oxygen in its gaseous form to generate the fire. In the *Naturphilosophie* of 1803–4, Hegel refers to 'phlogiston' without appearing to have adopted it for his discussion. *HGW*, 6, 153.

In *Hegel und die Chemie* von Enghelhardt discusses the debate between the phlogiston and the anti-phlogiston theories.

5 He does, however, discuss other kinds of combustible substances in Michelet's addition to this paragraph. In the early lectures of 1803–4, Hegel tried to combine all chemical processes under the physical element of fire as pure activity (*HGW*, 6, 143ff.).

6 Hegel developed both concepts in the logic of positing reflection, *WL HGW*, 11, 250–2; (Miller) 400–2; compare *On Hegel's Logic*, 67–8.

7 See Michelet's addition to §331: 'Because the new form which we introduce arises only for us (i.e., in the concept or implicitly), we have to take all that enter into the process as they naturally are.'

8 See the lectures of 1803–4, *HGW*, 6, 168: 'In general, the acidity of the acids or the causticity of the bases involves being directed to another, it is not matter; for matter is what is on its own account. Being directed to another, however, is what is not on its own account, it is the ideal (*ideelle*). Acid as such is as little matter as, for example, hardness.'

9 Berthollet had defined metals as inflammable because they could be oxidized. But metals do not burn; so Hegel distinguishes simple oxidation from combustion, which is a separate process (though in the first edition of 1817 he discusses combustion under the same number as the oxidation of metals, see §§251–4). Compare Michelet's addition to this paragraph: 'Only the concept, the inner necessity takes the process further; only implicitly is the process taken on towards the cycle of totalty.'

10 Although Michelet's addition to this paragraph talks about how air and water are at times involved.

11 §254. Only after this comment, and an earlier one about the break up of water in oxidation (§253), did Hegel in 1817 discuss the four chemical elements (§255).

12 But see the comments contained in Michelet's addition to this paragraph.

24: §332   c / Neutralization

1 See *WL HGW*, 21, 96–110; (Miller) 109–22; and *On Hegel's Logic*, 46–50.

2 On acidity as merely a quality, see the lectures of 1803–4: 'Acid as such is matter as little as, for example, hardness is' (*HGW*, 6, 169).

3 Compare Berthollet, *Essai de statique chimique*, I, 285, whose definition is entirely functional: 'Among the alkalis should be included all the substances which can produce by themselves a complete saturation of acids, while rendering their acidity latent, by an antagonistic property which constitutes their alkalinity.' He lists ammoniac, manganese, chalk, potash, soda, strontion, and baryte.

4 Since the modern chemical formulae were initially proposed by Berzelius in his *Lehrbuch*, and presupposed Dalton's atomism, which was a disputed theory

throughout Hegel's lifetime, they were not adopted by Hegel. I have therefore refrained from using them to characterize chemical processes.

5 'This opposition, once ignited, does not need to be first brought to activity by means of a third.' (Michelet's addition to §332.) Michelet concludes with a paragraph that discusses how air and water have a mediating role to play here as well.

6 The only clue in Hegel's text that might explain why neutralization is also a water process is the parenthetical comment, added in 1830, where he suggested that both acids and alkalis are 'blunted' in contact with air, and are reduced to a formal neutrality. When analysing the concept of a chemical process in the *Logic*, he used water (as well as language) to illustrate what he meant by a middle term that is formally neutral.

7 In 'Chemie und Dialektik,' Simon generalizes from the relationship between acids and bases: they show how nature follows the same dialectical processes as the social order. His argument builds more on the philosophies of nature of Engels and Lenin than on that of Hegel.

8 *WL HGW*, 21, 99–102; (Miller) 111–15. The first edition of the *Science of Logic* separated the two terms: reality was directly associated with the concept 'being-in-itself,' whereas negation was tied in with the limitations of finitude (*WL HGW*, 11, 63, 75–6).

9 *Systematisches Handbuch*, I, §853

10 Compare Berthollet, *Essai*, 285. The development of ordered series is discussed in Hegel's remark to §333.

11 See Michelet's addition to §329: 'The third is the process of what is thus animated, while the first is the positing of oxides and the second the positing of acids.'

12 *WL HGW*, 12, 149:27–31; (Miller) 728

13 *WL HGW*, 12, 149:34–6; (Miller) 729

25: §333   d / The Total Process

1 *Werke* (Weimar 1887–1919) I.20, 556. Cited in Snelders, 'Hegel und die Bertholettischen Affinitätslehre,' 91. Snelders' article offers useful background for this paragraph.

2 'Bergman studied extensively the relative ability of bases and acids to replace one another in salts. For example, when *caustic terra ponderosa* ($Ba(OH)_2$) was added to *vitriolated tartar* (K_2SO_4), *ponderous spar* ($BaSO_4$) was formed, leaving a liquor that contained *caustic vegetable alkali* (KOH); hence he concluded that the vitriolic acid (H_2SO_4) had a greater affinity for barytes than for potash' (Ihde, *Development of Modern Chemistry*, 94).

3 From Partington, *History*, III, 631
4 Partington, III, 676. Hegel cited this thesis in the remark to this paragraph and referred as well to Guyton de Morveau. Since Richter's term for the elements was *stoicheia*, ultimate chemical stuff, he called the measurement of definite proportions *Stöchyometrie*.
5 'I shall conclude by deducing from these experiments the principle I have set out at the commencement of this memoir: viz that iron, like many other metals, is subject to the law of nature which presides at every true combination, that is to say, that it unites with two constant proportions of oxygen. In this respect it does not differ from tin, mercury, and lead, and in a word almost every known combustible' (cited in Partington, *History*, III, 647).
6 Partington, *History*, III, 665
7 Berthollet, *Essai*, 77. As we have seen, Berthollet's evidence led Hegel to be cautious about using the term 'elective affinity' when talking about the natural process; he prefixed 'so-called' both here and in the 1831 edition of the *Logic*: WL HGW, 21, 355:13; (Miller) 357.
8 See *Essai de Statique Chimique*, I, 134–8. The original note can be found in C.L. Berthollet, *Über die Gesetze der Verwandschaft*, trans. E.G. Fischer (Berlin, 1802), 229–35.
9 This distinguishes it from amalgamation, which also is a process where presupposition and product are of the same class.
10 See Michelet's addition to this paragraph: 'Neutrality is here conceived as in struggle with itself, since the neutrality which is the product is mediated by the negation of neutrality.'

26: 2 / Separation §334

1 See chapter 14.
2 The discussion of abstract separation was introduced in 1827 and amended in 1830. In 1817, the abstract simple substances appear as components in the process of double affinity. In the interim, Hegel realized that the second logical moment of separation needed to have its own paragraph in the philosophy of nature.
3 See *HGW*, 8, 96 (this passage is reproduced in the addition to §330), and Snelders, 'Hegel und die Bertholletischen Affinitätslehre,' 97. The list of chemical substances Michelet provides in the addition to this paragraph does not reflect the classification according to the stage in the process as developed in the 1830 edition of the *Encyclopaedia*, but rather the point of view that characterized the Jena philosophy of nature, where chemical substances are co-ordinated with the physical elements. It does not represent Hegel's final position.

4 See Michelet's addition to this paragraph.

5 *Naturphilosophie*, I, 103–4

27: §335

1 See chapter 12.

2 See *WL HGW*, 12, 182–91; (Miller) 764–74.

3 *WL HGW*, 21, 94–5; (Miller) 106–8

4 In his remark in the larger *Logic* mentioned above, Hegel equated the passive participle to 'the ideal.' His spelling of this term (*Ideelle*) with a double 'e' and double 'l' showed that he was not referring to an ideal (*Ideale*) union of concept and object, but to something that is recognized and isolated only by thought. (Compare our note on 'real' in §333 above.) Whatever is *augehobene* is a moment that can be ignored, the negative moment left behind when one focuses on immediate reality. *Aufhebung*, then, is the dynamic in which mediation disappears and a new immediate is constituted.

5 *WL HGW*, 11, 166–85; (Miller) 461–96

6 See *WL HGW*, 11, 312–19; (Miller) 466–74; *On Hegel's Logic*, 94–9.

7 In his lectures of 1819–20 Hegel introduced his discussion of chemical process by calling it an analogon of life and then distinguishing it from the self-maintaining dynamic of the latter (Hegel, *Naturphilosophie* I, 82:28–30). Compare the end of Michelet's addition to §326.

8 Michelet spells out six ways chemical process is distinguished from life in his addition to §329.

9 Ritter, *Beweis daß ein beständiger Galvanismus den Lebensprocess in den Thierreich begleite*

10 See the remark to §334: 'Animal and vegetable substances belong to a quite different order; their nature can be so little understood from chemical process that they are rather destroyed thereby, and only the way of *their death* is grasped.'

11 Hegel had the logic of teleology or purposiveness between the logic of chemism and that of life. This led him to insert a remark here that describes the same process (of disproportionation), which he mentioned towards the end of the logic of chemism, in which a particular oxide will adjust the degree of oxidation of its various parts so that one part canunite with some other substance. See note 2 in Chapter 15.

28: §336

1 He used the noun form of 'absolute' primarily in the prefaces, lectures, or remarks with reference to an academic community informed by Schelling's phi-

losophy, or in the *Logic* when analysing the principles of Spinozism. Chapters 13 and 14 of *On Hegel's Logic* argue for the thesis contained in this note.

2 See *WL HGW*, 21, 124–37; (Miller) 137–50; *On Hegel's Logic*, 53–8. Compare the note on *Aufhebung* in the previous chapter.

3 Kant, *Kritik der Urteilskraft*, §64, B286; *Critique of Judgment*, trans. J.H. Bernard (New York: Hafner; London: Collier Macmillan, 1951) 217

4 *Kritik der Urteilskraft*, §65, B291–2; (Bernard) 220. My translation

5 Compare Michelet's addition to this paragraph: 'Bodies alter in chemical process not superficially but on all sides. Every property is lost: cohesion, colour, lustre, opacity, resonance, transparency. Even specific weight, which appears to be the deepest, simplest determination, does not persist ... The body shows the transience of its existence, and this its relativity is its being.'

6 See here Von Engelhardt, 'Das chemische System der Stoffe, Kräfte und Prozesse,' 133f: 'In der Chemie besteht kein unmittelbar zusammenhängenden Kreislauf synthetischer und analytischer Veränderungen. Die Einheit der beiden Prozesse ist in ihr nur eine gedankliche Vorstellung ohne Korrespondierende Realität. So wie Begriff und Wirklichkeit für die sich verbindende und trennende Stoffe auseinanderfallen stimmt auch der Begriff der gedanklichen Einheit von synthetischen und analytischen Prozessen nicht mit der chemischen Wirklichkeit überein. Jene beiden ersten Inkongruenzen der einfachen und verbundenen Stoffe heben die chemischen Prozesse auf, die Auflösung der zweiten Inkongruenz leistet ein neuer Prozess, der Prozess des Organischen.'

7 We could substitute any other chemical substance for 'metals' in this statement.

8 In our current environment, he might have included a discussion of the ecosystem. Since that is a unity that incorporates plants and animals, it would not replace the discussion of geology, but would come as a separate stage that integrates all the moments of organic physics into a totality. On Hegel's discussion of geology see Levere, 'Hegel and the Earth Sciences,' in *Hegels Philosophie der Natur*, 103–20.

29: From 1817 to 1830

1 On the differences between these three editions as a whole, see W. Neuser, 'Dokumente einer Entwicklung – Zu Hegels Naturphilosophie,' *Dialektik* 8 (1984), 245–57.

2 The word is *Vereinzelung*, not *Individualität*. In the first edition, Hegel sees chemical processes as leading towardsan integrated singular, or organism, and builds this into both the title and the preceding transitional paragraph.

3 (2) and (3) handled neutralization and double affinity.

4 This paragraph was substantially incorporated into the later §328. It would need

a separate study to explore the changes in Hegel's discussions of the chemical elements from the Jena manuscript of 1803–4 (where the fourth element is carbon dioxide) through the 1817 edition to the 1827/30 editions.

5 *Naturphilosophie*, I

6 The threefold pattern is now air-, fire-, and water-process, leaving double affinity on its own as 'process in its totality.'

7 It should be recalled, however, that the three basic processes of oxidation, combustion, and neutralization did fit (and perhaps instigated?) the threefold syllogistic pattern of combination in the *Encyclopaedia* Logic, §149 (1817) and §201 (1830).

8 *Systematisches Handbuch*, §1, p.1

9 *Lehrbuch der Chemie*, I, 1, p.1

30: The Remarks

1 See *HGW*, 13. An English edition can be found in *Encyclopaedia of the Philosophical Sciences in Outline and Critical Writings*, ed. E. Behler, The German Library (New York: Continuum 1990), 177. The remark is the second paragraph and is not separated from the main text.

2 In 1830 Hegel dropped a reference to the increased efficiency of acids as evidence of the variability of nature, and pointed out instead that some 'metalloids' were so unstable that they became oxides in air.

3 The specific wording changed from 1817 to 1827. 1817: 'Since further the chemical process has its determination in the concept, so (as with electricity) the empirical conditions of any of its particular forms are not so *fixed* sensible determinations, and not so *abstract* moments as one might imagine, for example, with elective affinity ...' 1827: 'Further, elective affinity itself is only an *abstract* reference of an acid to a base. But the chemical in general, and in particular the neutral body, is at the same time a concrete physical body of a determinate specific weight, cohesion, temperature, etc. These properly physical properties and the alteration in the process enter into a relation with the chemical moments of the same, hindering, making more difficult or easy, modifying its effectiveness.'

4 See Färber, 'Hegels Philosophie der Chemie,' 96: 'Die "Méthode de Nomenclature Chimique" bringt im Jahre 1787 als erste ein Einteilung der Chemie nach den elementen und deren Verbindungen, während vorher diejenige nach den Operationen wichtiger war.' And again on 109: 'Wir versuchen das Werden einzufangen in das Schema aus beharrenden Dingen, die einen gewissen Abstand, ein Umwandlungsverhältnis zueinander haben ... Hegel versucht sie statt aus solchen Stücken als Ganzes und begrifflich einheitlich zu fassen.'

5 See footnote 2 in chapter 15.

6 On the logic of teleology, see my paper, 'The Cunning of Reason,' to appear in *Final Causality in Nature and Human Affairs* (Catholic University of America Press).

7 Compare Collingwood, *The Idea of Nature*, 1960, 124–5: 'Nothing in nature fully and completely tallies with our scientific description of it; and this not because our ideas are in need of correction, but because there is always in nature a certain backlash, an element of indeterminacy, of potentiality (to use Aristotle's language) not yet resolved into perfect actuality.'

8 §329, Michelet's addition

9 This follows a pattern systematically developed by Hegel in the opening pages of the *Doctrine of Essence* in the *Science of Logic*. See *WL HGW*, 11, 144–57; (Miller) 394–408; and *On Hegel's Logic*, 63–72.

10 Remark to §330

11 In a similar way, Hegel may well have maintained the fourfold classification of chemical bodies, not only because metals, oxides, combustibles, and salts each had their own position relative to the various processes, but also because they could be described as abstract universals, singulars, particulars, and concrete universals.

12 On this relationship between the natural sciences and the philosophy of nature, see Gloy, 'Goethes und Hegels Kritik an Newtons Farbentheorie,' in particular 345–59.

13 Remark to §334

14 For more on the conceptual difference between Hegel's philosophy of nature and scientific theory, see Buchdahl, 'Conceptual Analysis and Scientific Theory in Hegel's Philosophy of Nature.'

15 Michelet's addition to §329; Suhrkamp edition 9, 300–1; Petry, II, 190:32

31: How Chemical Process Is Systematic

1 Although the paragraph was different in 1817, there was enough common ground that Hegel could incorporate the second half of the earlier §250 into the expanded text of 1827.

2 In the translation, to keep *Leib* distinguished from *Körper*, I have used 'flesh' rather than 'body.'

3 *Encyclopaedia*, §249. See Verra, 'Dialettica contra metamorfosi,' in *Letture Hegeliane*, 99–112.

4 Remark to §334

5 See Taylor, *Hegel*, 352: 'Necessity belongs to the Concept. We have to show its traces in nature, and this presupposes the empirical results of natural science. But

it is not an appeal to experience, for the structure of necessity comes from the Concept. We deduce its stages and then recognize them in empirical nature.' In our analysis, 'deduce' is not the right word for the intellectual operation involved.

Note as well this comment from Michelet's addition to this paragraph: 'In accordance with the concept, structure passes over into this third. But it is rather the first, out of which that, which previously was first, originally proceeded. That is based in a deeper, logical advance.'

6 See §245. The proper context for teleology is history, not nature.

7 That is, when nature is made the object of teleological concerns.

8 In this I distance myself from Findlay who wrote, in 'Hegel and the Philosophy of Physics': 'The argument of Hegel up to this point is most readily characterized as a progress guided by a conceptual ideal, which is also such that it cannot be reached or formulated except as the outcome of such a progress. The conceptual Ideal is one that is absolutely unitary in that it admits of no stark dualisms or pluralisms within itself, features which do not require one another, or which have nothing to do with each other, whose joint application is a mere fact, or a mere matter of experience rather than a necessary, conceptual fitting together' (86). In my analysis I have tried to show that the givens of empirical nature, though organized conceptually, are the constituents that determine the systematic advance as much as the conceptual, ideal framework.

Von Engelhardt, in *Hegel und die Chemie* also notes that the transitions to and from Chemical Process in the *Philosophy of Nature* are conceptual and not real: 'Die Einheit der chemischen Prozesse oder die Einheit von Differenz und Identität ist eine gedankliche Vorstellung, die sich in der chemischen Realität bildet, der in der Chemie aber keine Realität entspricht' (101).

32: Conclusion

1 Compare this with di Giovanni's 'More Comments on the Place of the Organic in Hegel's Philosophy of Nature,' where he argues that Hegel's philosophy of nature is a mistake, since the *Logic* on its own covers all the critical categories.

2 See here the useful article by Drees: 'The Logic of Hegel's Philosophy of Nature,' and his 'Das Werden des Philosophischen Wissens von der Natur.'

For Dieter Wandschneider (see 'Nature and the Dialectic of Nature in Hegel's Objective Idealism'), the move from the *Logic* to the *Philosophy of Nature* is a logical shift, a dialectical move from the ideal to the non-ideal. So the philosophy of nature becomes a series of logical categories derived a priori and has the potential of replacing the a posteriori development of scientific explanations and laws. Experience is needed only to determine the antecedent conditions for particular natural events.

Even logically, on this account, the absolute idea at the end of the *Logic* is not absolute, but only relative. So it is not surprising that Wandschneider finds Hegel's analysis flawed: 'I have already [shown how dialectic can be elaborated into a stringent product] for that part of the *Logic* which approximately covers Quality Logic, whereby, however, far reaching revisions of the Hegelian original are necessary' (40; 283). 'If a relation can be established [between a dialectic of nature and natural law], then it too must be obtained from the idealistic conception of nature developed. Hegel does not do this. I will therefore indicate some considerations which could be developed further within this framework' (42; 287). (See also Wandschneider and Hösle, 'Die Entäusserung der Idee zur Natur'; Wandschneider, 'Die Absolutheit des Logischen und das Sein der Natur'; and Wandschneider, *Raum, Zeit, Relativität*.)

This view of the *Philosophy of Nature* as simply a version of what has already been accomplished in the Logic has a long tradition. Thus Vera, in his introduction to his translation of *Philosophie de la Nature de Hegel*, wrote: 'Il suit de là premièrement, ainsi que nous venons de le voir, que l'idée logique est dans la nature, et qu'elle y est comme forme et comme contenu, et ensuite, et par cela même, que la nature est une idée, ou un moment de l'idée absolue, ce qui veut dire qu'il y a une idée de la nature, et que cette idée une, indivisible et systematique, constitue le principe vrai et suprême de la nature, et, en même temps, le principe qui unit la nature aux autres parties ou principes de l'univers' (I, 128).

A similar approach was taken by Cunningham, in *Thought and Reality in Hegel's System*: 'If the preceding considerations are substantially true, then we are forced to conclude (a) that the *Logic, Philosophy of Nature* and *Philosophy of Mind* are only three points of view from which one organic whole is observed and interpreted ... [and] (b) that in a sense the *Logic* comprehends the other two parts of the *Encyclopaedia*' (p. 58).

3 G.W.F. Hegel, *Vorlesungen über die Geschichte der Philosophie*, in *Sämmtliche Werke*, Jubiläums Aufgabe, ed. H. Glockner (Stuttgart-Bad Cannstatt: Frommann, 1965), xviii, 340

4 This reading too has a distinguished pedigree. Thus W.T. Harris writes: 'A proper statement of Hegel's endeavours would be more nearly this: he attempts to comprehend the world of actuality, and to explain all things through it. He has first investigated the validity of all thoughts and ideas (i.e. pure thoughts) in his Logic. Then he comes to nature with the insight into the FIRST PREMISE that leads him to look for certain realizations of those pure ideal forms. His great labour, however, lies in critically collecting and sifting the phenomena of nature, for he must correctly classify these phenomena according to the scale of concreteness and abstractness' ('The Philosophy of Nature,' 275).

Similarly Alexander writes: 'However abstract and difficult the process is, and however unacceptable particular conclusions may be, yet Hegel's Philosophy of Nature is an attempt to understand the forms of nature as they really are apart from the ordinary prejudices with which we approach the study of them ... The whole of the system may be described in fact as an attempt to arrange natural facts according to their logical function in the economy of nature' ('Hegel's Conception of Nature,' 510).

More recently, T.R. Webb writes: 'Philosophy of Nature accomplishes this task [viz: grasping nature as a whole] by giving an absolute form to the results of empirical research, and the "absoluteness" of this form is nothing *apart from* the empirical data, for it consists in just the comprehensive making sense of the data which thinks nature as a whole' ('The Problem of Empirical Knowledge in Hegel's Philosophy of Nature,' 184. See as well his dissertation: 'Hegelian Science and the Problem of Nature').

5 In 'Hegels Raum-Zeit-Lehre,' Bonsiepen discusses the development of Hegel's thought on space and time, as well as two different sets of notes from his 1821–2 lectures. On Hegel's analysis of space, see Stepelevich, 'Hegel's Conception of Space'; and two dissertations: Webb, 'Hegelian Science and the Problem of Nature,' and Peterson, 'Volcanoes in the Sky.'

6 See my article 'Concept and Time in Hegel,' in *Hegel on Logic and Religion*, 79–93.

7 *Vorlesungen über die Geschichte der Philosophie*, 341

Bibliography

BOOKS ON CHEMISTRY TO BE FOUND IN HEGEL'S LIBRARY

[From W. Neuser, 'Die naturphilosophische und naturwissenschaftliche Literatur aus Hegels privater Bibliothek,' in *Hegel und die Naturwissenschaften*, ed. M.J. Petry (Stuttgart-Bad Cannstatt: Frommann-Holzboog, 1987) 479–99]

Berthollet, C.L. *Essai de statique chimique*. Paris, 1803
– *Mémoires de physique et de chimie de la Société d'Ancueil*. 3 vols. Paris, 1807–1817
Berzelius, J.J. *Essai sur la théorie des proportions chimiques et sur l'influence chimique de l'electricité*. Traduit du suédois. Paris, 1819
Biot, J.B. *Traité de physique expérimental et mathématique*. 4 vols. Paris, 1816
Bischoff, G. *Lehrbuch der Stöchiometrie oder Anleitung die Verhältnisse zu berechnen nach welchen sich die irdischen Körper miteinander verhalten*. 1819
Fischer, N.W. *Das Verhältniss der chemischen Verwandtschaft zur galvanischen Elektricität in Versuchen dargestellt*. Berlin, 1830
Fourcroy, A.F. de *Chemische Philosophie; oder Grundwahrheiten der neueren Chemie auf eine neue Art geordnet*. Trans. J.S.T Gehler. Leipzig, 1796
– *System der theoretischen und praktischen Chemie*. Trans. C.G. Eschenbach. Leipzig, 1801
Pohl, G.F. *Ansichten und Ergebnisse über Magnetismus, Elektrizität und Chemismus*. Berlin, 1829 (presentation copy)
– *Der Elektromagnetismus theoretisch und praktisch dargestellt*. Berlin, 1830 (presentation copy)
– *Der Process der galvanischen Kette*. Leipzig, 1826 (presentation copy)
– 'Über den Gegensatz zwischen galvanisch-elektrischen Primär- und Secundärketten.' *Poggendorffs Annalen*, 14 (1828), 71–90 (presentation copy)
– 'Über die von Pfaff versuchte Bekämpfung meiner Theorie des Galvanismus' (presentation copy)

Trommsdorff, J.B. *Angewandte Chemie.* Erfurt, 1804
– *Geschichte des Galvanismus oder der galvanischen Elektrizität, vorzüglich in chemischer Hinsicht.* Erfurt, 1803
– *Reine Chemie.* Erfurt, 1800–1802
– *Systematisches Handbuch des gesammten Chemie zur Erleichterung des Selbststudiums dieser Wissenschaft.* Erfurt, 1800

WORKS CITED IN THIS STUDY

[Dates in square brackets indicate original publication when that differs from the publication used.]

Alexander, S. 'Hegel's Conception of Nature.' *Mind* 11 (1886), 495–523
Berthollet, C.L. *Essai de Statique Chimique.* Paris, 1803
– *Versuch einer chemischen Statik das ist einer Theorie der chemischen Naturkräfte.* Trans. G.W. Bartoldy with notes by E.G. Fischer. Berlin, 1811
Berzelius, J.J. *Essai sur la théorie des proportions chimiques et sur l'influence chimique de l'electricité.* Traduit du suédois. Paris, 1819. German trans.: Dresden, 1820.
– *Lehrbuch der Chemie.* Trans. F. Wöhler. Dresden, 1825
Biard J., D. Buvet, J.-F. Kervegan, J.-F. Kling, A. Lacroix, A. Lécrivain, M. Slubicki. *Introduction à la lecture de la Science de la Logique de Hegel.* 3 vols. Paris: Aubier-Montaigne, 1981–87
Bloch, E. *Subjekt-Objekt: Erläuterungen zu Hegel.* [Berlin, 1951; erweiterte Ausgabe, 1962] Frankfurt: Suhrkamp, 1972
Bonsiepen, W. 'Hegels Naturphilosophie: Selbstorganizationstheorie der Natur oder des Geistes?' In *Hegels Enzyklopädisches System*, ed. H.-C. Lucas and B. Tuschling. Stuttgart-Bad Cannstatt: Frommann-Holzboog, 1994
– 'Hegels Raum-Zeit-Lehre.' *Hegel-Studien* 20 (1985), 9–78
– 'Hegels Vorlesungen über Naturphilosophie.' *Hegel-Studien* 26 (1991), 40–54
– 'Veränderungen in der Einleitung zur Naturphilosophie 1823/4–1828,' *Hegel-Studien* 26 (1991), 213–18
Braun, H. 'Realität und Reflexion: Studien zu Hegels Philosophie der Natur.' diss., Heidelberg, 1960
Brecht, S.S. 'The Place of Natural Science in Hegel's Philosophy.' diss., Harvard, 1959
Breidbach, O. *Das Organische in Hegel's Denken.* Würzburg: Königshausen and Neumann, 1982
Browning, G.K. 'Transitions to and from Nature in Hegel and Plato.' *Bulletin of the Hegel Society of Great Britain*, 26 (1992), 1–12

Buchdahl, G. 'Conceptual Analysis and Scientific Theory in Hegel's Philosophy of Nature, with Special Relevance to Hegel's Optics.' In *Hegel and the Sciences*, ed. R.S. Cohen and M.W. Wartofsky. Dordrecht: Kluwer, 1984, 13–36

- 'Hegel's Philosophy of Nature.' *British Journal for the Philosophy of Science* 23 (1972), 257–66

- 'Hegel's Philosophy of Nature and the Structure of Science.' In *Hegel*, ed. M. Inwood. Clarendon, 1985, 110–36

Burbidge, J.W. 'Chemistry and Hegel's *Logic*.' In *Hegel and Newtonianism*, ed. M.J. Petry. Dordrecht: Kluwer, 1993, 609–17

- 'Hegel and Galvanism.' In *Hegel on the Modern World*, ed. A Collins. Albany: SUNY Press, 1995, 111–24

- *Hegel on Logic and Religion*. Albany: SUNY Press, 1992

- *On Hegel's Logic, Fragments of a Commentary*. Atlantic Highlands: Humanities, 1981

Butler, C. and C. Seiler, trans. *Hegel: The Letters*. Bloomington: Indiana University Press, 1984

Cohen, M.R. *Studies in Philosophy and Science*. New York: F. Ungar, 1949, 176–98

Cohen, R.S. and M.W. Wartofsky, eds. *Hegel and the Sciences*. Dordrecht: Kluwer, 1984

Collingwood, R.G. *The Idea of Nature*. [Oxford, 1949] New York: Oxford University Press, 1960, 121–32

Croce, B. *Cio che e vivo è cio che e morte nella filosofia di Hegel*. [Bari, 1907] In *Saggio sullo Hegel*. Bari: Laterza, 1948

Cunningham, G.W. *Thought and Reality in Hegel's System*. New York: Longmans Green, 1910

D'Hondt, J. 'La dialectique hégélienne de la nature.' Paper presented at Journée sur Idéalisme allemand et *Naturphilosophie*. Paris, March 1994

di Giovanni, G. 'The Category of Contingency in the Hegelian Logic.' In *Art and Logic in Hegel's Philosophy*, ed. W. Steinkraus and K. Schmitz. Atlantic Highlands: Humanities, 1980, 179–200

- ed. *Essays on Hegel's Logic*. Albany, SUNY Press, 1990

- 'Kant's Metaphysics of Nature and Schelling's *Ideas for a Philosophy of Nature*.' *Journal of the History of Philosophy* 17, no. 2 (1979), 197–215

- 'More Comments on the Place of the Organic in Hegel's Philosophy of Nature.' In *Hegel and the Sciences*, ed. R.S. Cohen and M.W. Wartofsky. Dordrecht: Kluwer, 1984, 101–7

Doull, J.A. 'Hegel's Philosophy of Nature.' *Dialogue* 11 (1972), 379–99

Drees, M. 'Evolution and Emanation of Spirit in Hegel's *Philosophy of Nature*.' *Bulletin of the Hegel Society of Great Britain* 26 (1992), 52–61

- 'The Logic of Hegel's Philosophy of Nature.' In *Hegel and Newtonianism*, ed. M.J. Petry. Dordrecht: Kluwer, 1993
- 'Das Werden des Philosophischen Wissens von der Natur – Natur, Naturwissenschaft und Dialektik in Hegels Naturphilosophie.' *Annalen der Internationalen Gesellschaft für dialektische Philosophie – Societas Hegeliana* 3 (1986), 325–33

Easton, L.D. 'The First American Interpretation of Hegel in J.B. Stallo's *Philosophy of Science.*' In *Hegel and the Sciences*, ed. R.S. Cohen and M.W. Wartofsky. Dordrecht: Kluwer, 1984, 287–99

Elder, C.L., III. 'Towards a Revised Hegelian Theory of Nature.' diss., Yale, 1975

Engelhardt, D. von. 'Chemie zwischen Metaphysik und Empirie zu Beginn des 19. Jahrhundert.' In *Biochemische Forschung im 19. Jahrhundert, mit einer Bibliographie der Quellen*, ed. E. Hickel. Braunschweig, 1989, 217–26
- 'Das chemische System der Stoffe, Kräfte und Prozesse in Hegels Naturphilosophie und der Wissenschaft seiner Zeit.' *Stuttgarter Hegel-Tage 1970: Hegel-Studien*, Beiheft 11 (1974), 125–39. English version: 'The Chemical System of Substances, Forces and Processes in Hegel's Philosophy of Nature and the Science of his Time.' In *Hegel and the Sciences*, ed. R.S. Cohen and M.W. Wartofsky. Dordrecht: Kluwer, 1984, 41–54
- 'Hegel on Chemistry and the Organic Sciences.' In *Hegel and Newtonianism*, ed. M. Petry. Dordrecht: Kluwer, 1993, 657–68
- *Hegel und die Chemie: Studien zur Philosophie und Wissenschaft der Natur um 1800*. Wiesbaden: Pressler, 1976
- 'Müller und Hegel: Zum Verhältnis von Naturwissenschaft und Naturphilosophie im Deutschen Idealismus.' In *Johannes Müller und die Philosophie*, ed. M. Hagner and B. Wahrig-Schmidt. Berlin: Akademie, 1992, 82–103
- 'Philosophie und Theorie der Chemie um 1800.' *Philosophia Naturalis* 23 (1986), 223–37

Engels, F. *Dialectics of Nature*. Moscow: Foreign Languages, 1954

Esposito, J.L. *Schelling's Idealism and Philosophy of Nature*. Lewisburg: Bucknell University Press, 1977

Färber, E. 'Hegel und Chemie.' In *Chemische Zeitung* 55 (1925), 873–4
- 'Hegels Philosophie der Chemie.' In *Kant-Studien* 30 (1925), 91–114

Ferrini, C. 'Framing Hypotheses: Numbers in Nature and the Logic of Measure in the Development of Hegel's System.' To be published in the proceedings of the 1994 meeting of the Hegel Society of America on the Philosophy of Nature, edited by Stephen Houlgate
- 'Logica e filosofia della natura nella "dotrina dell'essere" hegeliana.' *Rivista di Storia della Filosofia* 46, no. 4 (1991), 701–35; 47, no. 1 (1992), 103–24
- 'Meccanismo e Organicità nel Sistema del Mondo, dalla *Teoria del Cielo* di Kant al *Bruno* di Schelling.' *ANNALI – Sez. Germanica* Nuova serie 3, 1–3, 297–333

– 'On the Relation between "Mode" and "Measure" in Hegel's *Science of Logic*: Some Introductory Remarks.' *The Owl of Minerva* 20, no. 1 (1988), 21–49
– 'La teoria della misura nella *Scienza della Logica* di Hegel.' Tesi di Laurea, Facoltà di Lettere e Filosofia Roma, 1982
Findlay, J.N. *Hegel: A Re-examination.* New York: Humanities, 1958
– 'Hegel and the Philosophy of Physics.' In *The Legacy of Hegel*, ed J.J. O'Malley et al. The Hague: Nijhoff, 1973, 72–89
– 'Hegel and Whitehead on Nature.' In *Hegel and Whitehead*, ed. G.R. Lucas, Jr. Albany: SUNY Press, 1986, 155–66
– 'The Hegelian Treatment of Biology and Life.' In *Hegel and the Sciences*, ed. R.S. Cohen and M.W. Wartofsky. Dordrecht: Kluwer, 1984, 87–100
Geraets, T.F. 'Les trois lectures philosophiques de l'Encyclopédie ou la réalisation du concept de la philosophie chez Hegel.' *Hegel-Studien* 10 (1975), 231–54
Gies, M. 'Naturphilosophie und Naturwissenschaft bei Hegel.' In *Hegel und die Naturwissenschaften*, ed. M.J. Petry. Stuttgart-Bad Cannstatt: Frommann-Holzboog, 1987, 65–88
Gloy, K. 'Goethes und Hegels Kritik an Newtons Farbentheorie. Eine Auseinandersetzung zwischen Naturphilosophie und Naturwissenschaft.' In *Die Naturphilosophie im Deutschen Idealismus*, ed. K. Gloy and P. Burger. Stuttgart-Bad Cannstatt: Frommann-Holzboog, 1993, 323–59
Gloy, K., and P. Burger, eds. *Die Naturphilosophie im Deutschen Idealismus.* Stuttgart-Bad Cannstatt: Frommann-Holzboog, 1993
Greene, M. 'Hegel and the Problem of Atomism.' *International Studies in Philosophy* 11 (1979), 123–40
Grimmlinger, F. 'Zur Methode der Naturphilosophie bei Hegel.' *Weiner Jahrbuch für Philosophie* 3 (1970), 38–68
Haering, T. 'Hegel und die moderne Naturwissenschaft: Bemerkungen zu Hegels Naturphilosophie.' *Philosophische Hefte* 3 (1931), 71–82
Harris, E.E. *An Interpretation of the Logic of Hegel.* Lanham: University Press of America, 1983
– *The Spirit of Hegel.* Atlantic Highlands: Humanities, 1993
Harris, H.S. *Hegel's Development I: Towards the Sunlight 1770–1801.* Oxford: Clarendon, 1972
– *Hegel's Development II: Night Thoughts, Jena 1801–1806.* Oxford: Clarendon, 1983
Harris, W.T. 'Philosophy of Nature.' *Journal of Speculative Philosophy* 5 (1871), 274–282
Hegel, G.W.F. *Encyclopädie der Philosophischen Wissenschaften im Grundrisse 1830 II: Die Naturphilosophie mit den mündlichen Zusätzen.* Werke 9. Frankfurt: Suhrkamp, 1986

- *Gesammelte Werke.* Hamburg: Meiner, 1968–
- *The Jena System, 1804-5: Logic and Metaphysics.* Ed. and trans. J.W. Burbidge, G. di Giovanni, H.S. Harris et al. Kingston and Montreal: McGill Queen's University Press, 1986
- *Logica e metafisica di Jena (1804–1805).* Trans. and ed. F. Biasutti, F. Chieregin, et al. Trento: Quaderni di verifiche 1982
- *Naturphilosophie: Band I: Die Vorlesungen von 1819/20.* Ed. M. Gies. Napoli: Bibliopolis, 1982
- *La Théorie de la mesure.* Trans, and with a commentary by A. Doz. Paris: Presses Universitaires de France, 1970
- *Vorlesungen über Logik und Metaphysik (Heidelberg 1817).* Ed. K. Gloy. Hamburg: Meiner, 1992
Henrich, D. 'Hegels Theorie über den Zufall.' *Hegel im Kontext.* Frankfurt: Suhrkamp 1967, 157–86
Hoffmeister, J., ed. *Briefe von und an Hegel.* Hamberg: Meiner, 1952
Horstmann, R.P., and M.J. Petry, eds. *Hegels Philosophie der Natur: Beziehungen zwischen empirischer und spekulativer Naturerkenntnis.* Stuttgart: Klett-Cotta, 1986
Hösle, V. *Hegels System: Der Idealismus der Subjektivität und das Problem der Intersubjektivität.* Hamburg: Meiner, 1987
- 'Raum, Zeit, Bewegung.' In *Hegel und die Naturwissenschaften,* ed. M.J. Petry. Stuttgart-Bad Cannstatt: Frommann-Holzboog, 1987, 247–82
Ihde, A.J. *The Development of Modern Chemistry.* New York: Dover, 1984
Kant, I. *Metaphysische Anfangsgründe der Naturwissenschaft.* Frankfurt and Leipzig, 1794
- *Werke in zehn Bänden.* Ed. W. Wieschedel. Darmstadt: Wissenschaftliche Buchgesellschaft, 1968
Kröner, R. *Von Kant bis Hegel.* Tübingen: Mohr 1924
Küppers, B.-O. *Natur als Organismus: Schellings frühe Naturphilosophie und ihre Bedeutung für die moderne Biologie.* Philosophische Abhandlungen 58. Frankfurt: V. Klostermann, 1992
Lécrivain, A. 'Pensée spéculative et Philosophie de la Nature: Les rapports entre la *Science de la Logique* et la *Philosophie de la Nature* chez Hegel.' Paper presented at Journée sur Idéalisme allemand et *Naturphilosophie,* Paris, March 1994
Levere, T. *Affinity and Matter: Elements of Chemical Philosophy 1800–1865.* Oxford: Clarendon, 1971
Lucas, Jr., G.R. 'A Re-interpretation of Hegel's Philosophy of Nature.' *Journal of the History of Philosophy* 22 (1984), 103–13
Mabille, B. 'Sens de la contingence naturelle et liberté de l'absolu chez Hegel et Schelling.' Paper presented at Journée sur Idéalisme allemand et *Naturphilosophie,* Paris, March 1994

Maesschalk, M. 'Construction et Réduction: le conflit des philosophies de la nature chez Fichte et Schelling entre 1801 et 1806,' Paper presented at Journée sur Idéalisme allemand et *Naturphilosophie*, Paris, March 1994

Mathieu, V. 'Filosofia della Natura e Dialettica.' In *Hegel Interprete di Kant*, ed. V. Verra. Napoli: Prismi, 1981, 91–122

McCumber, J. *The Company of Words: Hegel, Language and Systematic Philosophy*. Evanston: Northwestern 1993

McMullin, E. 'Philosophies of Nature.' *New Scholasticism* 43 (1969), 29–74

Miller, A.V. trans. *Hegel's Phenomenology of Spirit*. Oxford: Clarendon, 1977
– trans. *Hegel's Philosophy of Nature*. Oxford: Clarendon, 1970
– *Hegel's Science of Logic*. London: Allen and Unwin, 1969

Moiso, F. 'Die Hegelsche Theorie der Physik und der Chemie in ihrer Beziehung zu Schellings Naturphilosophie.' In *Hegels Philosophie der Natur: Beziehungen zwischen empirischer und spekulativer Naturerkenntnis*, ed. R.P. Horstmann and M.J. Petry. Stuttgart: Klett-Cotta, 1986, 54–87

Mure, G.R.G. *The Philosophy of Hegel*. London: Oxford, 1965, 149–57

Nadler, K. 'Die Entwicklung des Naturbegriffs in Hegels Philosophie,' *Zeitschrift für Deutsche Geisteswissenschaft*, 1, no. 2 (1938), 129–42

Neuser, W. 'Einfluß der Schellingschen Naturphilosophie auf die Systembildung bei Hegel: Selbstorganisation versus rekursive Logik.' In *Die Naturphilosophie im Deutschen Idealismus*, ed. K. Gloy and P. Burger. Stuttgart-Bad Cannstatt: Frommann-Holzboog, 1993, 238–66
– 'Die naturphilosophische und naturwissenschaftliche Literatur aus Hegels privater Bibliothek.' In *Hegel und die Naturwissenschaften*, ed. M.J. Petry. Stuttgart-Bad Cannstatt: Frommann-Holzboog, 1987, 479–99

Partington, J.R. *A History of Chemistry*. Vols. 3, 4. London: Macmillan, 1962

Peterson, M.C.E. 'Volcanos in the Sky: Nature's Contribution to Hegel's "Philosophy of Nature."' diss., Toronto, 1988

Petry, M.J. 'Hegel's Dialectic and the Natural Sciences.' *Hegel-Jahrbuch* (1974), 457–61
– 'Hegel's Philosophy of Nature: Recent Developments.' *Hegel-Studien* 23 (1988), 303–26
– 'Hegel's Teleological Reconstruction of Newtonian Mechanics.' In *Metaphysik nach Kant*, ed. D. Henrich and R.-P. Horstman. Stuttgart: Klett-Cotta, 1988, 572–97
– 'Scientific Method: Francoeur, Hegel, Pohl.' In *Hegels Philosophie der Natur*, ed. R.P. Horstmann and M.J. Petry. Stuttgart: Klett-Cotta, 1986, 11–29
– ed. *Hegel and Newtonianism*. Dordrecht: Kluwer, 1993
– ed. *Hegel und die Naturwissenschaften*. Stuttgart-Bad Cannstatt: Frommann-Holzboog, 1987
– trans. *Hegel's Philosophy of Nature*. London: Allen and Unwin, 1970

Pitt, A. 'Die dialektische Bestimmung der Natur in der Philosophie Hegels und der statistische Charakter der quantenmechanischen Naturbeschreibung.' diss., Freiburg, 1971

Pohl, G.F. *Der Process der galvanischen Kette.* Leipzig, 1826

Renault, E. 'La Théorie de la science de la philosophie de la nature hégélienne.' Paper presented at Journée sur Idéalisme allemand et *Naturphilosophie*, Paris, March 1994

Richter, J.B. *Anfangsgründe der Stöchyometrie; oder Meßkunst chymischer Elemente.* [Breslau u. Hirschberg, 1792] Hildesheim: Olm, 1968

Richter, L.G. *Hegel's begreifende Naturbetrachtung als Versöhnung der Spekulation mit der Erfahrung.* Würzburg: Königshausen und Neumann, 1985

Ritchie, D.G. *Darwin and Hegel, with Other Philosophical Studies.* London: Sonnenschein, 1893

Ritter, J.W. *Beweis daß ein beständiger Galvanismus den Lebensprocess in dem Thierreich begleite; nebst neuen Versuchen und Bemerkungen über den Galvanismus.* Weimar, 1798

Rosenkranz, K. *Hegels Naturphilosophie und die Bearbeitung derselben durch den italienischen Philosophen A. Vera.* Berlin, 1868

– 'Die Knotenlinien von Maßverhältnissen.' *Studien* 2. Leipzig, 1844, 62–95

Ruschig, U. 'Chemische Einsichten wider Willen.' *Hegel-Studien* 22 (1987), 171–9

Santoro-Brienza, L. 'Aristotle and Hegel on Nature: Some Similarities.' *Bulletin of the Hegel Society of Great Britain* 26 (1992), 13–29

Schelling, F.W.J. *Ausgewählte Werke.* Darmstadt: Wissenschaftliche Buchgesellschaft 1967

– *Ideas for a Philosophy of Nature.* Trans. E.E. Harris and P. Heath. Cambridge: Cambridge University Press, 1988

– *Ideen zu einer Philosophie der Natur als Einleitung in das Studium dieser Wissenschaft. Erster Theil.* 2nd ed. Landshut, 1803

Schipperges, H. 'Hegel und die Naturwissenschaften,' *Stuttgarter Hegel Tage 1970: Hegel-Studien.* Beiheft 11 (1974), 105–10

Schmied-Kowarzik, W. 'Thesen zur Entstehung und Begründung der Naturphilosophie Schellings.' In *Die Naturphilosophie im Deutschen Idealismus*, ed. K. Gloy and P. Burger. Stuttgart-Bad Cannstatt: Frommann-Holzboog, 1993, 67–100

Simon, R. 'Chemie und Dialektik.' *Deutsche Zeitschrift für Philosophie* 23 (1975), 980–4

Snelders, H.A.M. 'Atomismus und Dynamismus im Zeitalter der Deutschen Romantischen Naturphilosophie.' In *Romantik in Deutschland*, ed R. Brinkmann. Stuttgart: Metzlersche, 1978

- 'Hegel und die Bertholletsche Affinitätslehre.' In *Hegels Philosophie der Natur*, ed. R.-P. Horstmann and M.J. Petry. Stuttgart: Klett-Cotta, 1986, 88–102
- 'The Significance of Hegel's Treatment of Elective Affinity.' In *Hegel and Newtonianism*, ed. M. Petry. Dordrecht: Kluwer, 1993, 631–43

Stace, W.T. *The Philosophy of Hegel*. [London, 1924] New York: Dover, 1955, 297–317

Stallo, J.B. *General Principles of the Philosophy of Nature, with an Outline of some of its Recent Developments among the Germans; Embracing the Philosophical Systems of Schelling and Hegel and Oken's System of Nature*. Boston, 1848. [See Easton, 'The First American Interpretation ...']

Steinkraus, W., and K. Schmitz eds. *Art and Logic in Hegel's Philosophy*. Atlantic Highlands: Humanities, 1980

Stepelevich, L.S. 'The Hegelian Conception of Space.' *Nature and System* 1 (1979), 111–26

Taylor, C. *Hegel*. Cambridge: Cambridge University Press 1975

Trommsdorff, J.B. *Systematisches Handbuch des gesammten Chemie zur Erleichterung des Selbststudiums dieser Wissenschaft*. Erfurt, 1800

Vera, A. *Philosophie de la Nature de Hegel*. Traduit et accompagnée d'une introduction et d'un commentaire perpétuel. [Paris, 1863] Brussels: Culture et Civilization, 1969

Verra, V. *Introduzione a Hegel*. Roma-Bari: Laterza, 1988
- *Letture Hegeliane*. Bologna: Il Mulino, 1992

Wandschneider, D. 'Die Absolutheit des Logischen und das Sein der Natur.' *Zeitschrift für philosophische Forschung* 39, no. 3 (1985), 331–51
- 'Natur und Naturdialektik im objektiven Idealismus Hegels.' In *Die Naturphilosophie im Deutschen Idealismus*, ed. K. Gloy and P. Burger, Stuttgart-Bad Cannstatt: Frommann-Holzboog, 1993, 267–97. English translation: 'Nature and Dialectic of Nature in Hegel's Objective Idealism.' *Bulletin of the Hegel Society of Great Britain* 26 (1992), 30–52
- *Raum, Zeit, Relativität: Grundbestimmungen der Physik in der Perspektive der Hegelschen Naturphilosophie*. Frankfurt: Klostermann, 1982
- 'Die Stellung der Natur im Gesamtentwurf der hegelschen Philosophie.' In *Hegel und die Naturwissenschaften*, ed. M.J. Petry. Stuttgart-Bad Cannstatt: Frommann-Holzboog, 1987, 33–64

Wandschneider D., and V. Hösle. 'Die Entäusserung der Idee zur Natur und ihre zeitliche Entfaltung als Geist bei Hegel.' *Hegel-Studien* 18 (1983), 173–99

Wattles, J.H. 'Hegel's Philosophy of Organic Nature.' diss., Northwestern, 1973

Webb, T.R. 'Hegelian Science and the Problem of Nature.' diss., Toronto, 1976
-- 'The Problem of Empirical Knowledge in Hegel's *Philosophy of Nature*.' *Hegel-Studien* 15 (1980), 171–86

Whewell, W. *History of the Inductive Sciences*. [London, 1857] London: Cass, 1967
– *On the Philosophy of Discovery*. 1849
Winterl, J.J. *Prolusiones ad chemiam saeculi*. Budapest, 1800
Wundt, M. *Hegels Logik und die moderne Physik*. Köln: Westdeutscher, 1949

Index